18⁹⁵

7⁵⁰

M

D0904941

THE
WANING
OF THE
WEST

BOOKS BY STAN STEINER

THE RANCHERS: A BOOK OF GENERATIONS

DARK AND DASHING HORSEMEN

SPIRIT WOMAN

FUSANG: THE CHINESE WHO BUILT AMERICA

IN SEARCH OF THE JAGUAR

THE VANISHING WHITE MAN

THE ISLANDS

THE TIQUAS:
THE LOST TRIBE OF CITY INDIANS

GEORGE WASHINGTON:
THE INDIAN INFLUENCE

LA RAZA: THE MEXICAN AMERICANS

THE NEW INDIANS

THE LAST HORSE

THE WANING OF THE WEST

STAN STEINER

EDITED AND WITH REFLECTIONS BY
EMILY SKRETNY DRABANSKI

FOREWORD BY JOHN NICHOLS

ST. MARTIN'S PRESS
NEW YORK

Grateful acknowledgment is made for permission to use the following:

"This Train Is Bound for Glory" ("Bound for Glory") adapted by Woody Guthrie. Copyright © 1958 (renewed) by Woody Guthrie Publications Inc. All Rights Reserved.

"66 Highway Blues" words by Woody Guthrie, music by Pete Seeger. Copyright © 1966 by Stormking Music Inc. All Rights Reserved.

"Chicken Sneeze" new words and new music adaptation by Woody Guthrie. TRO – Copyright © 1963 by Ludlow Music, Inc., New York, N.Y.

"Jewish Conquistadors" from *Dark and Dashing Horsemen* by Stan Steiner. Copyright © 1981 by Stan Steiner. Reprinted by permission of Harper & Row, Publishers, Inc. (World rights granted).

"The Chinese Railroad Men" from *Fusang: The Chinese Who Built America* by Stan Steiner. Copyright © 1979 by Stan Steiner. Reprinted by permission of Harper & Row, Publishers, Inc.

DESIGN BY DIANE STEVENSON, SNAP·HAUS GRAPHICS

Library of Congress Cataloging-in-Publication Data

Steiner, Stan.
    The waning of the West / Stan Steiner; foreword by John
    Nichols.
        p. cm.
    ISBN 0-312-03000-2
      1. West (U.S.)—Civilization. I. Title.
F595.3.S74 1989
978—dc19   89-30087
                                        CIP

First Edition

10 9 8 7 6 5 4 3 2 1

*Dedicated to the Santa Fe Writers' Co-op,
a group founded by Stan Steiner,
which continues the important work
of encouraging and promoting writers in the West*

*And history becomes legend
and legend becomes history.*
—*Cocteau*

CONTENTS

CONTENTS

FOREWORD

I liked Stan Steiner and admired his work long before I met him. *The New Indians* and *La Raza: The Mexican Americans* were among the first books to articulate the Southwest for me when I arrived in New Mexico at the end of the 1960s.

Stan was a writer and social historian after my own heart. He had a flair for the macroscopic overview made human, and his credibility was deeply rooted in research of a vast and telling scope. Still, facts never obscured the soul of Stan's place, or of his people, or of his subject matter. Reading him was always a moveable feast.

Stan was a populist and a storyteller, a conscience in touch with humanity, a moralist who always took a stand on the correct historical side. He let people speak their own truths, and it's a complement to his vision (and to his integrity) that their dignity always came through.

As a folklorist, Stan's sense of humor was always apparent; Carl Sandburg would have loved his stuff . . . and Mark Twain, also. Woody Guthrie and Studs Terkel are two other kindred spirits to the author of *The Waning of the West*.

Stan wandered a lot, he listened to people, he transcribed what they said with insight and compassion. On the one hand, his books are important scholarly documents; on the other, they are a moving tribute to people, earth, history. They are richly informed by the traditions of struggle; they elucidate our times and our roots.

The Waning of the West is no different from his other books. At work on it when he died, Stan's last book is a delightful smorgasbord of the West, a complex, crazy quilt of anecdote, myth-telling, history, romance, politics and cowboy panache. Imagine, if you can, *The People, Yes* and *Leaves of Grass* meet *Legends of the Fall*, as painted by Frederic Remington and Fritz Scholder—at least for starters.

After that, about all you can say is that any place as vast as the West must have a real kaleidoscopic soul. And it is that soul which Stan has captured here.

In these pages you'll find stories of old-timers, of mountain men on the Green River and of slick urban cowboys and corrupt Indian politicos. You'll find smatterings of Thoreau, Jefferson and Emerson in these pages, as well as a bit of Lyndon Johnson, Oriana Fallaci and Edward Abbey.

You can't pin down the West or its people any more than you can pin down this book. Stan Steiner's West is Jack Shaefer discussing *Shane* one moment, and Marxist rodeo freaks in Budapest, Hungary, the next.

If you don't like Sam Peckinpah's macho pronouncements about Western movies, just turn the page for a trenchant history of feminism in the West. Did you know that Wyoming was the first state to offer women suffrage and to prohibit discrimination based on one's sex? Likewise, did you know that a Jewish *conquistador* pal of Coronado's named Hernando Alonso was burned alive at the stake? And if you think there's no connection between the man who started a cowboy sperm bank and that cosmic *vaquero*, Chuck Yeager, you'd better think again: for they have both contributed significantly to the spirit of the West.

This book delivers a marvelous tapestry of myth and reality: a Navajo medicine man performing a blessing ceremony at a cocktail bash mostly attended by Ralph Lauren cowboys; Chinese railroad laborers pulling a locomotive over the Sierra Nevada by hand, in winter; a pair of Levi jeans helping to tow another train for miles; and, last but not least, a hydrogen bomb accidentally falling on Albuquerque, New Mexico, in 1957. And—guess what?—miraculously, it doesn't explode!

You can't label the West anymore than you can fit this book into a convenient slot. Inside these pages reside the Atomic Age and the death of small-town America, the sad demise of the family farmer and the struggle to stop the MX missile. One minute you'll be reading about a judge in Texas who is reelected to office weeks after he dropped dead. Moments later, you're reading about the Indian wars, sex in the old West and a woman doctor who wore a necklace of bullets she'd removed from her many patients over the years.

Though Stan was never a man to overly comment on his material, he's given a chance to speak up in two fine interviews included at the back of this volume. I suppose his attitude toward it all can be summed up in the words of Lou Attebery, an Idaho professor, whom Stan quotes: "There ought to be a resonance between man and the earth."

It is that resonance that this book celebrates.

Stan gave us many books that I cherish—*La Raza*, *The New Indians*, *Fusang*, *The Ranchers*, *The Vanishing White Man*—and this one is certainly the equal of any of those. Full of life and thoroughly eclectic, *The Waning of the West* moves around in history, place, culture and vision. Its contradictions reveal all the important truths. What's more, the book was composed on an old Olympia portable typewriter, no electricity, the kind you haven't been able to buy parts for for at least twenty years. It happens to be the same make of machine I use, although Stan neither willed me his when he died, nor did I steal it when nobody else was looking. We just shared certain perspectives about the proper sort of rhythm to seek in this turbulent modern world.

At the time of his death, Stan felt the West that he loved was dying. I'm not so sure. For as long as this vast area can produce folks like Stan to write about it from the heart, then the West has certainly got as good a chance as any other place on earth to glory in its living, changing, volatile, amusing, tragic and beautiful destiny.

This book is a serious history. It's also a lot of fun. It is a marvelous character study of marvelous characters. And I hope there are other books like it hiding in Stan's trunks, or down in his basement, or in manuscript form in a library somewhere, awaiting another nod from some perceptive editor. It would give me great joy to see continued this fine writer's—and the Westerners'—remarkable legacies.

—*JOHN NICHOLS*
Taos, New Mexico
October 1988

INTRODUCTION

In the summer of 1945 Stan Steiner hitchhiked from Manhattan to the West in search of America. It was a trip that would forever change his life. He developed a love at first sight that would grow into a passion. That is when this book was born.

For years, Stan traveled the back roads of the West meeting and talking to people, from the Mississippi River valley to the Pacific Ocean. Yes, he even interviewed the paniola cowboys in Hawaii. Stan loved the grandeur of the wide-open spaces, the exhilarating fresh air and diversity of the landscape, and he went wherever his thumb would take him. He rode the rails and bunked at ranches and on Indian reservations in search of the Old West.

More than the land itself, the Western people totally captured his heart. Their spirit, rugged independence and sense of heritage infatuated him. Following his arrival in the West, he went on to write twenty books and numerous articles, many dealing with the West. But it was always this book that was in progress. Throughout the years, he would clip articles, read histories of the West and talk with its people.

All the while, his books were becoming literary landmarks. He wrote histories of the forgotten people who built the West, as well as the prominent contemporary leaders of our time. Where others thought of the West merely in terms of Hollywood stereotypes, Stan saw the West as being composed of a rainbow of peoples. His book *The New Indians* introduced readers all over the world to contemporary Native American leaders who treasured their heritage yet were powerful forces in modern society. The book challenged prevailing stereotypes of Indians that were conveyed in the majority of books and movies about the West.

Equally powerful was Stan's book *La Raza: The Mexican Americans*, which chronicled the emergence of Hispanics as a dynamic force in the 1960s through the voices of everyone from farmworkers to social activists.

Other books by Stan challenged our perceptions about that most hallowed of Western stereotypes, the cowboys themselves. One of his last books, *The Ranchers*, took us to ranches across the West to listen to the real men and women who rode the range in the West. In fact, many of the thoughts and issues that first surfaced in *The Ranchers* intrigued Stan, and led him to pursue them further in this book.

This last collection was a difficult task—a challenge for Stan. The West he knew and had fallen in love with in 1945 had changed radically over the years. He believed he was witnessing the passing of the Old West, a period that he sometimes likened to the fall of the Roman Empire. And he knew he could not let the Old West slip by without pausing to pay homage to those people who were part of its vanishing culture. Yet, while he was heartsick about the passing of something he loved, he was also encouraged by the birth of a New West.

As is customary in most of Stan's writings, he most often allows Westerners to speak for themselves. He was especially careful to orchestrate different voices with varying opinions on what the Old West was all about and where the New West was headed.

On January 12, 1987, Stan was working at his manual typewriter on this book in his studio in Santa Fe. He was struggling with a chapter on the newest man of the West —the cowboy politician—when the sentence on the piece of paper in his typewriter was cut short by a heart attack. That last sentence was: "Who was this new man?" It was a question he grappled with most of his life, and one he attempts to address in this book.

In cooperation with his widow, Vera John-Steiner, I've compiled and edited this collection, including in it a blend of essays and interviews he had completed for the book, and complementing those with a few other pieces he had written about the West. Needless to say, the task would have been impossible without the constant attention, encouragement and support given by Vera, a well-known psychologist, educator and author in her own right. Together, we spent hours poring over notes, manuscripts, articles and tape recordings. In addition, in order to write the introductions and edit the various sections, I interviewed Vera about Stan's perspectives on the West. In the process, we learned a lot about Stan, ourselves and each other. But most of all we learned about this place we call home—the West.

—*EMILY SKRETNY DRABANSKI*
Editor, New Mexico Magazine
December 1988

PART I

❖

IN
SEARCH
OF THE
OLD WEST

For Stan Steiner, the search for the Old West was the quest to find America and what it meant to be American.

The son of Viennese emigrants, he grew up in New York, and came to believe that the West was the transforming experience for Europeans. It was through the West that they could become true Americans. At the same time, Stan personally felt a tension between the hope and promise of the West and its reality. In the end, he believed that only by discovering its reality could he become a true native son of America. Happily for the reader, Stan lovingly recounts the beginning of that journey of discovery in the first chapter, "Going West."

Just as Stan had embarked on his own personal quest, he was fascinated by others who sought out the Old West. In the second chapter, "Bound For Glory," he looks at some of those vagabonds headed

for the modern-day frontier of the West. These folks were lured by the blacktop pavement that snaked through the mountains as surely as the homesteaders who sought the washed-out and rutted trails were a hundred years earlier. True, the new pioneers stashed their worldly possessions into the backs of beat-up trucks and moving vans instead of the back of a covered wagon. But, like their pioneer counterparts, they, too, sought a land of opportunity, rugged individualism and adventure.

As part of his personal quest to determine what the West really represented, as well as what it meant to be Western, Stan engaged in an ongoing dialogue and exchange of ideas with everyone from academics to ranchers. Shunning the term "oral history," Stan preferred to call these conversations "testimonials," and included a sampling of them in most of his books because he felt it was vitally important to listen to a variety of voices and opinions on a topic. Many of the testimonials included herein are part of that ongoing dialogue. Some began with relationships formed years ago, whereas others were a natural progression from his writings of *The Ranchers* and *The Vanishing White Men*. The testimonials themselves took many forms. Often they were face-to-face conversations that lasted several hours or days. Other times they were the result of a lengthy correspondence.

Many of the people in this collection wrote letters to Stan. Some wrote out of isolation and loneliness. For others, the written word was a means of maintaining a connection and exchanging ideas. In either case, Stan loved the written word and valued the correspondence he received, realizing that few people today have the time or inclination to write letters. The chapter "The Present Is the Past" is the result of his long-term correspondence with Ray Allen Billington, "the dean of Western history." Though the two never had the opportunity to meet face-to-face, their letters to each other formed a strong bridge across the vast expanses of the West.

Stan treasured his hours spent talking with old-timers. The courtesy and grace of Westerners who had lived hard and rewarding lives seemed to sustain him in his own isolation as a writer. Not surprisingly, in almost everyone of his books he has paid homage to these people, as well as to the fact that they still endure. This book is no exception, with his chapter "The Old-Timers" based on the many interviews he had with old-timers of the West over the years.

One of Stan's favorite old-timers was a rodeo cowboy named Rex Bundy who also wrote about the West. They first met at a Western Writers' conference, and Bundy immediately impressed Stan as a true Westerner writing about the West. Stan was intrigued by such people, and thought the act of writing about their own experiences made them people of integrity and wholeness. A conversation with Rex Bundy is included in this section for that reason.

Often Stan was frustrated with interpretations made by various academics who wrote with scant firsthand knowledge of the West itself. In his mind, such people preferred to remain in their ivory towers while avoiding places where they might step in a cow pie or actually meet real Westerners. Stan, on the other hand, always delighted in finding academics who were in touch with the rural roots of the West. Lou Attebury was one of those rare people, and Stan was especially impressed with the work Attebury was doing with the College of Idaho as part of an organization to study Western farm and ranch folklore. Stan was impressed with the dialogue between academics and ranchers on a variety of issues. To Stan, these people in Idaho were pioneers attempting to overcome the sociological barriers between academics, townsfolk and ranchers, while at the same time trying to deal honestly with environmental concerns and other local issues.

Another academic who was in touch with the West's rural roots was Howard R. Lamar. When Stan interviewed him in 1983, Lamar was then the dean of Yale University. They had been introduced by Peter Decker, a rancher whom Stan had interviewed for his book *The Ranchers*, and their conversation took place at Decker's ranch. Lamar completed his six-year term as dean in 1985, and continues to teach at Yale as the Sterling Professor of History. His testimonial concludes the first part of Stan's book.

GOING WEST

❖

On a quiet day in the summer after World War II ended, there was a peace that came over the city that made young men restless. Not having anything to do and no money to do it with, I walked out of Manhattan with a bedroll, an Army-surplus blanket under my arm. Not knowing where I was going, I walked down to the waterfront, to the docks of the old Hoboken ferry, and I headed West. The end of the war had brought an emptiness onto the streets of the city and I, too, was restless. And I set forth to discover the West.

But where was the West?

❖

The silent year after the war ended the highways of the country were crowded with wandering youths, the soldiers and survivors of the war searching for the peace they had won, or escaping from it. Some said there were a million young men and women on the road that year. Some said there were two million. No one knew how many.

And I was one of them.

In my mind the covered wagons still rode into the sunset. The old trails had become superhighways. The pioneers were children who had become veterans. The new seekers after that Golden Fleece on the road to the West were runaways from the war and dropouts from the peace.

Maybe the prairie schooners were now semi-trailer trucks and recreational vehicles, but their destinations were not that different from what they always had been. The new immigrants to the West were searching for the same freedom from their past that their ancestors had sought. And these children of the old emigrants became the new immigrants.

It was the Jewish prophet of the ghettos, Abraham Cahan, who had voiced the quest of the old emigrants that was to become the cry of the new immigrants, the sons and daughters of the second generation: "America! To go to America. My spirit soared to reestablish the Garden of Eden on that distant land. I was for America."

Along the highways lay the solutions to my discontent. If I could find them.

Going West!

To reach the West I had to cross the Hudson River. And so I booked passage on the old sagging ferry to Hoboken, that gateway to the prairies, for a nickle, and on the far shore of New Jersey I would lift my thumb and point it in the direction of the Rocky Mountains, waiting for a covered wagon to come down the highway.

The smell of the musty river, rotting wooden piers, grimy freighters and the odors of garbage that floated past the Statue of Liberty mixed with the polluted breezes from

New Jersey. The foul odors were like a sweet nectar to me, an elixer that promised unknown adventures. I was like Christopher Columbus upon the decks of the *Santa Maria*, or at least Henry Hudson steering his *Half Moon* on the river to China, only to land at the site where Albany now sits. Myrrh and incense could not have smelled sweeter than that morning breeze. It had blown, I was sure, all the way from the Rocky Mountains to guide me West.

The aged ferry waddled upon the water as if uncertain that it would reach the other shore. On its wet decks I stood watching the city disappear in the fog, its luminous towers like a mirage. In the distant harbor the Statue of Liberty arose from the murky waters, not welcoming but bidding farewell to a young emigrant.

I waved good-bye. The shimmering fog made it seem as if the Statue waved back.

❖

And why was I going West? I was not sure. Nor did I know what I was looking for; how could I know what was unknown to me when I had no idea where I was going or what it was that I was seeking. The pioneers of old may have known no more of their destination when they headed West than I did on that summer day in 1945.

Never had I been west of the Hudson River before, and in my mind I was no less of a pioneer than those whom had gone before me.

❖

On safely landing at the ferry dock in Hoboken that morning the exhilaration I felt cannot be remembered in words. Nor can it be relived with the same intensity. I had finally left New York. The pioneers were no more awed and excited by their discoveries of the New World than I was in reaching the shore of Hoboken.

I remember writing a postcard to my mother in which bravely I said FAREWELL in big letters. The postcard had a black-and-white photograph on it of that ancient Hoboken ferry that had been tinted in rosy hues.

To my father I boasted, "America, here I come."

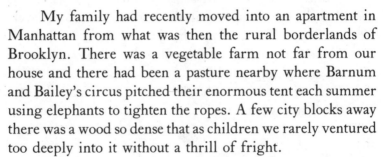

My family had recently moved into an apartment in Manhattan from what was then the rural borderlands of Brooklyn. There was a vegetable farm not far from our house and there had been a pasture nearby where Barnum and Bailey's circus pitched their enormous tent each summer using elephants to tighten the ropes. A few city blocks away there was a wood so dense that as children we rarely ventured too deeply into it without a thrill of fright.

Brooklyn was then a land of "beautiful hills and pastoral souls," as Walt Whitman said in "Crossing Brooklyn Ferry." He then asked if in a hundred years "will it not be the same?"

Not far from our house in Brooklyn were the old, abandoned railroad tracks of the Sheepshead Bay Line, which ran for miles through the sand dunes to the sea. Many times I spent my days walking the rails to the fishing villages on the shores of Long Island instead of going to school, wishing that my eyes could see across the horizon into the world beyond the Eastern shore.

On Long Island I once found a tree that Walt Whitman had sat beneath, dreaming of the West. And I sat where he had—dreaming his dream.

And so I grew up as a country boy in the city, and a city boy in the country. That was less of a paradox than it seems in the 1930s. It was a common reality to millions of city children with rural dreams.

During the summers my family lived in the small farm town of Spotswood in the piney woods of central New Jersey.

The sign on the road that told travelers they were coming to the town said POPULATION 906, but I think that probably was an exaggeration. It was not really a town at all, but more of a country crossroads with a general store surrounded by the obligatory post office, gas station, railroad depot and American Legion post.

On the outskirts of the town there was a Grange Hall where the farmers had a dance once a month, and in the midst of a cornfield down the road there was the Roadhouse, a mysterious place where children were not allowed. It said so on the doors. My childhood girlfriend, who lived next door, was the daughter of the town constable; he was an Irish tenor and worked nights in the Roadhouse as a singing waiter. In our town there was little or no crime and not much for the constable to do, he said, but to sing for his supper.

It was a town where people sat on their screened porches on summer nights, listening to the radio or reading the Wishing Book, the Sears catalogue. There was sometimes nothing to do but talk.

And then there was the two-room schoolhouse where one autumn I attended class when there was a polio epidemic in the cities. Of my schooling in that country school, what

I mostly remember is the recess. If I ran across the single railroad track into the cornfield I was home free. The teachers would not chase a pupil into the cornfield.

There are times when I think I have made up that memory of the country. Memories of childhood always seem more like fantasies as one gets older. But being a country boy is not merely a memory—it is forever after a part of your fantasy and your reality.

One day many years later I took my wife to visit that farm town of my youth. It had disappeared. The general store had been replaced by a suburban supermarket, the old railroad depot had been torn down, the single railroad track had been torn up, the two-room schoolhouse had been closed and nailed shut and the Grange Hall was an antique shop.

And yet, I was not willing to relinquish the memory of my town to history. I was determined to find some remnant of my youth. There was one place, I told my wife, that had to be unchanged by time. On the edge of the piney woods down by the old creek was a huckleberry swamp that only the locals knew about. In the Depression the WPA had built a cement highway to nowhere, as they sometimes did, that halted at the wooden bridge that led to the huckleberry swamp. When I was a boy I hunted for sand turtles in the swamp. No one knew the swamp as I did.

The old creek was still there. And so was that wooden bridge with its rattling planks. My wife and I walked across the bridge hand in hand, a boyish excitement in my heart. But the swamp was gone. It had been bulldozed to the ground for a subdivision.

On the construction site there was a sign that warned us: NO TRESPASSING.

My youth was gone.

◈

To me, my family's move into the city was a difficult and painful one.

My father had bought a shabby Victorian building on the Upper East Side of Manhattan between Lexington and Park Avenues, a middle-class tenement with solemn halls and baroque rooms where the night traffic in the streets would keep you awake most of the night. By day everything seemed to be permanently gray: the sidewalk, the streets, the buildings, the faces of the people, the air you breathed. Even the sun was gray most of the time. The sun didn't rise in Manhattan. It fell.

In those years millions of young men and women were brought by their families into the cities. Many of them had come during the war and even more came after the peace, abandoning the Spotswoods of America. The rural neighborhoods of Brooklyn disappeared as well, becoming the suburbs of post-war urban life.

And this, to me, was not the America I had known. And I left my father's house to search for the memory of youth that I had known as a child. My youth had been taken away from me and I wanted it back and I set sail on the Hoboken ferry and headed West to find the America that I had loved and lost. I was not alone.

After all, Billy the Kid had been born in Brooklyn, too.

BOUND FOR GLORY

❖

On the back of a pickup truck piled high and tied down with furniture and mattresses a woman sat tightly embracing her children. They rode into the cold dark night holding onto one another, trying to get as warm as possible in the face of the highway winds and not fall off the truck. Even so, the darkness chilled them and she could not stop the shivering of her children.

They were going home.

In the early years of the war they had gone to California for jobs in the war industries and earned some money. Now the war was over and they were going home again.

But why go back to Oklahoma?

The woman said, "Grandpa, when he died before we left, asked that he be buried sittin' up in his favorite chair. And that's how we buried him, wearin' his old cowboy hat. He said that way he could still hear what was goin' on. He didn't want to be alone in his grave, he said. He was part Cherokee, you know. Me and Pa, we liked to be buried that way, sittin' up in our favorite chairs on our own ranch. On our own land."

"Not in some foreign country," she added, "like California."

And as the pickup truck drove through the Texas panhandle the woman peered across the silent fields. She could not see them in the darkness but she knew them in her memory, her hair blowing in the wind and her eyes smiling. "I guess that is maybe why we're going home again, to be buried on our own place.

"We'd like to be buried sittin' up, like Grandpa," she said.

❖

"Movin' on," he said. "Where am I goin? I'll know when I get there."

On the roads to the West there are nowadays more modern pioneers than there were in the days of the covered wagon trains. They come in station wagons and rented trucks, customized vans and recreational vehicles, mobile homes on wheels and jet planes. And, as always, these pilgrims and refugees from the East have come "Bound for Glory," seeking the Promised Land; they have forever changed America and the West.

> *This road don't carry no rustlers,*
> *Whores, pimps or side-street hustlers.*
> *This road is bound for glory.*
> *This road!*

On the old roads to the West in the Great Depression of the 1930s, "Bound for Glory" was a gospel hymn of hope. Sometimes Woody Guthrie sang it as a church spiritual and sometimes he sang it with the bitter twang of the homeless

farm boy he was. The song is still full of both sorrow and salvation. And it points the way to the Promised Land of the
West that is not on any road map at the local gas station.

> *This road don't carry no gamblers,*
> *Liars, thieves and big-shot ramblers.*
> *This road is bound for glory.*
> *This road!*

In the quiet and uneasy peace that fell upon the land
in the years after the end of World War II there was a
restless discontent. The wars in Korea and Vietnam deepened
the sense of unease in the veterans of the war, and of the
peace. By the 1970s there were millions of people on the
roads leading from South to North, from East to West, a
modern migration that had begun years before and was
changing the entire country. No one seemed to have noticed
them at the time; they were an unseen and silent army
searching for their share of the peace, and they did not line
the roads, they rode on them in their own cars.

"Nowadays folks got wheels instead of feet," said a
motel owner in western Nebraska. "But they ain't as free
as they may think. They got to go where the road goes."

One old Montana rodeo cowboy by the name of Rex
Bundy compared himself to a lone "tumbleweed that just got
blown out of Dakota and into Montana." In his life he had
gone everywhere and tried his hand at everything, like any
Westerner. He had been a horse wrangler, a sheepherder, a
working cowboy, an oil-rig jockey, a truck driver, an historian
and a writer. "If a man is free to believe he is free, it doesn't
much matter if he is or not, or what road he rides, or whether

he gets to where he's going," he said. "Being free is knowing you don't know where you are going. That's the West."

Another favorite Bundy saying went something like: "A man has got to go wherever the wind blows him. But a man's got to be able to land on his own feet."

"Movin' on" has been a way of life in the West. The lure of the frontier sprang from the belief in the freedom to be whomever you wished to be and to go wherever you wished to go. Whether it was true hardly mattered.

Nowhere do people move as often as they do in the West. One family in every four moves each year from state to state, from city to city, or just within the cities where they already live—as if they were nomads on the road to nowhere.

The cowboy writer Eugene Manlove Rhodes described Westerners as "fiddle footed"; they were forever "sniffin'" the "sweet scent" of the breeze from the next county, wondering what lay beyond the hills on the horizon, forever movin' on. It was not merely the lust for land and gold, though they sought both. What drove them farther and farther West was a quest for freedom from the East. To go West was to "make danger kind of a mystic ceremony, or rite, or crucible," as Ernest Hemingway later wrote—it was a test of the American spirit to be free. It was a kind of patriotism.

On the roads to the New West the immigrants no longer come in Ma Joad model T Fords, ailing pickup trucks and creaking farm wagons piled high with grandma's dowry chests and grandpa's rocking chairs, the belongings of generations. They are not the adventurers and pioneers of old. Nor are they the misfits rejected by the society back East. Instead, they have rejected the society that no longer needs them. And they come seeking nothing more than a new job and a new home, for unlike the earlier emigrants who came in covered wagon trains and caravans of dust-bowl refugees, they come alone.

"Now all you need to go West," said a man in a mobile home park in Rock Springs, Wyoming, "is your credit card."

In a palm tree and cactus—fringed mobile home court in Tucson, Arizona, named something like the Royal Palm Tree Court, a little white-haired lady with a girlishly mis-chievous smile told me, "Coming across the country from Iowa we used a credit card. Then when we'd got here we threw the damned thing away."

She smiled with delight at the memory. "Yes, sir, we threw the damned thing out the car window into the desert. We felt freed."

One young man asleep in a bus terminal in Logan, Utah—or was it Boise, Idaho—late enough at night it's hard to tell the difference—woke long enough to say, "Why did I come West? I came out here to be free. To be clean. To begin again. To be born again. It don't matter much where I am at, what town I'm in. I got wheels. A Ford Mustang that goes anywhere I tell it to. Nobody knows me here. Nobody knows who I am. So I can be anybody I want to be."

At an all-night gas station in Loveland, Colorado, a young woman said, "No, I don't know where I'm at. I come from Maine. All I know is I'm not going home again. There's nowhere to go home to. My family sold the farm. My husband disappeared. There's nothing for me back East anymore."

Her baby in the front seat of the car began to cry. She comforted the child and got into the car and pointed it toward Nevada.

Where was she going? "I think I need a change of life. Maybe I'll become a call girl." She laughed and drove off.

16

In a desolate neon-lit convenience store on the highway in the middle of the night in Lubbock, Texas, a weary middle-aged woman mused, "We come from Scranton, Pennsylvania. My husband lost his job. The bank took our house. We had to go somewhere, anywhere.

"Lubbock, why Lubbock? Why not?" she shrugged.

Maybe these new immigrants do not know their destination any more than did their ancestors who came West on the old Indian trails, but that doesn't stop them. They have no choice. On the road they come in growing numbers, from the decaying ghettos of the cities and the monotonous suburbs, from broken families and busted-up marriages, from the abandoned factories and dying industries, the mortgaged farms and empty small towns of the East.

"No one's hardly moving anymore from the West to the East," said a cross-country moving van driver in Lincoln, Nebraska. "Except'n the politicians in Washington. Them dudes."

In fact, the migration to the West is the largest in the history of our country, surpassing that of the old covered wagon days. Not by the millions but by the tens of millions the new immigrants have gone West since the end of the Second World War, as many people as had come as emigrants from Europe at the turn of the century trying to escape the same conditions of poverty and despair that these new immigrants to the West seek to escape.

"It's like the Exodus in the Old Testament," said a woman from West Virginia in a laundromat on a highway in Oklahoma. "No one I know is planning to go back East. If'n Moses tried to part the waters of the Red Sea once more to lead his people back into bondage, Lord, who would follow him?

17

No, Lord, we can't go home again when we got no home to go home to," continued the woman. "We's don't even know if we's the Egyptians or the Jews. And if this here is Egypt or Israel.

"If this is the Promised Land like they say, somebody broke his promises to me," she said, putting her husband's socks into the dryer. "I pissed my monthly blood into every state and what good's it got for me? Nothing I can see."

A small-town banker in New Mexico shook his head. "I see these folks come and go every day. And I'd guess two of every five don't stay. Because they are looking for a romantic West, a Promised Land that doesn't exist. Probably never did. And never will.

"So they move on. Next stop Los Angeles," he said.

On old Highway 66 it was said that the reason people settled in Albuquerque and Phoenix was that their cars broke down in the desert on their way to California. It was a joke, but it was true. In those days California was called the "seacoast of Iowa." And if that was so, then Phoenix and Albuquerque were the "suburbs of Des Moines." The Corn-belt retirees who settled in the Sunbelt cities changed the nature of the West as much as did the unemployed steel workers and engineers who came later.

One old man in Horizon City, which is situated in the desert of northern Arizona, put it this way: "We started out to reach paradise and we got as far as purgatory."

His wife laughed. "That's halfway."

On one of the roads heading West there is a place they call "the Truckers' Heaven." From the highway it looks like any other motel. But its parking lot is full of dozens of huge trucks and semi-trailers that resemble beached whales. And this highway oasis offers truck drivers their every fantasy. It has an all-night café and porno movie theater, a bar and lounge with exotic dancers as nude as possible and a monastery of a motel with every imaginable room service. The entire wall of the motel's lobby is built in the shape of a truck's hood. Its gigantic grill opens to reveal a darkened bar where truckers sit alone in the dark world they have entered, one by one, like Jonah being swallowed by the whale.

Truckers' Heaven is a monument to the loneliness of the road.

> *There is a Highway from coast to coast.*
> *New York to Los Angeles.*
> *I'm going down that road*
> *   with troubles in my mind.*

And that road had no beginning and no ending. It was a way of getting from somewhere to somewhere else. Anywhere. Nowhere.

Not that it ever mattered much where the road led. In days gone by, the road had no destination but was merely a means that justified its end. On the road, the road became its own destination.

> *Been on this road for a mighty long time,*
> *Ten million men like me.*
> *You drive us from yo' town*
> *   and we ramble around,*
> *And got them 66 Highway Blues.*

If you traveled down the road far enough you eventually came to the town of Why, in Arizona.

Bound for Glory! This train?
    Ha!
I wonder just where in hell
    we're bound for.
Rain on, little rain, rain on!
Blow on little wind, keep
    blowin'.

And yet, the road did sometimes lead to the Promised Land. Even if it did not, all was not lost. To the refugees on the highways to the West, Woody Guthrie had some good old-fashioned words of advice (Copyright © 1963 by Ludlow Music):

If you want to go to heaven
Let me tell you what to do.
Just grease your feet in mutton stew,
And slide out of the Devil's hand,
And come over to the Promised Land.
Take it easy,
An' go greasy.

On the cement walls of a highway overpass just west of Laramie, Wyoming, where hitchhikers have waited patiently for passing cars year after year, a despairing and anonymous wanderer has written an ominous message of warning to those who will come down the road after him and wait in vain as he did for a car to stop and give him a ride farther West. In bold letters he has written:

GO BACK!

WHERE IS
THE WEST?

◆

The summer heat shimmered on the highway. It was a hot desert day.

Against the barren hills, the old ranching town of Socorro, New Mexico, was an oasis. I had driven all morning through the desert to talk to the Association of University Women at the mining college in town. The women had gathered for a picnic under the cottonwood trees by the Rio Grande, where it was a little but not much cooler. My talk that day was about "Manhood in the Old and New West." It had attracted fifteen women and two courageous men.

Not many men will come to hear a talk about "manhood." Not in the West. It isn't something men like to talk about, or listen to.

After my talk one of the men, an old-time Westerner, came up to me and said, "That was real interesting what you were saying what it was like being a man in the Old West. When I was a boy back in the 1920s, I used to go see the Western movies starring Tom Mix on a Saturday afternoon, and I always wanted to live in the West like Tom Mix. So one day I said to my daddy, 'Daddy, why can't we live in the West, like Tom Mix?' "

"My daddy, he looked at me and he smiled at me and he said, 'But, son, we are in the West.' "

THE PRESENT
IS THE PAST

❖

TESTIMONIAL BY
RAY ALLEN BILLINGTON

A distinguished gray-haired man, Ray Allen Billington seemed taller than he was. Most men resemble their reputations, and Ray looked like the "dean of Western history," a term he disliked. In his own mind he liked to think of himself as a down-home country-boy who saw the history of the West from the ground up standing ankle deep in cow manure, as he once said.

The perfect Westerner, a friend once called Ray Allen Billington. One of his old friends said he was more like Gary Cooper in High Noon; his favorite phrase of praise was to say that something was "Jim Dandy!"

Nonetheless, in spite of his good-old-country-boy pose, he was indeed one of the great historians of the West. He had as panoramic a view of Western history as a Lord Toynbee or

23

Lord Bryce. After all, he was the Senior Researcher at the Huntington Library. And the books he edited for his Histories of the American West *series will long remain classics, as will his own books,* America's Frontier Heritage *and* Land of Savagery, Land of Promise.

And until his dying days "the dean" and the country boy remained one and the same. The last book he wrote before his death was the joyous and irreverant Dirty Limericks.

RAY ALLEN BILLINGTON:

These voices are of the present but out of the past. And probably the future. In the West today, people live but they give the past the credit for their ways. And this is an important indication of their manner of thinking. And perhaps the manner of thinking of most frontier people over their three centuries that they were moving Westward.

Folks talk of pickups and tractors, or going to town and buying store goods and using today's conveniences. But they talk also of doing things their fathers and grandfathers did. Of the unchanged way of life on the Western frontier.

Just, I suspect, as did the pioneers who moved westward into the Great Valley of the Appalachians or over the Cumberland Gap into Kentucky and on over the Mississippi Valley and across the Big Muddy onto the Great Plains. Each succeeding generation had a new way of life forced on them by the different environments in which they lived, but each thought of themselves as bringing "civilization" to the wilderness, and living and thinking of himself as had his father and grandfathers back in England, back of the Tidewater, back in the Piedmont.

Whether in the shadows of the Appalachians or the Rockies, men and women tried to live as their parents and grandparents had lived "back East." They modeled their territorial government and state constitutions on those they had known in their old homes. They started schools and literary societies and thespian groups and circulating libraries to perpetuate and keep in touch with the culture that was familiar to them. They sought Eastern capital to develop their new country. They kept their ties to the East strong —culturally, politically, socially, religiously.

Yet they lived different lives and thought different thoughts than had their ancestors and Eastern contemporaries. The new country put its stamp on them and on their institutions. They might try to rewrite the constitution of the state they had left behind, but here and there a clause was modified to provide for the greater degree of democracy possible on the frontier, where social mobility was higher. They might practice the old-time religion but conditions were different, so the camp meeting and circuit rider and a few theological changes were needed. They might subscribe to Eastern literary journals, but their writing and speech was touched by their wilderness experience. They might establish schools on the patterns of the East, but in those schools surveying became more important than Latin grammar. Frontiering was a demanding experience and changed men and women whether or not they wanted to be changed.

So [it was] with the ranchers and 'steaders and miners and all the others who pioneered the Far West and whose descendants now boast of their frontier backgrounds. Their ways of life and thought were different from those of Easterners in the pioneer period. And their ways of life and thought today differ from those of their ancestors.

Yet each group clings to the past. The Far Western pioneers to a past that lay in the East. The current sons and daughters of the pioneers to a past that lay in their ancestor's life patterns.

This mere fact is important if we are to understand the Western "character." Their veneration of tradition alters their view of the modern world. They still think of themselves as rugged individualists, even though their lives are shaped by government regulations—some of which they support without realizing their inconsistency. They boast of their self-reliance, yet lean heavily on the group. So it goes.

The pioneer tried to associate with a *spatial* past (the East he had left); the modern Westerner tries to associate with a *chronological* past (his ancestors, the pioneers). Neither is able to do so completely, but his politics and social views are shaped by that insistence.

Here is a vital segment of the American past, perpetuated in the views of the present. We can better understand Lord Bryce's belief that the West is the most important part of America.

THE
OLD-TIMERS

❖

There are few real Westerners left. And they, too, are dying out.

One of the last of the breed was the soft-spoken, gentle-eyed, warm-hearted but tough-minded old gentleman rancher of the mountain village of San Cristobal, north of Taos, New Mexico, who was slowly dying of emphysema. As though he knew he was an endangered specics, he held onto his life tenaciously, surviving for years after the doctors said he should have been dead.

He refused to die. If he was going to die he would die in his own way and in his own time. No one was going to tell him when or how to die. For years he was kept alive by inhaling oxygen through a tube in his nose. At the same time he continued to chain-smoke the cigarettes that were killing him. It was a wonder he did not explode.

The old rancher was as ornery and stubborn as the

high mountains he loved. His father had been a country lawyer on the Western slope of the Rocky Mountains of Colorado. And he, too, had a lawyer's tongue.

Mountain politics were in his bones and blood. But it was the politics of the old populism, which were giving way to new politics of the West. The eye-to-eye politics of his beloved mountains were the politics of village gatherings, county commissions and rural ditch committees. His brand of politics did not operate in committee rooms but instead was fought out around the huge round table in the kitchen of his ranch house. There he presided like an old-fashioned *patrón* (Hispanic political boss), telling endless "shaggy village" stories that enforced ancestral laws. And he fought for every lost cause he could find. It was the battle he loved as much as the victory. He loved a good fight.

In the village a neighbor said, "He is his own man." "Nobody owns him," said another. He was as independent as the mountains.

The old-timer knew that the old times were dead and that he soon would be, too. Nonetheless, he fought down to the wire and conceded nothing to death, for nothing could ever conquer the mountains of the West. Or him.

One night, late, before he died, he and an old friend were sitting around the table in his kitchen resolving the problems of his mountain valley and the world when he suddenly stood up and walked out of his ranch house and into the night. After a few moments he returned and was asked where he had gone.

"To piss," he said.

"Why don't you use the toilet in the ranch house?" he was asked.

And with a mischievous smile in his eyes he solemnly

replied, "If the time ever comes when a man can't go out on his own land and piss at the moon, New Mexico is dead!"

Oh, bury me, baby, in the lone
parking lot of the K Mart,
Where the tourists and land
developers roam free—

The old saying was: "Anyone who had come to town the day after you had was a newcomer and anyone who had come to town the day before you had was an old-timer, and anyone who was a newcomer yesterday would be an old-timer tomorrow if he stayed over."

The newcomer and the old-timer were the same person in the Old West because historians had not yet separated them into the past and the present. No one had become a footnote buried in the history books. In the early days old-timers were living history who walked the streets of all the small towns of the West. As an old-timer mused, "I may be dead but no one bothered to tell me. So I keep on living."

Not so long ago, no more than about seventy years ago, the *Frontier Times* published an appeal to old-timers to RESCUE HISTORY—their memories—before they died. The notice read: "We are glad to receive reminiscent sketches from old frontiersmen and we urge that every old pioneer send in his recollections, write in your own style and if we find it necessary we will cheerfully correct all grammatical errors. Send us your history."

Of those forgotten old-timers who responded to the plea in that January 1925 issue of the magazine, many were eighty, ninety and over a hundred years of age. That so many "old frontiersmen" and "old pioneers" were still alive was amazing. Not only were they tough and strong old folk, but they had survived their own lives, no small feat of endurance in the Old West.

These old-timers sat on their front porches or on the wooden benches before the county courthouse and peered with squinting and judicious eyes at the townspeople that passed by on the sidewalk. In the old days every small town had its old-timers who sat in judgment upon it to see if its present lived up to its past. It seldom did.

"Not that the old'n days were any better. But the people were," an old-time newspaper editor in Nevada said. "Folks were quieter."

In silence they measured the passage of time. The old-timers were the grandfathers and grandmothers of the small towns, a silent Greek chorus that eyed the empty stores on Main Street and the new popular fast-food franchises on the highway with equal scorn.

The small towns needed these old-timers. Not only did they foretell the coming of the seasons, they were their towns' historians, giving their communities the feeling of a continuity with the past and a sense of belonging to the present. Every town was proud of its old-timers and boasted of their age and agelessness, as though their wisdom had come with their years. In some ways the old-timers were like the elders of an Indian tribe.

"An old-timer? That's a fellow that's got a memory so good that he remembers things that never happened to him," an aging cowboy said, laughing.

More recently, the wisdom of the old-timers has become the oral history of scholars. Their knowledge of the past has become folklore that seems of little practical use to the New West except as exotic and folksy nostalgia.

One old-timer scoffed, "That oral history sounds to

me like some kind of social disease. It's like a hoof-in-the-mouth disease that cows used to get. The cows are lucky they can't talk."

The memories of these old-timers have become as suspect as their factual accuracy. But old-timers are storytellers, not scholarly historians. In their fantasies and fables they are creative artists, and their tall tales and exaggerations are an "art that lies like the truth," for they improve on reality.

"If God didn't want for us to use our imaginations, He wouldn't of given it us," one old-timer said.

No personal history was more objective than the diaries and journals from the old days. They had a quality of literature that was fitting to the Old West, where folklore was a way of life, a native art form that went with the territory; it was larger than life.

"Once a man cuts a folktale down to a realistic size he's lost its power to surprise. It's got to be a convincing lie," a storyteller in Montana said. "If you want the facts go and buy a computer." Then he grimaced. "They are too dumb to lie."

An old-timer was once asked why he told such lies. He knew his stories weren't true. Why couldn't he stick to the facts? The old man thought about it for some time and smiled.

"Cows is pretty boring," he said, "if you don't exaggerate its tits a little bit."

The way the old-timer preserved the past was very different from the methodology of historians. The old-timer remembered it. He did not write it down, analyze it, research it, verify it with a footnote. Even if it had happened generations ago he remembered it as if it had happened yesterday. The old-timer told the story as though he had been there. He did not remember and repeat it as his father and his grandfather had told it to him; he told it as he thought it might have, or should have, been. In his own words he elaborated and exaggerated their words.

"Hell, I don't make it up," said an old-timer, grinning. "I just *improve* on it." "A little imagination never hurt anyone," he said.

The memories of the old-timers were "half-historical, half-legendary," wrote Frank Dobie, the Texas folklorist. But they were also half-wishful thinking. First among them were legends of buried treasure, which gradually gave way to legends of lovers, of lovers' leaps and lovers' ghosts, the latter often supernatural tales of seductive, mysterious women who appeared with the "midnight music" of the lonely prairies.

The legends of the gunmen and lawmen came later. In the early days the legends were as romantic as the men who told them. But with the coming of settled towns and the appearance of gunmen and lawmen, the romantic legends of women all but disappeared in the West. The gunfighter replaced the lover. The "midnight music" was shattered and silenced by gunfire. The romance of the West gave way to its conquest.

Not that men consciously knew what they were doing. They did not. It was rather the necessity of equality—in their sharing of work and of beliefs—on the covered wagon trains giving way in the fledgling towns to the older, more traditional roles that these settlers had brought with them from East to West. The old ways persisted. But the memories of equality that developed on the wagon trains lingered in the minds of these men. And so they reshaped it into the adoration of women, the "pioneer mothers," whose statues to this day dominate many a town square in the West. Curiously, there are no statues of "pioneer fathers."

And yet, the old-timers almost always have been portrayed as men. Until recently, in fact, the deeds and words of women had been forgotten or ignored, as if women had not existed in the Old West. Nor was there a siren song of "midnight music."

More often than their men, women remembered and wrote about their family and community, about how people lived and survived by those little acts of heroism in their home that made life more humane. On the other hand, men seemed to remember, if not prefer, their memories of real or imagined gunfights and battles with Indians. Men rarely wrote about family life, and even less often about their wives.

One woman old-timer recalled that "folks in those days were real friends. I had a spell of typhoid-pneumonia and old man McAdam and his wife took me and my children in their home and cared for us. He hired the threshers and fed them and never charged me a cent.

"That's the way everyone did," she added. One's neighbors were "like family."

"Most of our homes were made of logs. There were no windows of glass," another woman old-timer remembered. Then she vividly described her own lonely world and that of her community. "We cooked on an open fire in huge iron pots . . . and a woman needed no rouge to render her complexion in a carmine shade. . . . Our candles were manufactured at home by first killing a beef for tallow. . . . Our soap was made at home from lye from wood ashes. . . . I made my husband an entire suit from cloth that I wove by hand, as I had no sewing machine. We had no luxuries. . . .

"And I marvel when I now look back and wonder how I did it," said the old woman.

The source of her endurance was that she was not alone. On the frontier, she said, "We all were like one family, a neighbor was a real friend and whatever we had we were willing to share with those folks less fortunate."

On the earth that was parched and sparse, the old-timers were proud of their endurance. The hardships they faced and overcame toughened and strengthened them. Of course, they boasted of these obstacles, exaggerated and celebrated them nearly as much as they did their triumph over these obstacles. They had an obstinate pride in their ability to suffer adversity and did so with a shrug of their shoulders. And few of them complained; it was thought to be unmanly and unwomanly, a sign of moral weakness.

Instead, they endured hardships in silence. The old-timers were people of "the finest type, good and strong" men and women, as one settler remembered, who "hadn't the time to get sick, because it was too far to the doctor, being forty miles distant."

One old-timer, a rodeo cowboy, personified this attitude. In a state fair rodeo he was thrown by a bull that stomped on him and nearly crushed him to death. The morning after a newspaper reporter came to interview him as he lay wrapped in bandages like a mummy.

"Tell me, how're you feeling today?" the reporter asked.

Lying on his hospital bed the cowboy grinned, or winced. It was hard to tell. "Well, I guess I broke darn near every bone in my body," he said through the bandages.

"But it don't hurt much," he added, trying to laugh.

The men and women of the old days suffered their hardships as a matter of belief. And pride. It was a face-to-face struggle with nature that made them feel they were part of nature. Few of these old-timers would cry out with pain, in public, any more than the earth and the stone would have done.

If the old-timers often talked of "makin' do" by their

own hand it might have been because there were so many things they *had* to make by hand. Most general stores were a long journey away, by wagon, and even then there were few "store-bought goods to be had between the coming of the trains." Most things had to be homemade out of necessity, not out of any philosophy of a "work ethic."

Not that the old-timers were opposed to machine-made things. But they were suspicious about the effect store-bought things might have in dulling and diminishing the senses if men depended on them rather than their own spiritual and physical resources.

One old-timer sadly recalled, "In those days a man had to have good hearing. He had to have good eyes. Now you have to use a flashlight to find your hat at home."

Nowadays, he continued, "the young do not realize the deprivation that old-timers endured, and I fear the present generation will not leave civilization as good as they found it. The new age has pushed the pioneers aside. As to civilization—we know it from the tallow candles to electicity and from the ox cart to the automobiles."

"Our frontier passed away," he lamented, because these newcomers cannot survive the hardships of the old-timers.

Each past generation of old-timers thought that it would be the last. In mourning their way of life they lamented their passing with eloquent eulogies, as if the newcomers would never become old-timers.

An old Montana rancher voiced his sadness angrily, as many old-timers had done before him. His words sound more like a threat than a plea: "We are going to be the last generation of Western men!" he bristled. "When we die, America dies."

Even so, similar announcements of the old-timers' mortality and demise were premature. Ironically, the old-timers survived in part because of the revival of the Old West's way of life by the New West; the newcomers were strengthened by the memory of the old-timers. The past was the present and the present was the past. In the old-timers' survival, the Old West was like a newborn infant, adopted by each succeeding generation. It was a blessing and a curse. Modern machinery made life easier, if not better, but was still greeted with a mixture of enthusiasm and suspicion. Nevertheless, the machinery brought by the urban Easterner always fascinated the rural Westerner.

"Lord created machines," said a Dakota farmer, "but He don't do no repairs."

None of those mechanical wonders brought from the East into the West had as profound an effect upon the old-timers as did the coming of the railroads. The "iron horse" opened the West to manufactured goods and city ways, and the economic influence of the railroads forever changed the rural isolation of the small towns and farms. But they did more than change the way of life of the old-timers. They also changed his character. He was no longer the loner, the man on horseback, the individualist who was dependent on himself, that self-reliant pioneer on the frontier who created the West in his own self-made image.

Benjamin Taylor, in his book *The World on Wheels*, written in 1874, described the old-timer as "quiet, civil, self-reliant." He was "peripatetical to the Bill of Rights. He was his own Legislature," Taylor wrote. "He is at home on horseback. He is at home anywhere. . . . He gives the stranger a square look with both his eyes.

"There you have him and *isn't* he cool," concluded Taylor.

As the interstate highway was to do generations later, the railroad changed the old-timer socially and physically. The passing of the horse and buggy and the stagecoach was the symbol not only of the new way of life but of a new way of looking at life as well. For the old ways were dying. On a stagecoach the old-timers had sat facing one another. The passengers rubbed their knees and shoulders together. Even strangers got to know "each other well" after a single trip. Taylor wrote: "Fifty miles [of] battering in a stagecoach used to shake people out of their shell [and made] more life-long friends than a 5,000 mile voyage by rail."

On the train, on the other hand, all the passengers could see was the back of the head of the person in front of them. It was as friendly as "contemplating the bumps of compativeness" on their heads, a sight "as merry as a catacomb and about as conducive to friendship," Taylor wrote. No one could talk to the back of someone's head. Passengers remained strangers as distant from one another as the countryside that passed before their eyes.

The coming of automobiles and interstate highways increased the isolation of travelers from one another. Any human contact seemed more distant still. On the plains and in the mountains the convenience of modern means of transportation was welcomed with uncertainity and unease. In fact, some of the more obstinate counties in the West refused to accept federal highway funds. One interstate highway ended at a county line. There was another that ended in a cornfield.

Old-timers distrusted the highways even after they were built. In Arizona, the Cattlemen's Association and Farm Bureau printed a little booklet titled *Corralling A Problem; Cattle and the Interstate Highways* to reassure ranchers that there would be under and overpasses, exit ramps and cloverleafs, to facilitate the safe passage of their cows from one pasture to another.

And yet, the old-timers were not convinced. Nor were their cows. The new-fangled highways were like old-fashioned barbed wire fences.

In Lordsburg, New Mexico, an old-timer, a woman rancher, decided to protest the building of a highway exit ramp in her cow pasture. She built a wooden hut in the path of the highway bulldozers and halted the construction of the interstate. "My cows don't need any exit ramps," she said. "Exit ramps! Not on my pasture, by God!"

She guarded her cows' pasture with a shotgun. It was as though she had walked out of the Old West with gun in hand and stopped the interstate and personally held up the highway's bulldozers face-to-face. The newspapers called her "the Little Old Lady Billy the Kid."

"I haven't done anything any self-respecting rancher wouldn't have done in my place," she sweetly said. "My cows got rights."

The highway that went nowhere was oddly silent. Its bulldozers and highway machinery stood still, immobilized by the old woman who sat in her hut with her shotgun across her lap. Nothing stirred but the desert breeze. Her ranch was in the nearby ghost town of Shakespeare, where the stagecoach from Lordsburg to Silver City once stopped. Now, she was riding shotgun, at least in her mind, upon the abandoned stagecoach sitting on the front porch of the old general store of the ghost-town ranch. The stagecoach was one of the Overland stages that went into Silver City in the days of Billy the Kid.

The local sheriff was dispatched to disarm the old

woman and end her solitary vigil. He obeyed reluctantly. It embarrassed him, the sheriff said, to have to arrest the old woman and force her to leave her own land. But he had to. She had broken the law by halting the interstate. He had no choice but to arrest her.

She wept in anger. The bulldozers tore down her hut. And the building of the highway began again as if nothing had happened. The exit ramp into the cows' pasture became famous throughout the county.

Not long after her arrest the old woman died. They buried her near her ghost-town ranch.

The sagebrush on the banks of the River Jordan had not changed in a hundred and fifty years.

In a remote valley near the Idaho border with Oregon, the family settled in a land so empty that there were hardly any Indians. The land was too hard. The water was too scarce. The weather was too harsh. The ranching was too poor. But the family survived.

On the lawn of the new, modern ranch house, with its picture windows, color television and electronic kitchen, there was a shrine to the old-timers.

It was the old sod house that their pioneer ancestors had built on the barren land. Earth brick by earth brick, stone by stone, blade of grass by blade of grass, they had moved the ancestral sod house onto their lawn and rebuilt it as if they were reconstructing their history.

And why did they do it?

"To remind us of who we were," the old-time rancher said. "So we don't forget."

LEGENDS
OF THE PAST

TESTIMONIAL BY
REX BUNDY

Old Rex Bundy was a "real man," he liked to say of himself, and "damned independent." He was right on both accounts. In spite of his gruff voice, his mean demeanor, his fierce orneryness, his magnificent curses, his piercing eagle-like eyes, his unshaven stubble and his defiant Wild Bill Hickok mustache, he was, secretly, a gentle man with a soft heart. Still, he successfully hid his tenderness as best he could. Few people saw through his disguise.

One of the last of those old-time cowboys, Rex was proud of his manhood. Before he died he had several heart attacks and strokes, but they could not kill him. He shook them off and pretended they had not happened. Not to him.

After his first heart attack he was asked what he intended to do. "Go fishing," he said. The doctors told him he ought to jog or run or walk. He snorted at the thought and blew the snot out of his nose. "I can hardly walk to the garden gate," he scoffed. "Walk! Cowboys don't walk. They ride."

In his youth he had been a cowboy, both a working and rodeo cowboy, and he knew the difference. Back in the 1920s, "You got a dollar for a bareback ride," he remembered, "if you stayed on the horse." As a "dumb cowboy" he worked at any job "where all that you needed was a strong back. And a weak mind."

That was why he became a writer, he said: it was easier than working with cows.

That and, the way he told it, because he got sick and tired of writing about the West that "didn't have a lick of truth in it." His friend, the Montana novelist A. B. Guthrie, told him to quit bellyaching about all the lies that bothered him in writing about the West and "write the truth himself."

And so he did.

REX BUNDY:

My God! I wasn't dumb enough to go West. I had no choice. I was born here.

Back East they don't know what the West was. If a story isn't about Wyatt Burp or Will Bill Hiccup those Eastern publishers aren't interested. They got the idea that the West was, and is, full of Indians, buffalo and outlaws. And it isn't safe to cross the Mississippi.

All I can say is that they read too many goddamned wild-and-woolly stereotyped books about the West. I have read some goddamned dillies.

And in the movies they got so poor a concept of the

West that it amazes them to see a concrete highway out here. Cours' it amazes the hell out of me, too.

And I can never understand why the American people hero-worship these crooks! You take outlaws, these Western outlaws. By far, more is written about them than the peace officers. There is a Western writer and I who're pretty good friends, but I accused him of it. Every time he found out Jesse James had another hangnail he wrote another story about it. And he said, "Goddamn it! I get paid for it!"

There are thousands and thousands of plots for books where they could tell what happened in the West realistically, as it actually happened. But people like to read these shoot'em-ups. Now I don't know what their conception of the West is, the people from the East.

Now, I was writing a story of Liver Eating Johnson. You've seen that movie, *Jeremiah Johnson*, with Robert Redford, who was supposed to be Liver Eating Johnson. No connection whatsoever between the two of them. I don't know where they come up with this Jeremiah Johnson. I can find no trace of him in Montana. At any time. The guy who was called Liver Eating Johnson, he jumped ship in 1860 in San Francisco and he came out here. He never married a Crow. He never killed a Crow. He never ate a liver.

Who was the guy who wrote that *Liver Eating Johnson: The Crow Killer*? That was the goddamndest mess I ever read. And I researched it and researched it. It never happened.

The way he got his name was over there on the Musselshell River. Whites killed some Indians. Some Sioux. And he pretended he was eating one, and the only reason he did that was that the guy who was with him at the time

42

was only nineteen and he knew that would make the kid sick. I got a letter he wrote, or had someone write for him, to the *St. Paul Pioneer Press* in which he stated he never had an Indian wife, that he'd never eaten an Indian liver and that he'd never killed a Crow Indian.

One time I got into quite an argument with a historian about that. I told him flatly that Johnson never had an Indian wife, never killed a Crow Indian and he never had eaten an Indian liver, and I had a letter to prove it. In fact, he didn't even eat game liver. He didn't *like* liver!

Now that Johnson, he had lived right over here at Lodge for years. He raised cabbage on an island in the Yellowstone River. And one time the farmer took his cabbages to town to sell them and they offered him a cent a pound, but, by God, he'd dump them in the Yellowstone River before he'd sell them at one cent a pound. He'd sweated over those cabbages all summer long.

And so he hauled them down and dumped them cabbages in the Yellowstone River. And some guy will write a wild fantasy about that.

Maybe not. I guess riding herd on a cabbage patch isn't very heroic. Or is it?

MAN COMES
FROM THE SOIL

❖

TESTIMONIAL BY
LOU ATTEBERY

On the Boise River near where it and the Owyee River enter the Snake, just across the state line from Oregon, is the town of Caldwell, the "Potato Capital" of Idaho. It is a down-to-earth town, as you would expect of a town that depends for its survival on growing potatoes and other crops. The urban sprawl that has been spreading across the West has not come to Caldwell. Not yet.

People in Caldwell are close to the earth, Lou Attebery says. And he is right.

The son of an Idaho stockman-farmer, Attebery embodies the sense of not only being dependent on the land, but of being part of the land, of America itself. And that feeling lingers in the minds of the town's people, though they may now live in suburban homes and shop in the nearby shopping centers built on the ranchlands of their ancestors.

A modest, soft-spoken and shy man, Lou Attebery is a professor of folklore and literature at the College of Idaho. His quiet manner, however, disguises his strong belief in the spirit of the land that shaped the Westerners and made them unique.

LOU ATTEBERY:

Man comes from the soil. The human body, when reduced to its ashy components, is pretty much earth. And man is made of the same stuff that the earth is made of. There ought to be a resonance between man and the earth. It is physical and metaphysical. There is something in man that is metaphysical.

Man is like a clod of earth; but he is different. He is like a rock; but he is different. He has a soul, and that transcends the purely physical.

And I think these things are fairly consistent with Thomas Jefferson's idea of the yeoman farmer, the man who, working with the land, was a partner in a happy marriage. By marriage I mean—and this is going to sound incestuous—that man is happiest tilling his mother earth. Perhaps it would be best just to say, a happy partnership between man and the soil.

So, I am not sure that the great myth of Eden doesn't have in it a lesson for the ages. Everything man needs, certainly for his physical life and for much of his spiritual life, is right here on the earth. Food. Shelter. Clothing. If he takes care of it.

45

The earth, in this sense, is the Garden of Eden. And when man violates it, violates his partnership with the soil, he is going to be eliminated. He will eliminate himself.

In that sense, I would like to say something about ranching as a way of life: Even though ranchers may not begin their declamations about why they stay on the ranch by talking of their way of life, everyone of them, when they get down to it, says this is what keeps them on the ranch. Sometimes they use these very words, *a way of life*, but they just slip out unconsciously.

And I really think it is time that the case was made for ranching as an authentic way of life. Maybe it is the only one there is in this country.

"By way of life" I don't mean things like law or medicine or teaching or motorcycling or skiing or surfboarding. I don't even mean the "American way of life," which is a way people describe our democracy, or free-enterprise system. The corporate existence is not a way of life; it's a way of making money and exerting power, but it isn't a way of life. Banking certainly is not a way of life. By way of life I mean the agrarian impulse in this country.

Ranching as a way of life makes a total demand on the person who lives it. And it's the only calling, besides farming, where the person who lives it lives where he works, with his work, twenty-four hours a day. The miner doesn't live in the mine, the pilot in his plane, the banker in his bank. I don't know how many times I hear ranchers say, "There's work here for beyond my lifetime, long after I'm gone." And that's because ranching demands the total emotional and intellectual energies of the person who lives it.

And yet, if ranchers had their druthers, they'd rather be ranching than doing anything else. They do have the kind of freedom that often accompanies necessity. They have that satisfaction.

These things, too, are fairly consistent with Thomas Jefferson's idea. Of the spirit of independence. Of doing for oneself. Of self-reliance.

I seem to remember it was Aristotle who said: "For the best material of democracy is an agricultural population." There is no difficulty in forming a democracy if the mass of people live by agriculture and the tending of cattle.

THE
COVERED WAGON
IN THE BARN

TESTIMONIAL BY
HOWARD R. LAMAR

The spires poke through the Connecticut mist. They seem to be the offshoots of a Gothic castle gray with the salty patina from sea and harbor. On the campus of Yale University, the seemingly ancient buildings are elegant imitations of the past, the bastions not of knights but of scholars residing in a fantasy world of reconstructed history.

But they are fakes.

Seen more closely, the buildings appear to be a mixture of Medieval and Gothic styles. The ivy-covered walls offer a *brooding and somber countenance that does not entirely silence the campus but hushes its more youthful enthusiasms.*

Here, in his office, Dean Howard Lamar presided over Yale University with a judicious eye, balancing the worlds of academia and contemporary America, for this dean is neither a scholarly monk nor a Don Quixote of knowledge. He is, first and foremost, an historian of the American West.

It is not easy to imagine Howard Lamar amid the cow manure on the ranch of his friend Peter Decker, who lives on Colorado's Western Slope of the Rockies. But he is no armchair historian. Lamar does not merely delight in the vast horizons of the West; he also knows the earthy hardships of ranch life.

As a scholar of Western history, Lamar has been president of the Western History Association. In 1985, he completed a six-year term as Dean of Yale. He is now the Sterling Professor of History. He is also the author of The Far Southwest *and* Dakota Territory, *and has served as editor of* The Encyclopedia of the American West.

He has not only studied the Old and New Wests. He has also, as they say, gotten his boots dirty.

HOWARD R. LAMAR:

My first trip West was in 1947. I caught a ride with some North Dakotans who went on and toured parts of Montana. Up a little mountain road they found a log cabin in an isolated area where there was a family who had gone there in 1912 in a covered wagon. They simply had not come out again. They had lived undisturbed through World War I, and in World War II they registered their sons, but did not send them off.

49

And their covered wagon was still in the barn.

That kind of ability to be able to stand still, a timelessness that Willa Cather caught in New Mexico, fascinates 'us about the West. That kind of ability to build a Shangri-la and survive in it is an extraordinary achievement that few people could accomplish.

It seems to me this is the jack-of-all-trades quality that we see in Benjamin Franklin and Daniel Boone and Davy Crockett. The quality of self-sufficiency, the ability to do everything alone. All of this suggests that a man in the West realized himself through the necessities of life. In this, he can understand not merely himself better, but everybody else as well.

These are people with a certain perspective on our country. These are people with horse sense about our country. These are people with the real energy that drives our country. These are real Westerners.

And so it is refreshing to hear somebody say, "Down with electricity!" One is reminded of the Southern lady who said she refused to vote because, "It only encourages them!" And this attitude is becoming more evident in America every day. These people are getting tired of being controlled by computers, contraptions, rules, monthly bills and technology. These people want to be free. But this is not a Luddite resistance. It is a placing of things in perspective so that people are not ruled by things that are not of their own making. From that comes a kind of possessiveness about the land and a sense of character that outsiders have admired without knowing how that feeling came about.

It is that understanding of the real nature of the land and that sense of place that gives Westerners an edge on the rest of the population. For they have engaged in an essential confrontation with the spirit of America that they, and we, have never forgotten.

Yes, the pioneers wanted to be helped by the government, but as their handmaiden, not as their boss. Indeed, that was the older role of the government in the development of the country westward to the Mississippi River, and later to the west of the river.

And that reminds me of a theme I think we do not fully appreciate: There are people in the West who we associate with large ranching empires and a rugged independence, who looked like the kings of everything around them, but who were actually the *managers* of cattle companies, not the real owners. It was rugged individualism in a business context.

Those were the "good old days" of isolation when people got together with a sense of community. But that was destroyed by the coming of roads and automobiles. In that sense, technology was a kind of destroyer of communities.

Here was a profound thing. The ability to move about so easily made the Westerner a wanderer in his own land. Once, cowboys were known as drifters. The West was famous for its mobility. But in the old days the pace of life was slow enough so that people could build new communities that could not be destroyed as easily as they are today.

There is an invisible community in the West that is often unseen by those who see only the wide-open spaces. It still exists.

PART II

❖

MANHOOD, ROMANCE AND THE MYTH OF THE WEST

Most of our cherished images of the West are masculine—worn leather saddles, wide-brimmed hats with drenched sweatbands, dirt-covered, shit-kickin' boots and blazing guns. But Stan Steiner always treaded beyond the superficial trappings of the West to find out what was in the hearts and minds of the real men and women of the West.

Stan loved the contradictions and ironies of life in the West. He was fascinated by the paradox of the independent man who rides into the sunset and the steadfast woman who provided a foundation for the maintenance and development of community life. He was equally intrigued by the merging of contrasting cultures as native groups came into contact with newcomers from the East.

He found that most of our ideas about Western masculinity were based on myth, fantasy and romantic images. In his quest to understand the manhood of the

West, what emerged was not only a tough, independent male but also a strong female who provided a sense of courage and a yearning for stability. He discovered this strength in the indigenous people, the Native American and Hispanic women of the West, as well as in the Eastern women who traveled across the country to start new lives.

Stan struggled for many years to come to terms with the issues of male and female strengths. For that reason he began working on a book on manhood in 1982, but was unable to get it published. His wife, Vera John-Steiner, thought that part of his difficulty was that he began the book too early: It was a time when male voices were not yet being sought out in the rethinking of gender roles. (Stan was often identified as a specialist on minorities but was unrecognized for his interest in masculine and feminine roles.)

Personally, he always believed that there was a profound connection between Western and gender issues. He thought the exploration of what it was like to be a man or woman in the early years of the frontier West would provide insights into contemporary male and female interactions. During the last year of his life, Steiner, with his wife, co-taught a course at the University of New Mexico titled "Male and Female: the Continuing Dialogue." That, along with a course he taught on cowboy culture, provided him with ongoing exchanges with students. The first two chapters of this section, "The Frontierswoman's Man" and "Love in a Covered Wagon" are from writings that resulted from those experiences.

The creation of a mythology about the West in films

and literature also fascinated Stan. In the spring of 1981, he was a participant in a symposium at a Western film festival in Santa Fe. He loved the idea of film stars, scholars and real cowboys convening to discuss the West face-to-face. The chapter "Real Horses and Mythic Riders," first published in the September/October 1981 issue of *American West* magazine, resulted from that exchange.

The myth and romance of the West is not strictly American, having developed a global appeal. In his chapter "The Global Cowboy," Stan looked at the international images of the West and cowboy culture. For those whose lives are steeped in European or Oriental tradition, the idea of the American West offers an alternative. It represents the opportunity to be free and independent. The son of European emigrants himself, Stan grew up immersed in the Viennese society of his elders in New York and was often torn between his own prim European upbringing and the more feral alternatives of the American West. Eventually, he felt that to become a true, native son of America, it was essential to combine his past with the present. For him, going West provided that. It intrigued him how the West also provided this for others.

Stan's final chapter in this section, "Space Cowboys: Notes on the Cosmic Cowboys," was written in 1984 for *Across the Board*. It's fitting that this piece be included within a section on manhood, for it examines further some of the issues that were raised in Tom Wolfe's book *The Right Stuff*. In light of the tragic explosion of the *Challenger*, some of the material will seem dated. Yet our country's continued fascination with new frontiers draws much of its inspiration from the ideals of the Western frontier.

Perhaps the pendulum has swung once again, however. After a barrage of space epics in the late '70s and early '80s and the almost total disappearance of the Western film genre, we're now seeing the Western come back into its own with the popularity of films such as *Silverado, Lonesome Dove* and *Young Guns*. At the same time, men continue to relate to the manhood of the West by donning Ralph Lauren's line of Western apparel and splashing on Santa Fe cologne. Of course, as Stan knew, it's never been the clothes that make the real men and women of the West, but an inner strength and spirit that can't be bought in department stores.

LOVE IN A
COVERED WAGON

❖

"Our grandfathers had a species of indomitable directness in making roads and making love. . . ."

That masculine boast was made by Benjamin Taylor,
the son of covered wagon–train pioneers. He proudly remembered: "They did not believe in the line of beauty.
They went by the square and compass." In building highways and marriages they went "straight over the hill and
through the big timber—and plump into the swamp."

"Making roads and making love . . ." The nature of
manhood described by this grandson of pioneers told as
much about his attitude toward feminine and manly love as
it did about his grandfathers.

On the covered wagon trains the men and women were
expected to follow the straight and narrow path of necessity.
It was a difficult enough journey without the luxury of excess
emotional baggage. The life was tough and cruel. And

though the settlers often brought the puritanism of New England with them, it evolved into a religion more concerned with day-to-day survival than sin. The pioneer practices a practical puritanism, and he reshaped it to fit his day-to-day needs. Even love in a crowded covered wagon had to adapt to what Ralph Waldo Emerson had called "the useful good."

On the trail men suffered hardships and endured pains they never had experienced back East as schoolteachers, clerks or small-town farmers. It both hardened and weakened them. And, as their wives sadly noted in endless diary entries, the deprivations and humiliations of the journey seemed to be more traumatic for the men than the women.

As if to protect themselves, men adopted a new image of manhood; it was tough, vigorous and taciturn. They were influenced, in many ways, by the behavior of the Indian men whom they met, and imitated. Romance, to the pioneer man, might have seemed a sign of vulnerability. And the frailty of passion might have seemed an indulgence amid the austerity of life in a covered wagon, where starvation and thirst threatened everyday life.

Not that there was no romance in the covered wagons or settlers' camps. But it had to be muted and hidden from sight in those small-town societies on wheels, where one's private life and almost everything else was shared. The fact was, there was little privacy available for passion on the trail.

There was also a shortage of space. In the covered wagon a family stored all its possessions, from its furniture and household pets to children and chickens. The prairie schooners were like the Biblical "ark of old," said John Greenleaf Whittier; they transported "the truth of God" to "make the West as the East," and that, understandably, led to some overcrowding.

Evenings, the covered wagons often formed a circle so that man and wife might sleep alone—under a blanket on the ground. The circle of wagons was less for protection against curious Indians than for the protection of marital harmony and loving.

On the open and endless horizons of the West the pioneer men and women were probably more closely crowded together than they had been on their farms and in their towns back East. Each covered wagon had "to sleep a small family" for many months, as J. M. Shively recalled of his trek across the Oregon Trail in 1846. For "the emmigrant caravans creeping on their slow procession" moved "inch by inch," as historian Francis Parkman wrote in 1849 in *The Oregon Trail*, and the crowded conditions only could be survived by the muting of emotions and subduing of passions.

Romance on the wagon trail may have survived the journey but not likely the confines of these "schooners" of the prairie. The wagons were not only as plodding and clumsy as the oxen who pulled them, but also were unromantic and as foul-smelling as the cloven beasts. And men seldom rode in or drove the wagons; that was considered to be "women's work."

The sod huts and log cabins the pioneers built at the end of their journey were no better. In a prairie home "the sleeping arrangements [were] of a somewhat perplexing character," was the laconic comment of William Fowler in *Woman on the Frontier*, in the late nineteenth century. Few had a private bed. And husband and wife often "had to repose on the floor, with buffalo robes for pillows and with their feet toward the fire," while the children "played like kittens" in their communal bed. In the corner of the room stood the family cow, several dogs and perhaps a prize sow. Managing such a one-room household, the pioneer mother was soon as "thin as a shadow, pinched and wrinkled by hard labor," wrote Fowler—and perhaps by lack of sleep.

"The plainness of the habitation" of these pioneer men and women was more than a way of life; it became a moral code. Plainness of behavior "was suited" to the frontier and became "the costume of women"; they wore clothes of "homespun, linsey-woolsey and buckskin," not only because, often, that was all they had, but also as a matter of principle. The woman in a sod hut and log cabin was not "a doll to carry silks and jewels, not a puppet to be dandied by fobs, an idol of profane adoration"; she was "useful," wrote Fowler.

The men behaved with the same plainness as did the women, creating a manner of laid-back courtship and romance that reflected and expressed the austere life they lived on the frontier.

Plainness became a religion on the frontier. The austerity of daily life resulted in a philosophy in which poverty became a virtue and modesty became the measure of morality. "It is the iron band of poverty, of necessity, of austerity, which excluded them [the settlers] from sensual enjoyment," wrote Ralph Waldo Emerson in *Society and Solitude*. It also made them, "despite themselves, reverers of the grand, the beautiful, the good."

There was a touch of shame, Emerson said, in enjoying the sensual pleasures of love and wealth. In his belief in the virtue of self-reliance there was an element of self-denial; for poverty was "a miracle" of democracy that led to living the "heroic life." Besides, our country's wealth came from our poverty, not from our inheritance. So, he concluded, "Let us build altars to beautiful necessity."

For all that, these were robust and lusty men and women. The crossing of a continent and the settling of an unknown and frightening land could not have been done by timid souls. If their plainness and modest behavior was forced upon them by frontier society, it hid a flamboyant individualism and a quietly arrogant sense of self-confidence.

The plain men and women on the frontier were bold, daring, adventurous, passionate, strong-willed, determined and conceited. If they were to survive, they had to be. And in living as close to the earth as they did, as though they were married to it, they became as earthy and sensual a people as the earth itself.

On coming home to the East from a journey "through the garden of the West," an ecstatic Walt Whitman, that "singer of Adamic songs," as he called himself, was so enthused by the rigorous masculinity he found in the West that he depicted it by "singing [to] the Phallus." On the prairies, he said, men became "lusty, phallic, with potent original loins," and he celebrated their manhood "by bathing my songs in [the] sex" of the frontier.

As for the women on the frontier, the Old Gray Bard from Long Island envisioned them as Eves who had "return[ed] to paradise." In "Ma Femme," the poet lovingly named the land "My Woman," and claimed that it taught the settlers "robust American love."

Nonetheless, love in the West was the creation of pioneer men and women who worked together. The bonds of love were those of survival for both; and they were strengthened by the perils that threatened both. As Fowler wrote of the wilderness, it "is a scene where love springs out of [that] close companionship which danger enforces."

If the puritan way of life on the frontier muted and subdued passions, it intensified them at the same time. As a result, there arose two very different, if not opposed, ways of looking at love in the West. One was as romantic as the other was laid-back, bold as the other was timid, as openly passionate as the other was quietly embarrassed, and as feminine as the other was masculine. Both were as uniquely Western as the frontier.

No wonder Emerson was unnerved by the "excess of virility" that he sensed in frontiersmen and women. The sensuality of the earth permeated the settlers' lives.

The settlers in the West and the original colonists in the East had that in common. For the physical limitations imposed by the austere wilderness were more than equalled by "the freedom to be discovered" there. In going West the pioneers found a way of life that was as free as the East once had been, and was free of what the East had become.

In the West, on the other hand, the settlers sought and found that sense of freedom once again. It was the rediscovery of America—for them, an America even farther from the shores of Europe and therefore more American: "the most American part of America," Lord Bryce called it, because the land was most beautifully preserved in its native freedom by the native people, the Indians, and here men and women were freed once more of European constraint.

In New England the passions of the colonists may have been outwardly muted by their Puritan patriarchs, but they were not wholly exorcised. The spirit of the land could not be entirely subdued. Not even the orderly theology of Salem and Boston could completely suppress the vigor and vitality of those earlier, earthier pioneers.

So bawdy and ribald were the early colonists, in fact, that one year after the *Mayflower* had landed, Sir Georges arose in the English House of Commons to condemn the "licentious" acts of the New England Puritans, who, he said, were "in manners and behavior worse than the very Savages, impudently and openly lying with the [native] women," and who were "teaching the men to drinke drunke." The Puritan "Saints," said William Byrd sarcastically, "as Jews of old [were] drawn into idolatory by Strange women."

The colonial dames and daughters of the American Revolution were as open and direct in their passion as the men, wrote Alice Morse Earle in *Colonial Dames and Good Wives*. "Consorts and Relicts," she called these colonial women, who behaved like "Double-Tongued and Naughty Women." From the time the first shiploads of English wives arrived, "Oh, what a glorious and all abounding courting and mating time was straight away begun."

And if these colonial women were unsatisfied by the "halting lovemaking" of their men with its "scanty fruition," they turned to "other amusements" for their enjoyments, as Mrs. Earle said. They were the original "daughters of liberty."

Even in the "love literature" of the eighteenth and early nineteenth centuries, as seen in the popular love manuals and homilies of the time, there was an explicitness "that contrasted sharply to those of the later Victorian period," as Robin and John Haller note in *The Physician and Sexuality in Victorian America*. More than that, women in the post-colonial East shared a reciprocal and equal love with men, as Orson Fowler wrote in 1846 in his *Love and Parentage: Suggestions to Lovers Concerning the Most Sacred and Momentous Relations in Love.* "Almost any wife whose husband is not repugnant can be persuaded of all the intensity of emotion necessary or desirable," Fowler said, an idea the Victorians would have rejected as emasculating to man, if not blasphemous to God.

On the frontier these women and men rediscovered their earlier freedoms. They renewed their muted sensuality. In spite of the difficult physical environment in the covered wagons and trail camps, these pioneers were freer in voicing their emotions and acting upon them than they had been back East. There were fewer institutions to inhibit them. And the vast open spaces of the West were a place so free that "men live[d] rapidly—a whole month in a day, a whole year in a month," marveled the *Marvels of the New West.*

Nonetheless, the settlers were shocked—even as they were tempted—by the free and uninhibited way of life they found. Especially was this so in the Southwest, where, in Mexican and Indian villages, they encountered a freedom and independence of behavior that both startled and intrigued them.

Susan Magoffin, one of the first Eastern women to reach New Mexico, in 1846, was amazed and appalled to see women who not only smoked cigarettes, gambled like men and broke the Sabbath, but who managed saloons and businesses. Not only that; these same women wore neither corsets nor undergarments and were "perfectly free" in their behavior. "It is truly shocking," she said.

The men were equally shocked and titillated by the

"boldness" of the native women, said Lewis Garrard in *Wah-to-yah and the Taos Trail*; he thought them immodest and yet fascinating. So, too, George Rutledge Gibson, who noted, in 1848 in his *Journal of a Soldier under Kearny*, the attractions and disturbing independence that the native women displayed.

Taking a sardonic view of this paradox, Janet Lecompte, in her study of *The Independent Women of Hispanic New Mexico, 1821–1848*, wrote of the confusion of the settlers. The freedom of the native women equalled their familial importance. On marrying, a New Mexican woman "retained her property, legal rights, wages, and maiden name, while the Eastern woman lost almost all of her legal rights; her property and wages both belonged to her husband." And since the Eastern woman "was believed to have no sexual urges, from which arose a double standard of behavior . . . she was expected to be pious, chaste and self-sacrificing," recognizing that "her place was in the home."

By contrast, the Mexican census did not have a word for *housewife*; the woman who worked at home was called a *costerera*, or seamstress. Similarly, women were listed by profession—as weavers, gold panners, shepherds, midwives, healers, *cantina* owners, laundresses, ironers or prostitutes. Not surprisingly, the native woman seemed free of the usual guile and hypocrisy. Nor was she "measured by [a] double standard of sexual behavior," wrote Lecompte.

Even the forever chaste and virginal schoolmarm of legend did not, it seemed, always stay upon her pedestal. The story was told in the *New Mexican* of Santa Fe, New Mexico, of how a parish schoolmistress proudly invited her students' parents to an "examination day." She asked her pupils to recite what they had learned of the love of Christ.

"Now children, who loves all men?" she asked.

"You, missus," came the unexpected reply.

And the newspaper editorialized with fitting vulgarity considering the circumstances: "New Mexico is not the only place where the schoolmaster is a broad."

While the passions of the women on the frontier were as well guarded as their lustiness, the men of that time celebrated them with an understandable affection and enthusiasm.

Said one traveler on the Santa Fe Trail in 1841: the native women "make tortillas and dance at the same time, for they do whatever they wish." "The standard of female chastity is deplorably low," said author W. H. H. Davis, in 1857, in his novel *El Gringo*, with a somewhat suspect self-righteousness. Another chronicler of the time, George Kendall, observed, not without some begrudging admiration, that these women, as well as the men, did not abide by the "cold, conventional rules" of "feminine" behavior.

On the frontier, before the puritanism of the settlers led to the prohibitions of Victorianism, life was austere but sensual, hard but easygoing, frugal but freewheeling. The idyll did not last very long, however.

The Mexican and Civil Wars brought with them changing attitudes among men toward themselves, as well as women. In the aftermath of both these wars, a pained, more martial concept of manhood began to develop. Of the hundreds of thousands of men who were conscripted into the Union and Confederate armies and survived, the boldest, most adventurous headed West. Their ideas of masculinity, bloodied and hardened in battle, began to replace the earlier concepts of cooperation and equality between men and women that the necessities of frontier life had instilled in the first pioneers.

In the decades after the Civil War the settlement of the West was replaced by its conquest. The pioneers' attempts at friendship with the native people were doomed by "wars of annihilation" and the inevitable playing out of the expansionist impulses that united under the banner of "Manifest Destiny." In the minds of many Easterners, they were destined to dominate the native land and native women; the U.S. Army adopted the figure of the "kneeling squaw" as its target in rifle practice.

In the East the belief in the inferiority of women became institutionalized in Victorian "scientific" tracts and practices. The changing attitudes of men were heralded in 1857 by the publication of *Functions and Disorders of the Reproductive Organs* by Dr. William Acton, who declared that, in matters of love, men had to dominate women for medical reasons. He expressed that if a woman was not passive or indifferent in such matters, her passion might be a "drain" on a man's "vital energies" and damage his nervous system, as well as his manhood—a belief that caused much concern among Eastern physicians of the Victorian era.

"No matter who else may sleep together, husband and wife should not," wrote Dr. J. H. Greer at the end of the century. The emotions of women, the good doctor continued, had become not merely the means of usurping a man's potency, but also the enemy of his manhood.

While men of the Victorian era might have thought women to be inferior, however, they feared them nonetheless. So the great French historian Jules Michelet warily wrote in his *Woman's Love and Life* in 1881 that a woman "does nothing as we do. She thinks and acts differently." That mysterious difference resulted, he said, from her blood, which was a "foaming mountain torrent" of passions, for a woman "yearns with her very bowels." Michelet warned: "The deep cup of love is a sea of varying emotion hindering the regularity of the nutritive functions."

Of the late nineteenth-century believers in the primitive evil of a woman's lovemaking, none was more influential and articulate than the Italian sociologist Cesar Lombroso. In the evolution of the species, he claimed, women had been retarded; they were "semi-civilized." Scientific research had proven that in "female animals, aboriginal women and women of our time," the cerebral cortex, particularly in its psychical centers, is less active than in the male." Because of this, women really were "big children" and had "traits in common with children"; they were incapable of mature emotions.

"In the normal woman love is weak," Lombroso explained, and it "only becomes intense when it has reached the state of pathological phenomenon," a condition that drove women "mad." The cure for this madness, he wrote, was pregnancy, which he called the "moral prophylactic."

The "primeval" passion of a woman was therefore dangerous to a man. Once it was unleashed it could not be controlled. "Sensuality has multiple and impervious needs which absorb the mental activity of woman," Lombroso explained, and this "exaggerated sensuality" was evidence that in her heart every woman was "always a prostitute."

Even though a woman had these grievous faults, the faults were not hers. She was predestined by history and heredity to be inferior to men, Carl Vogy of the University of Geneva wrote in 1864 in his *Lecture on Man*. A woman was a "constantly growing child" and "in her brain, as in so many parts of her body she conforms to her childish type." Not only was the brain of a woman more "infantile in quality than that of the male," but she lacked "civilization in respect to morals." Sadly, Professor Vogy concluded, the "inequality of the sexes increases with progress."

Fortunately for men, "the majority of women (happily for society) are not very much troubled by sexual feeling of any kind," Dr. Acton claimed. The *Transmission of Life*, a love manual written in 1881 by a George Nathan, was even more reassuring. Most women were "entirely frigid," he wrote, "and not even in marriage do they perceive any real desire." Such beliefs, said the editors of the *Alkaloidal Clinic* in 1899, had turned the women of the East into "a race of sexless married nuns."

The Purity Department of the Women's Christian Temperance Union was delighted by this medical evidence. Its superintendent, a Dr. Mary Wood-Allen, agreed that women "have comparatively little sexual passion." She counselled that if a woman was forced to accept her husband's embrace she should do so "without a particle of sexual desire." In the *Relations of the Sexes*, first published in 1876, Mrs. E. B. Duffey confirmed the worst prognosis and dire warnings of Victorian doctors: "All the train of evil which follows masturbation attends only in a lesser degree to the too lustful marriage bed."

In his study of sexual relations, written in 1903, the New York physician Frederic Sturgis lamented that Eastern men no longer knew how to make love to their women. The man "goes through the performance as rapidly as possible and the act is begun, continued and finished, before a woman has had the time to realize what is going on." The woman, he continued, is "the passive instrument of the man and she often feels resentment and anger against the man who treats her merely as a machine."

None of these admissions of an Eastern malaise originated in the West. Few of these books were even known beyond the Mississippi. And few of the sad theories of love without women—or, at the very least, without their participation and passion—that so troubled men in the East made much sense in the West.

Even so, the later immigrants to the West brought these ideas with them, and sought to impose their Victorian beliefs about femininity on the proud and independent women of the frontier. In the eyes of these men, the women of the West had to be fitted into the masculine stays and mental corsets of the women of the East. The reality of life on the prairies and in the mountains, however, did not easily bend itself to fit these male myths.

As a result, the images of women in the West that took shape in the minds of men were anachronisms. They did not match the real relationships of men and women, either on the frontier or in the small-town settlements that followed.

The myths, in time, became the reality, and the reality began to resemble the myths. The open, unfenced lands of the frontier began to disappear, as did the necessity of equality and less inhibited emotions that flourished on them. But as the reality faded, it grew in memory, and a new, romantic image of the West was created.

By the end of the century, romance *in* the West had become inseparable from the romance *of* the West. Many of the ideas and beliefs about love on the frontier came from the pens of Eastern writers seeking to glorify love in a covered wagon and romance on the frontier in order to satisfy their own need for the passion they had expurgated from their lives; it was a paradox of puritanism. The daring and bold romance of the pioneers, whether real or imaginary, made them seem larger than life to those in the East. And their heroic stature among Easterners was increased by the recognition that these mythic Westerners had once been ordinary Easterners like themselves.

"So amid the rude scenes of frontier life, love and romance peep out," William Fowler wrote. The act of lovemaking "was conducted in log cabins" and even more "untoward places," he said. By "untoward places," Fowler meant the deepest forests and open meadows, where the bold and amorous "gallantry" of lovers was "repaid by the sweetest rewards."

The pastoral idyll of lovemaking upon the "sweet face" of nature captivated the imaginations of many Easterners. In New England the prohibitions of Puritanism and Victorianism had turned lovemaking into an "austere and almost cruel duty," Fowler said; it was as "graven" as the forbidding and "stern features on Plymouth Rock."

Not so in the romantic West, Fowler rhapsodised; there "the mind is uncramped and unfettered" and the "heart beats more freely, and warmly, when its current is unchecked by conventions." And so, "Life is more intense in the West."

"The western country seem(ed) naturally fitting in many ways for love and romance," he said.

Nature, in the wilderness, intensified the passions. It offered "thrilling scenes of Love's melodrama, acted and reacted on different stages, but always with startling effect,"

Fowler wrote. And pioneer women seemed to be more affected by the romantic beauty of nature than men; the "effects of the romantic incidents in the lives of pioneer women are heightened by the extraordinary and ever-changing scenery of [the] wilderness."

In the freer society of the frontier, "impulse largely governs," Fowler wrote. That openness favored the emotions of women, he said. "The cooler and more selfish faculties of man's nature [are] less dominant" in the West, and the emotions of women were therefore more freely expressed and enjoyed.

"Man's work is one of destruction and subjugation," Fowler said. "He must level the forest, break the soil and fight all the forces that oppose him"; while "woman is the preserver of life. . . . Her mission is peace" with the land. But, he added, "We are speaking now of the sex as it is seen in the new country and in remote settlements. In crowded cities we see too often selfish, frivolous females," but these women "are hardly known on the border."

"The romance of border life," Fowler concluded, "is inseparably associated with a women."

In the eyes of Europeans, the romance of the West assumed an even more idyllic dimension. The English observer of "American beauty," Henry Theophilus Finck, in his London publication *Romantic Love and Physical Beauty*, stated unequivocally in 1891 that after studying love around the world he was convinced that "Romantic Love [is] more ardent and prevalent in the United States than in any other part of the world."

The passion for romance was stronger in America, Finck believed, because of the nature of its women. In this country there existed an "intellectual culture of women" that surpassed that of other nations, and women were more "open to ideas" and "freer" in their choices than elsewhere in the world. Because of this they were more "individualized" and independent in expressing their love and desire. And besides, Finck said, "no country has as many beautiful girls" as America.

"There is more Love," Finck declared, "among the women of America than among those (women) of any other country."

But the romanticizing of love in the West came after the puritanical and Victorian beliefs had changed the lusty frontier into respectable small-town societies. The celebration had come too late. And the vehicles of romance, the covered wagons, now lay abandoned, covered by time and legend.

On the back pasture of a Nebraska farm and along the riverbeds in eastern Oregon, the rutted trails of the wagon trains can be seen beneath the grasses. And from time to time an old covered wagon, stripped of its canvas by the years like a beached ship, is found behind a barn or abandoned in some forgotten woods, patiently waiting to be discovered by an antique dealer in nostalgia who will put it to the more commercial uses of romance.

In his boyhood in Kansas, remembered prairie editor William Allen White, he and his schoolmates stumbled on an aged covered wagon abandoned in the woods near his home in Eldorado. The old wagon had become a haven for the kind of lovemaking that might have shocked its pioneer owners. The prairie editor fondly reminisced about the ironies of romance:

"And one summer day we discovered a camping place deep in the woods above the town where there was often a covered wagon and some strange girls. We used to peek through the brush at what was going on there, until Merz Young, who was the protector of the innocent came and chased us off with yells and curses. . . . And the knowledge of good and evil came to us, even as to the Pair in the Garden."

There was, after all, love in a covered wagon.

THE
FRONTIERSWOMAN'S
MAN

COME TO POPEASIA, PLENTY OF WHISKEY AND WHITE WOMEN.

On the abandoned wooden hut at the fur trappers' rendezvous site on the Green River someone had written this invitation in charcoal. The news spread through the hills like the beat of an Indian drum. And the mountain men came out of the woods with a raunchy exuberance to greet the wives of the missionaries who were heading West.

These mountain men had darkened faces caked with dirt that was itself like a brown wrinkled skin. Most of them were drunk, unwashed, foul smelling, hairy as beasts and danced around the party of missionaries' wives hooting and hollering "like savages," half naked and laughing and making explicit and obscene gestures.

75

One of the women, a Mrs. Myra F. Eells, wrote in her diary: "Last night twelve white men came, dressed and painted in the Indian style and gave us a dance. No pen can describe the horrible scene they presented. Could not imagine that a white man brought up in a civilized land, can appear to so much imitate the Devil." Needless to say, she was horrified.

Of course, the missionaries' wives, who had demurely ridden sidesaddle across half a continent, never had seen such "white Indians" before. Yes, they had come to Christianize the heathen, never dreaming that the heathen might be white. It came as a shock to find themselves surrounded by licentious white men posing as Indians.

On the frontier, a "confrontation between pious, virtuous, sober Eastern women and obstreperous, uninhibited men of the West would happen many times," commented T. A. Larsen in the *Women's Role in the American West*. That meeting of missionaries' wives and mountain men on the Little Wind River in the summer of 1838 was to establish the pattern that would prevail for much of the rest of the century whenever Western men and Eastern women met. Each of them, the men of the forests and prairies and the women of the cities, had created a unique mating ritual; for it was not the men alone who performed a dance. The women, too, on their English sidesaddles, were part of a Western drama that was just as unreal and theatrical.

To dress and dance as an Indian was not as strange a thing for white men to do as it may have seemed. For these frontiersmen the Indian was the symbol of virility and manhood; he was the man of nature who had not been tamed by society. As Thomas Jefferson had said: "From my childhood . . . I have felt an interest in the Indians," because upon them alone "English seductions will have no effect." They were the "beasts of the forest." They were, at the same time, "true" men.

And so the fascination with and foreboding of Indian men arose from the nature of their manhood. The fear was not wholly due to religious beliefs and culture differences; it was caused as well by a deep and unspoken sexual taboo. If white men wished to "secure our women" from "tomahawk and scalping knife," said Jefferson, they will do so only by "removing those [the Indian men] who excite them."

The men of the forests thus danced as Indians. For what better way to entice and frighten the "virtuous" wives of missionaries than by displaying the naked masculinity of "true" men.

In the wilderness the frontiersmen possessed an "excess of virility," thought Ralph Waldo Emerson. "Here is *man*," he said with some celebration and some trepidation, for, "as if to stimulate our energy, on the face of the sterile waste," the nature of the frontier creates new images of manhood. "The earth is shaken by our energies. We are feeling our youth and nerve and bone," Emerson wrote; he was both enthralled and made uneasy by this American man who grew "like grass" in the West.

The forests were "the realm of men and their erections," wrote Henry Thoreau in the same vein of admiration and disquiet. He neither elaborated, nor explained, whether he was referring to architectural or phallic creations. Either way, both Emerson and Thoreau seemed to sense that the men emerging from the wilderness were different from the men who had entered that wilderness—an as yet undefined man who was as peculiarly native to the land as he was to

America itself, and one who was in the process of recreating himself.

Since the pioneering men of the West had come at first without families and without wives, it sometimes was believed that they lived in a world without women, where men ruled and enforced their own rules. The West was often referred to as a "world of men."

But was it?

"No one has ever questioned, let alone analyzed, the masculinity of the frontier society," commented Richard Bartlett in *The New Country*. But then, no one had to, for the male domination of the frontier West was "as obvious as the sun." In the early settlements white men dominated both in numbers and authority. The codes and morals of the little mining and cow towns were deeply masculine, and they had a male ambience that became symbolic of the West. So, too, on the cattle trails and in the ranch bunkhouses, where the physical presence of men permeated the atmosphere like the "male" smell of old boots and leather. The range was "no place for a woman" went the popular saying.

And yet, from the earliest explorations of the West, wherever white men went there were women to guide them. If these women seemed invisible to later historians, one of the reasons might have been because they were often Indian women, nameless and forgotten by historians who, in the effect these women had upon the history of the West, could see nothing of significance that was worth mentioning.

Frederick Jackson Turner, in *The Significance of the Frontier in American History*, mentioned a woman only once, and that in a sentence where he noted that "the mother of Kit Carson was a Boone." Nearly a century later the recognition of the vital role played by frontierswomen had increased so greatly that Ray Allen Billington, in *Westward Expansion*, mentioned three women by name, and one of them was an Indian.

There was a "scarcity of women" on the frontier, explained historian Robert G. Athearn and Robert Riegel in *America Moves West* (1971). But the opposite was true. The authors were referring solely to white women, for in the censuses of the nineteenth century only white women counted and were counted. So, if the census of 1850 showed one woman to twenty-three men in California and the census of 1860 showed one woman to thirty-four men in Colorado, the ratio was more racial than actual. As late as the census of 1870 the white men of the West outnumbered the white women by a ratio of two to one, though once again Indian women were not counted.

In actuality, however, it is likely that white men were outnumbered by native women on the early frontier by as much as they outnumbered emigrant women from the East—a state of affairs none was known to have complained about in his memoirs. In fact, if white men desired female companionship, they most often found it among native women, a fact the census did not report anymore than it tabulated the resulting statistics. But it was not the sheer number of native women that captivated white men—it was their independence and freedom, most of all in affairs of the heart.

Spanish and English men in particular, coming as they did from societies with patriarchial and restrictive mores, were amazed by the freedoms of Native American women. And they rediscovered what the original discoverers had found—the profound effect of the native land and native peoples, most of all the native women, on the European man's idea of his manhood and his machismo.

"One of the significant but little known aspects of the Indian-white relationship was the sexual one," wrote the Smithsonian's historian, Wilcomb Washburn, in his unusually earthy treatise on the men and women of the frontier, *The Indian and the White Man* (1964). "Though unreported on the whole, enough evidence exists to show that the sexual attraction of the dark-haired native was one of the major forces inducing whites to push on into the interior," he wrote. More than merely amorous adventures of curious men and women, however, these matings were often the union of two very different societies and cultures, and helped shape the attitudes of each toward the other, as well as themselves.

Neither the men of England nor Spain could morally accept such freedoms without fear of chastisement and damnation. But their persuasive sins did not dissuade them. Instead, they made them question their old beliefs and behavior toward women and seek a new understanding of a changing morality.

Even as they wished to condemn native women, "as Eve had seduced Adam," European men sensed they were projecting their own fantasies upon those same women. One French explorer by the name of Pierre-Antoine Tabeau said of the Arikara women, "The word modesty is not even known"—a curious comment considering the notoriously promiscuous behavior of French fur trappers and squawmen on the frontier.

So, too, said David Thompson in his happy lament *Narratives of His Explorations in Western American: 1784—*

1812. "The curse" of the Mandans, Thompson said, was their "almost total lack of chastity." But, he added, since "the white men who have hitherto visited these villages have not been examples of chastity [either], we could not preach chastity to them. . . . Christianity alone can restrain the passions and desires," Thompson added, but the native women were not Christians. Nothing could be done. And so, Thompson had to endure the sorrowful fate of a man among the Mandan women, "each of [whom] takes the Man she chooses by the hand, he rises and goes with her, where she pleases and they lie down together. . . ."

Not all white men were subjected to such feminine attention. But, in one way or another, the confrontation between the Indian and white worlds had a human face before it assumed the faceless guise of clashing civilizations.

The men on the frontier were supposed to be tough, vigorous and self-reliant. Life in the West demanded these qualities. And if life called for "men to match the mountains," then it required women who could match the men. So animalistic and hardened were the images of themselves that frontiersmen liked to boast that one company manufactured a "Buckskin Undergarment," the hair shirt of the West. These garments of masculine self-torture were advertised not only for rough-skinned men but "For Ladies" as well. For these men projected their image of themselves onto their women, and the women not only accepted the challenge but often surpassed their men in meeting it.

Romantics have long believed that the "scarcity of women" on the frontier caused lonely white men to place white women on pedestals, like Greek goddesses, and clothe them with "adoration" and "exaggerated respect," as the Western historian Riegel wrote. But neither in the memoirs of pioneer men nor the newspapers of the day is there much evidence to support this romantic idea. In fact, the views of women held by frontiersmen were often quite the opposite.

In reality, there was another, quite different tradition on the frontier, a tradition of liberty and license for both men and women. For these were lusty people who enjoyed shocking and mocking the puritanical morality of the East.

The rambunctious and deliberately vulgar Davy Crockett was a popular representative of this new tradition of Western lustiness, voicing the freewheeling, devil-may-care licentiousness of his frontier constituents. In his campaign for Congress he chided those who had accused him of having morals as loose as his rhetoric by saying, "Friends, fellow citizens, brothers and sisters: They accuse me of adultery! It's a lie! I never ran away with any man's wife who was not willing to come with me."

His "brothers and sisters" on the frontier evidently believed him, or did not care, for they elected him to Congress. Maybe it was because, in the wilderness, human passions were more honestly, and directly, expressed than in the circumspect societies back East. The tongue-tied, shy and self-suppressed attitudes of Western men came later, for they were an Eastern invention.

In Crockett's day the "uninhibited men of the West" were not as laconic and laid-back as they were thought to be. In fact, they were a wild, raucous bunch. One of the ways they celebrated their masculinity was with their ear-rattling and exaggerated "cowboy yells"; this one originated in the Southwest and was recorded in New Mexico: "Who-ee-o-ee! I'm a bad man! Raised in the backwoods, suckled by a polar bear, nine rows of jaw teeth, a double coat of hair, steel ribs, wire intestines and a barbed-wired tail, and I don't give a dang where I drag it! Whoopee-whee-a-ha!"

In our own day the "barbed-wired tail" has been interpreted to mean these men were proclaiming the awesome prowess of their penises. Not exactly the words of shy men who were modest about their masculinity.

Few men ever quite equalled that claim to a "barbed-wire tail" or penis, though Davy Crockett came close. On the floor of Congress he let loose with this frontiersman's yell of his own: "Who! Who! Whoop! Bow! Wow! Wow! Yough! I say, Mr. Speaker, I've had a speech in the soak these six months and it has swelled in me like a drowned horse; If I don't deliver it I shall burst and smash the windows. I've soaked my head and shoulders in Salt River so much that I'm corned. I can walk like an ox, swim like an eel, yell like an Indian, fight like a devil, spout like an earthquake, make love like a mad bull and swallow a nigger whole without choking if you butter his head and pin back his ears! Yough! Yough!"

Make love like a mad bull! Not the most endearing or tenderest declaration of love a man has offered a woman, but it honestly described how the frontiersman felt about his manhood. The metaphor, of a mad bull, was fitting and telling.

The pioneer women who went West were more than a match for the "mad bulls" with their "barbed-wire" penises. Many crossed the country with their husbands, but many others came alone as heads of families, settling on homesteads they themselves built. And these women were often as daring and adventurous as the men; they were not simply the widow ladies, virtuous schoolmarms and whores depicted in Eastern stereotypes, but were often professional women, lawyers and doctors, wagon drivers and female soldiers.

There were hundreds of women who had fought in the Civil War as soldiers on both sides, for example. Some had boldly dressed in feminine military uniforms of their own design, while others disguised themselves in the uniforms of men. But all of them helped create not only a new role for women, but a new attitude in which, as soldiers and veterans, they judged and questioned the leadership of men. "The lessons of the war were not lost on the women of this nation," said Elizabeth Cady Stanton, a prominent suffragist of the time, for the women "beheld the danger of a 'male' government forever involving the nations of the earth in war and violence."

More than that, these female soldiers had taken part in that most masculine of all professions, fighting. And they had acquitted themselves well. "Like the soldiers of the armies," Frank Moore wrote in 1867 in *Women of the War*, the women exhibited "courage in times of danger, patience in suffering and by adventures romantic and daring, the best qualities of our nature"; they were "heroic women" and created a new femininity. Even though these women "do not figure in official reports" and "are not gazetted for deeds as gallant as ever were done," Moore believed "the nation holds them in equal honor with its brave men."

Neither on the covered wagon nor in town meetings were such women likely to take a back seat to their men. They were women who had proven themselves to be the equals of men, and the frontiersmen dared not patronize or belittle them the way they would the ladies of later Eastern fictions.

And then there were the professional women whose

presence in the West strongly affected the attitudes of men. These lawyers and doctors, journalists and businesswomen, had come across seeking to escape the restrictions that Eastern society placed on educated women. Many of them were independent and headstrong feminists.

So many of these women came across, in fact, that, by 1890, there were 452 women doctors and surgeons in the West. Though only 5 percent of the population and 4 percent of the women in the nation lived in the West, the western women professionals made up 15 percent of the female writers and "scientific persons," 14 percent of the lawyers and 10 percent of the doctors and journalists. These women "were tackling every profession," reported a rueful Western writer named Bill Nye.

The rugged frontiersmen, unfettered and free men, might have resented these professional women as they became civic and social elders in towns across the West. But they needed them and they developed a begrudging respect for their feminine contribution to the "masculine West."

Not only did these women perform in traditional "male" occupations, they also often dressed the part. One woman doctor, Lillian Heath, of Rawlins, Wyoming, carried two pistols in her belt on house calls and wore men's clothing "to avoid talk," she said. Another women doctor in Texas, Sophie Herzog, wore a necklace made from the bullets she had dug out of the cowboys and outlaws she operated on.

Such women were as tough as the trails they rode. And many men might have been somewhat intimidated by the boldness and prowess of their new style of femininity, which was as uniquely and distinctively Western as the men.

One such woman was Mrs. E. J. Guerin, better known

as "Mountain Charley," a fur trapper and saloon owner who had also been a second liuetenant in the Civil War. After the war, she packed her children into a covered wagon and headed for the goldfields of California dressed as a man. Along the way she rescued one woman who had been left to starve by a wagon train, another woman and her two children who had been abandoned by a wagon train when her husband died, and found still another woman who was riding to California, on a mule, all alone.

These deserted and abandoned women on the frontier touched her heart. She "longed to disclose my sex and minister [to the women] in that manner in which only a woman can another," she said; but "I did not dare." The men only accepted her when she was disguised as "one of them."

Some of the women who drove covered wagons across the country—and on the wagon trains many of the oxen drivers were women—later became freight haulers and stagecoach drivers. One such woman was Mary Fields, an ex-slave, who became not only a freight hauler but a pony express rider in Montana in 1880, and who was fired because she used her rifle to fight off a wolfpack in violation of company rules,—it was "unladylike," they said.

But perhaps the exemplar of feminine courage on the frontier was Nancy Rogers, a Kansas nurse, who diagnosed herself as having breast cancer, then performed a mastectomy on herself using a kitchen knife—after cooking supper for her family.

If men "to match the mountains" were needed on the frontier, so were women. The editorials and broadsides that urged and cajoled women to come West were aimed at down-to-earth women whose heroism was practical: Send us women who have the strength of Indian women and the skills of white women.

The *Laramie Boomerang*, in Wyoming, described the kind of women the frontiersmen wished for: "Wyoming wants women, and wants them bad. But there is no very clamourous demand for sentimental fossils. There are very few households here as yet that are able to keep their own private poet. We [want] to encourage a class of women to come to this region who would know enough to construct a buttonhole on an overcoat so that it wouldn't look like the optic of a cross-eyed hog. . . ."

The strength and self-confidence of most frontier women was so great that they sometimes treated their men with what seemed to be a motherly tolerance. Men were often described in women's diaries as boyish and awkward. If the strutting and boasting of men was viewed with more amusement than annoyance by women, this might have been one of the reasons.

And so the Mormon suffragette Emmeline Wells wrote in 1897: "Certainly we could not have settled the West without them [men]. We could not do without them. They built the bridges and killed the bears. . . .

"But I think women worked just as hard," she added.

In Colorado, the old saying was that pioneer women guarded the homestead, raised the crops, managed the livestock, taught the children, fed the family and stood guard with their rifles, while the men were out on the range moving a fencepost from one place to another, or—as one version has it—"pushing a stone from one place to another."

The ranch and homesteading women "made the West," said Roberta Cheney, the daughter of a fifth-generation pioneer family and author of the *Women Who Won the West*. ".Maybe it's time to remember [those] women who have really made the West," and not the stereotypes of the "dance hall girls or wife of an Army officer, or 'Lady' from Philadelphia. That's foolishness," she said. Instead, in the West there was a "strong line of women" who won their rights by hard work and independence.

Back East, as the pioneer women continued to head West, their sisters were building a women's rights movement of their own. It was not coincidence that these two movements began at about the same time. As the westward migration was reaching its pre–Civil War peak, the first "Women's Rights Convention in World History" was gathering at Seneca Falls, New York, in the summer of 1848. The new and independent lives of their Western sisters encouraged and strengthened these Eastern women. In time, in the decades after the Civil War, these two movements would merge—much as they had emerged—together.

The response of many men to the women's movement was, predictably, outrage. Men seemed confused, troubled, threatened, angered—sometimes all at the same time. Patriarchs of the Eastern establishment often spoke out against these women with a furiousness that may have surprised even them.

Of all the condemnations of women's rights none was more countemptuous than that of James Gordon Bennett, the urbane editor of the esteemed *New York Herald*. In 1852 Bennett compared white women to black slaves who ought to be "contented" and "happy" that white men were protecting them; it was "nature's law" he editorialized. "How did women first become subject to man, as she now is all over the world?" Bennet asked rhetorically. "By her nature, her sex, just as the Negro is and always will be to the end of time inferior to the white race, and therefore doomed to subjection; but she is happier than she would be in any other condition, *because* it is the law of nature."

The comparison of black slaves and white women was not as unrelated as it might now seem. From their beginnings the women's rights and anti-slavery movements had been closely entwined. After all, at the World Anti-Slavery Convention in London, in 1846, Lucretia Mott, Elizabeth Cady Stanton and Mrs. Wendell Phillips first attracted international attention to the American woman's battle for equal rights. The Englishmen who chaired the convention were so startled by the appearance of these formidable women that they refused to let them register as delegates and forced them to sit behind a curtain in the balcony, where the abolitionist leader William Lloyd Garrison sat with them, in protest.

Eastern newspapers ridiculed what they scorned as the "Petticoat Revolt" by portraying the women as "handmaidens" and "free lovers" of black men and white abolitionists. They advocated a "female socialism," said *Harper's* magazine in 1853, that divided the power of the white man among his inferiors; this was "opposed to nature and the established order of society. . . ." These women were "hermaphrodites," declared another newspaper. Still another suggested that they were not women at all, but were "Aunt Nancy's Men."

In Philadelphia, the usually staid *Public Ledger and Daily Transcript* went further when it published in 1848 that women had no rights, as women. "A woman is nobody," the editor intoned, but "a wife is everything. A pretty girl is equal to ten thousand men, and a mother is next to God, all powerful. The ladies of Philadelphia are resolved to maintain their rights as Wives, Belles, Virgins and Mothers, and not as women." Needless to say, the editor who wrote this was a man.

Emotionally unnerved by these "new women," the editors and publications of the East tried to idealize the old-fashioned women of bygone years. They created and perpetuated the image of the crinoline-clad, shy and "always pure" lady of the West, whether a schoolmarm or a whore, as Roberta Cheney has said. If these new women would not behave properly, then men's fantasies would take their place. But the fantasies did not fit the reality of the West.

Men and women worked together on the frontier, hard and with a quiet degree of natural equality. That was the only way they could survive. And so as Ernest Groves wrote in *The American Women*, the old and rigid "theory and assumption of male supremacy melted [as] men and women were welded together by their ordeals. . . . The woman who participated in nearly all of the basic means of livelihood, even in its perils, demonstrated her personality with a certainity that no one was inclined to gainsay." The necessities of life "were bound to upset the social scheme that had so long maintained women's social inferiority."

The importance of women in the society of the West and their spirit of independence fascinated the Eastern leaders of the women's rights movement. "Let us go to the untouched Western states," Elizabeth Cady Stanton wrote to Susan B. Anthony. "Pioneers are progressive folks. We will get *state* suffrage." And they did.

On her tour of the territories and states of the West, Susan B. Anthony promised each, as she did the Washington state legislature, that when they granted women the right to vote "the most gratifying results" would occur—"the immigration of a large number of good women." There was no evidence that such an immigration ever happened, but Wyoming became the first state, in 1869, to offer suffrage to women, and others soon followed. Similarly, in 1869, Wyoming passed the first law to prohibit "discrimination on account of sex." California, in 1873, enacted a similar law. (These were important steps, even though some of these laws were later repealed.) From then on Eastern women who demanded equal rights were told "to go to Wyoming."

Such legislation merely acknowledged in law what had long been true of life on the frontier. Men in the West recognized the importance of women not because of their "scarcity," or because of a romantic "adoration" of their femininity, but because of women's contributions to their own survival in the wilderness.

So tough was the average frontier woman, in fact, that many men may have exaggerated their own masculinity in order to neutralize women's power over them. Such men might have acted the stoic, undaunted by pleasure or pain, to demonstrate to women that they had little influence upon them, and they may have strutted and hollered for the same reasons: to dispel the new femininity, which to many men seemed frighteningly masculine.

This begrudging admiration of the frontierswoman on the part of the frontiersman was best summed up in the most unlikely of places, Thomas Dimsdale's book on the *Vigilantes of Montana*. Dimsdale lamented: "A woman is queen in her own home; but we neither want her as a blacksmith, a ploughwoman, a soldier, a lawyer, a doctor, nor in any such professions or handicrafts. As sisters, mothers, nurses, friends, sweethearts, wives, they are the salt of the earth, the sheer anchor of society, and the humanizing and purifying element in humanity. As such they can not be too much respected, loved and protected.

"But from Blue Stockings, Bloomers, and strong-minded she-males generally, '*GOOD LORD DELIVER US!*' "

And yet, the frontierswoman's man became the man he was because of the woman she was; his masculinity was shaped, in part, by her frontier femininity.

REAL HORSES
AND MYTHIC
RIDERS

MA, DO COWBOYS EAT GRASS?

NO, SON,

THEY'RE PART HUMAN.

"Ranch life isn't anything like a Western movie," said New Mexico rancher and farmer Cleofes Vigil. "It's more honest. Western movies are a bunch of lies," he told several hundred Beverly Hills cowboys, Hollywood Western superstars and directors, screenwriters and starlets in cowboy boots who had gathered for the Western Film Festival, in 1981, in Santa Fe, New Mexico. Mostly, the Westerns are about "greed and selfishness, cheating and killing," Vigil said; "but on a ranch, life isn't like that."

The rancher waved his fist in a friendly way at actor Charlton Heston, who was seated beside him on a panel assembled to discuss the question "Did the West Really Exist?" But Heston, who had defended "mythic Westerns," went on to say, "Since there is no 'truth' about the West, what is the responsibility of the filmmaker to tell the 'truth'?"

"I don't believe in lies," the rancher replied.

Rarely does an ordinary rancher come face-to-face with his or her idealized Hollywood image. Even rarer is the occasion when "men who push turds around with their toes," as one rancher said of his fellow cowmen, get to voice their feelings about the cops-and-robbers heroics of so many cowboy movies or question their own Marlboro Man media image. Yet that kind of face-off was the unique achievement of the Western Film Festival, as conceived by Bill and Stella Pence of Telluride, Colorado.

Before the silver screen was tarnished with realism, it portrayed no hero more luminous than the cowboy. "He was a shining knight," Jack Schaefer, the author of *Shane*, told the festival audience. "As the knight-errant of the sagebrush, he was 'immortal.' " The celluloid cowboy was nothing less than a "god," added screenwriter Miles Swarthout, who wrote *The Shootist*, John Wayne's last film. "Not a religious god," he hastily added, "but a mythic god; he was like the hero of a classic Greek tragedy."

Now, that was not quite the way contemporaries of the old-time cowboy perceived him. In his heyday the ordinary cowboy had a more realistically low public image. So poor was his reputation in the nineteenth century, in fact, that in *Marvels of the New West*, published in 1888, William Makepeace Thayer felt obliged to reassure his readers that "the cowboy was a member of the human family." To convince dubious Easterners, Thayer said he knew of cowboys "who were graduated at Harvard and Yale," and offered a drawing of a cowboy in a three-piece vested suit to prove he was "civilized." "Cowboys are not the desperados and cutthroats which many Eastern papers present them to be," said Thayer.

The romantic dime novels and spectacular Wild West shows of the turn of the century changed the cowboy's image. But it was the Western movie that transformed that image into a legend. On the endless plains of New Jersey, "cowboys" from the laboratory of Thomas Edison made what was probably the first Western, *The Great Train Robbery*, in 1903. It is fitting that the new image of the "heroic" cowboy was born in an off-Broadway production. And it is significant that this new cowboy was not a cowboy at all; he was, instead, a train robber, a "desperado."

In many of these early Westerns, "the West" was painted onto plywood flats, and so were the characters of the cowboys—flat, that is. "Bronco Billy" Anderson made hundreds of these Westerns, which were really "Easterns"; his specialty was the "good bad man," the gunfighter with a heart of gold. Not surprisingly, the high and low point of the Eastern-Western came in a post–World War I film in which, it was said, a mechanical horse was used. Apparently, the star's horse was asked to jump off a cliff, but it wisely refused to comply. And so a mechanical horse was built and pushed into oblivion.

Several old silent Westerns, preserved by the University of California at Los Angeles Film Archive, were shown at the festival, including films by D. W. Griffith

95

and Thomas Ince, among others. Favorites were the Gold-Rush epic *The Argonauts of California* and William S. Hart's *The Return of Draw Egan*, both made in 1916. The surprise was how innocent and gentle they were. And there was a poignancy about them that was both humane and funny, with little violence. It was just this naive quality that the Grade B Westerns and Saturday matinee serials of the 1930s so happily captured.

If there was conflict between Indians and whites in these old movies, it was likely to be romantic rather than martial. In fact, the romantic stars of these early films were often Indians, as in *Little Dove's Romance* and *A Squaw's Love*. The idea that Indians ought to be the villains of the Westerns came much later. And yet, remembering the hundreds of Westerns he had seen or acted in, that stereotypic Indian actor Iron Eyes Cody could think of "maybe ten" that were not insulting to Indians. Though he defended Westerns, King Vidor, a veteran of sixty years of directing (*Cimarron, Billy the Kid, The Big Train*), had to admit he had created "fake" Indians in his movies. "I am guilty," he said quietly. At a panel discussion devoted to the question "Was the Western Hero Really an Indian?", the Mohawk anthropologist and writer Shirley Hill Witt startled the film audience by suggesting that the cowboy hero may have been an Indian in drag. His modesty and self-effacing manner, his laconic, soft-spoken stoicism, his my-word-is-my-honor pledge and his laid-back and low-key behavior did not fit with his boisterous European heritage; these were Indian characteristics that the cowboys had learned, she said.

As troublesome to the lover of Westerns as the treatment of Indians was their seeming addiction to violence. When the historian Frederick Turner wondered if gunplay in Westerns had not "inculcated a tolerance for violence in American culture," he was quickly challenged by Charlton Heston. "I disagree! Violence is endemic; it isn't unique to Westerns," said Heston.

No less sharp was the response to *Los Angeles Times* movie critic Sheila Benson, who had plaintively asked, "Was there always the guy with the gun?" "Oh yes, baby," Lee Marvin shot back, "and there still is." It was the audiences' fault, he said; they "get hypered up by a certain amount of dead guys per film." So, it wasn't the problem of the Western; it was a "sociological problem."

The glorification of gunplay is at once the most singular and dubious part of the Hollywood Western. It has become an element of the genre as essential as the chase and the confrontation of good and evil. But, in the process, this glorification has paradoxically transformed the villains into heroes. Outlaws and lawmen become interchangeable, as in fact they were in reality. For the gun is an amoral tool of morality.

Buster Crabbe, star of forty *Billy the Kid* movies, put it bluntly. "We tried to make him into a hero. Actually he wasn't," Crabbe recalled. "He was a little s.o.b."

Evil has not triumphed; it has been transformed into entertainment. And the myth becomes the reality. "The public doesn't want its heroes debunked," said screenwriter Swarthout. "They don't want to see what a jackass Buffalo Bill really was."

"That's why I filmed *Buffalo Bill and the Indians* as a fantasy," said director Robert Altman, nodding in agreement.

"Bambi with guns is not what audiences want to see," said one screenwriter. "They want to see blood." Nonetheless, the shoot-out and shoot'em-up are the most historically dubious elements of the Western. In the vintage horse operas of William S. Hart and Tom Mix, it was horsemanship, not gunmanship, that won the fight and the maiden. Cowboys in those days displayed their manly prowess by their skill as riders and ropers, not gunmen. Sadly, the emergence of the gun as the decisive and dominant expression of manhood may be more symbolic of our own century than of the nineteenth.

That irony provoked a discussion about the validity and accuracy of the Western. Philip Garvin, director of *Siringo* (an attempt at an historically realistic Western), recalled a study of violent deaths in the five principal trailheads during the fifteen years of the largest cattle drives. In all those years, Garvin reported, merely forty-five people were killed. "That many people have died by accident *making* Western films," he said. "The Western isn't at all accurate," Garvin concluded, "but I don't know that it really matters."

Pursuing that theme, the obstreperous Jack Schaefer snarled like a cornered wolf and proclaimed that even his *Shane* was a fake. It never happened, and it never could. The old gunfighters, Schaefer said, did not face-off in gunfights. "They shot each other in the back." In fact, he had once offered a hundred dollars to anyone who "would send proof of a real-life shoot-out. No one ever did," Schaefer grumbled triumphantly.

(Now, Jack was not entirely correct. I remember reading about one face-to-face shoot-out. It happened in Denver, and if I remember right, the gunfighter, an Irish Jew named Levy who had recently arrived from Dublin, probably did not know that you were supposed to shoot your enemy in the back.)

"The future of the West[ern]: If Any" was, fittingly, the final topic of discussion. It was said by some of the moviemakers there that only the clothing and location of the Western hero had changed; that, in fact, he had reappeared in detective stories (Bogey as the Lone Ranger wearing a trench coat) and science-fiction shoot'em-ups. Cowboys now wore space suits and rode in space ships, not on horses. "*Star Wars* is a Western as completely as it could be," said the writer Tom McGuane (*Rancho Deluxe*). It represented the Western "of the future."

And so the Western Film Festival ended as it had begun, with a requiem and a rebirth. The movie that was perhaps the symbol of both of these was writer Edward Abbey's painfully angry *Lonely Are the Brave*, in which the cowboy hero is no longer a cowboy; he does not work on a ranch; and he has nothing to do with cows. But he *acts* like a cowboy. He is, above all, alone, an individualist, the misfit who is attempting to escape from urban life with the only things he trusts—his horse and his gun.

And so he rides off with his horse and gun into the mountains, escaping the jeeps of the police and the helicopters of the Air Force, only to be run down by a huge semi on the superhighway in the dark of night. He cannot ride off into the sunset, for the truck has disemboweled his horse.

In *Lonely Are the Brave*, the end of the trail was to become even more symbolic than its makers intended, for the truck driver in the film, Carroll O'Conner, in time became Archie Bunker. And, as in Peckinpah's *Convoy*, truckers became "the new cowboys." The Western had once again become, at its ending, the "Eastern" that it was at its beginning.

No one could have closed this festival better than did the Indian composer Louis Ballard, who spoke the last words. Quoting his fellow Oklahoman Will Rogers, Ballard said, the "only way the Western movie could be improved would be to run it backwards."

THE GLOBAL
COWBOY

❖

On a moody afternoon along the Danube, the Hungarian state television network was broadcasting a French documentary on the National Rodeo Finals in Oklahoma City. Prominent Budapest intellectuals had gathered reverently around the television set to watch the rodeo cowboys. As far as I could tell, they were fanatical rodeo fans who had never been to a rodeo. When the finals were over one of the Marxists turned to me.

"Tell me," she said, "why do the horses jump like that?"

A group of engineers, professors, book editors and scholars sat in the urbane apartment. They were meeting, as they regularly did, to watch films on the American West, which they loved with a platonic, faraway and unrequited passion.

Sipping brandy and delighting in their obscenely sweet

101

Budapestian pastries, these gentlemen and women were enthralled by the mountains and deserts of America. They watched as cowboys and Indians bit the dust with childish and ecumenical glee. In that comfortable, even bourgeois, living room, they were surrounded by relics of the West —a chandelier that was made from an old wagon wheel, Colt .45s mounted on the wall and coffee tables littered with the shards of ancient Indian pots.

And where in Budapest, Hungary, does one obtain relics of the American West? One makes them.

One year the owner of the apartment had built a thirty-foot birchbark canoe in his living room. The Mohawks had never built a more beautiful one, he said; but the canoe was so big it could not be carried down the stairs and had to be lowered by rope from the fifth-floor window. The canoe maker now paddled his canoe up and down the Danube, a lost Mohawk.

The men, it seemed, were members of an "Indian Club." In the summer they abandoned the city for an island in the Danube, where they stripped down to their loincloths, ornamented themselves with homemade Indian jewelry, erected their own teepees, ate beef jerky and tried to act as best they could like a tribe of socialist Indians. In the winter they changed into cowboys. Either way, these men of the East became men of the West, a new breed of man, half Indian and half cowboy.

In fact, across the entire continent of Europe there had been a spread of "Western" and "Indian" clubs. There was the "Dakota Trading Post," near Frankfurt for example, with its frontier fort and Indian village. And the *"Camp Indien"* and *"Le Cercle Peau-Rouge Hunkta"* (Huntka Redskin Circle) outside of Paris. There was the *"Trois Tribus*

Indiennes Campent sur les Bords du Rhin," with its powwows and fertility dances, at Strasbourg, near the Rhine. And, of course, those Hungarian cowboys and Indians on their island in the Danube.

These and similar encampments of earthen lodges and teepees, Indian villages, trading posts and frontier forts of European "weekend" Westerners could be found as well on the banks of the Elbe near Berlin, outside of Cologne and Munich in Germany, Århus in Denmark, Oslo and Porsgrunn in Norway and Göteburg in Sweden.

Of all of these countries, however, the mystique of the Old West seemed strongest among the people of West Germany. There, Western clubs were estimated to number 120, with a combined membership of 3,500. So great, in fact, was the fascination of men in that highly industrialized and densely populated country with the wide open horizons of the American West that there were 25,000 lending libraries circulating nearly 700,000 "Western" books yearly, while publishers had printed an unbelievable 91,000,000 copies of books on the subject in just one year. By far the "most virulent" interest in the West, as Ray Allen Billington said, has existed in West Germany.

Not to be outdone, East Germans had made a series of cowboy-and-Indian films. Of course, their cowboy heroes were blond-haired East Germans, and their Indians black-haired Rumanians.

But it was not just the Germans. . . .

Many years after Westerns had all but disappeared from the movie and television screens of the United States, they were still popular around the world. It was estimated that they had an audience of a quarter of a billion viewers. Some programs ran and reran for up to twenty years. And

103

their public ranged from Asian merchants and Arabian oil workers to European statesmen. Obviously, in the increasingly industrialized and suburbanized world of the late twentieth century, the cowboy was no longer the sole symbol of Americans. He had become, instead, a global symbol for a form of manhood that had universal appeal; for in evermore complex societies where the individual had less and less of a sense of identity, the cowboy retained an image of independence and freedom.

The "rugged individualists of the twentieth century could bask in the belief that frontier America was better suited to their talents," Billington once noted. In their fantasies, the organization men and factory workers of Eastern Europe "could escape the pressures of modern society" by riding off, alone, on their horses (even if they could not ride), with six-guns blazing to protect their independence (even if they could not shoot).

"Here was tonic for tired blood," Billington said, for it offered "a new sense of manhood." This new cowboy was a man of "personal vengeance, bloodshed and freedom"; he was "unrestrained by either civilization or savagery."

Who was this new cowboy? He was Everyman's dream.

The cowboy soldier who belonged to no battalion, no division, no army but his own. The cowboy policeman who took no orders from any officer (with the possible exception of Clint Eastwood). The cowboy factory worker who tightened no bolts or nuts unless he felt the desire to do so. The cowboy politician who belonged to no party, owed no campaign debt and had no outstanding loan from a bank. The cowboy actor who did not read the script because he could not read, but made up his own lines and said whatever was in his heart. The cowboy criminal who was as noble, honest and innocent as his victim.

These were men as no modern man could ever hope to be. Perhaps that was what made them so popular and imitated; they had not existed in history and did not exist now. They were a fantasy, an unobtainable dream, the creation of men's imaginations and wishful thinking. Because they were not real men, they were no threat to the reality faced by men.

And where were the cowmen and cow women of the "real" West? They no longer existed as they had. Nor did the squaw men, the mountain men and women, the fur trappers and fur traders, the homesteaders and settlers, the Mexican and Indian *vaqueros*, the old cowhands who smelled of cow manure.

No, men did not have to become cowhands to become cowboys. Nor was it necessary to ride a horse, tend to cattle, brave a prairie storm, freeze at night, bed down with lice or eat soured beans. The new urban cowboys merely put on their cowboy hats, cowboy shirts with pearl buttons, cowboy jeans with proper labels and cowboy boots from Italy. And maybe slouched.

The chronicler—if not creator—of the urban cowboy, Aaron Latham, wrote in "The Ballad of the Urban Cowboy," in *Esquire*, that "When a city cowboy dons his cowboy clothes he dons more than garments. He dons cowboy values. These values evolved among people who lived fifty miles apart. While they were away from everybody else, they *had* to be independent and self-reliant. And now these values, forged by people who lived too far apart, are serving people who live too close together."

If the Parisian cowboy could boast of his French designer jeans, the Budapest cowboy could boast of the jeans factory that Levi Strauss had built on the Danube. And while the cowboys of Moscow were without an authentic jeans factory of their own, they did have a brisk black-market trade in genuine labels, which could be sewed onto the back pockets of their Russian imitations.

And so did the urban cowboy become the old cowhand; with the purchase of his cowboy hat and jeans he "[drove] from his head the memory of his job," Latham wrote. "He had his armor on."

Ralph Lauren, the pioneering designer of a line of high fashion imitation cowboy clothes, believed his clothes remade the man. For the cowboy's way of dressing had an "American identity," he said; "It has the pioneer look. It has an earthiness. It has a realness . . . [that is] rugged American."

If the clothes alone did not transform the urban man into a rural boy, there were other ways to change his masculinity. Even perfuming the man with a cologne called Chaps, which made him smell like old saddle leather, might help, and if it didn't, there was always a deodorant by the name of Macho.

Cowboy clothes were becoming artifacts, not exhibited in glass museum cases but worn by human mannequins, the living images of an older fantasy. It was like a black stockbroker wearing an African mask to his Wall Street office. Nevertheless, the cowboy costume's incongruity seemed to increase the popularity of the disguise, for the further it was from the everyday reality of the wearer, the more profound the effect it had on him. And the less the urban cowboy knew about how a real cowhand dressed—not to mention what he did—the easier it was to transform the image of a cowboy into his own. The paradox was self-evident. If Easterners, in attempting to look like Westerners, donned an illusion that fitted them, Europeans were now donning an image that did not fit at all.

It was, above all, a masquerade of time and place. The global cowboy moved through space, as though into a time warp, and into another man's body, in another century. As a result, no man in our time has achieved the planetary popularity of the cowboy of the Old West, unless it is the spaceman of the future.

Most essential to the image of the cowboy, however, even more so than his clothes, was his sense of freedom. He was not a refugee; he was a self-exile. And he carried all of his belongings in his saddle bags.

A man who seemed free of society was first of all a man who did not have to work in that society. The "Westerner is *par excellence* the man of leisure," wrote Robert Warshow in *The Immediate Experience*; and so cowboys "were rarely represented as working at all," noted John Cawelti in *The Six Gun Mystique*, for the image of the working cowboy was that of a man who would pack his bag and leave *whenever* he wanted to, for *wherever* he wanted to go. As the famous Western writer Ernest Haycox, talking about his wandering cowboy, put it in *The Man in the Saddle*: "That's your trouble. Always goin' off to take a look at another piece of country . . . Fiddlefooted. Always smellin' the wind for scent. . . ."

Of course, the old cowhands' wanderlust on a ranch

107

was something less carefree than that. One old-time rancher, Spike Van Cleve, recalled in his book *40 Years Gatherin'* that cowhands often would take their wages, maybe twenty dollars a month, go into the nearest town, buy new outfits, get as drunk as they could and then "get word to the boss to come and get them.

"Actually, if a man worked for an outfit long enough, the boss would know about when to come and get him," added Van Cleve. The cowhands could not get far on their wages.

Still, the image of the lone cowhand riding the open range from ranch to ranch persisted in the imaginations of urban cowboys. In reality, however, the ranch was often a cowhand's only home. He was not about to leave it unless he was thrown off. In fact, though these cowhands "damn sure had bark on them," as Van Cleve said, and weren't particularly noted for their social graces, they were not loners. In the bunkhouse most men had the only family they knew, and, like most men, they usually stayed home, going into town no more than "maybe two or three times a year, was all," said Van Cleve. The cowhand was not a drifter, if he could help it, at least not by choice.

Lone rider on the lone prairie, forever searching for his lost dream, the Don Quixote of the range—that was the image that appealed to urban cowboys, not that of the cowhand. He had no love for sleeping on the hard, hard ground. After all, loneliness is a virtue only to the over-crowded.

Even stranger was the irony of history by which cow-boys became the heroes of romantic ecologists. In Europe they became the symbol of the "back-to-nature" movement, and were eulogized—as the Indians had been—as men of the earth who lived close to nature and whose natural and old-fashioned rural way of life was to be emulated—no easy task for an urban cowboy from Munich, Paris or Dallas.

Of course, the cowhands of reality fought nature all of their lives—as had the Indians—in order to survive. If they respected nature it was because they were in fear and awe of it as a friend and as an enemy; its beauty could be deadly, for its cycle of life was the cycle of death as well. In fact, the utopias of the "back-to-nature cultists" who believed that nature was as innocent as the cowboys were "the direct opposite" of Western reality, says Billington.

On the mountains and in the deserts settlers and cowhands, Indians and Mexicans, lived on the edge of survival. It was a fact of the life, and deaths, they shared. And there weren't too many ecologists among the starving.

Not so the back-to-nature enthusiasts who traveled to the West by the millions. In gourmet restaurants in Santa Fe, New Mexico, and luxurious motels in Jackson Hole, Wyoming, they sought a oneness with the earth, a spirituality with nature and a space in history. And in their cowboy hats and boots they came to watch Indians dance in reverence to the earth and flew hundreds of miles in jet planes to ride for a few days on the back of a tired horse.

Of all the many attempts, however, to transform the nineteenth-century cowhand into the urban cowboy of the twentieth century, none was as foolish, amusing, ridiculous, vain, glorious, sad and frightening as the politicians who used the *macho* image of the Old West to justify their rhetoric, especially in matters of war and patriotism.

These political cowboys are oddly apolitical; they are liberal and conservative, Republican and Democrat, from the East and West. Neither their political programs, nor their ideologies are as important as their *macho* images. Once these politicians mount their white horses, it did not matter that they cannot ride; what seemed to matter to the public, instead, is that they exhibited the qualities of cowboy *macho* and performed like cowboys. So have the presidents since the end of the Second World War tried to act. There are even some for whom it wasn't an act at all.

The code of honor that guided President Dwight D. Eisenhower in the military, and later in politics, was that of "a man named Wild Bill Hickok," said Ike. His was the code of the shoot-out on Main Street in the movie *High Noon*. Not the code of the real-life gunman but the remembered one of the imagined West. Many years later, Eisenhower recalled it vividly:

"I was raised in a little town of which many of you may never have heard. But out West it is a famous place. It is called Abilene. We had as our marshall a man named Wild Bill Hickok. Now, that town had a code, and I was raised as a boy to prize that code. It was: Meet anyone face-to-face with whom you disagree. You could not sneak up on him from behind. If you met him face-to-face, and took the risks as he did, you could get away with almost anything. . . ."

No doubt this code—real or imagined—of the Western gunman did guide Eisenhower in his political and military life. And even though no "face-to-face" shoot-out ever took place on the dirt streets of Abilene, it became a powerful image in the mind of the president.

The "New Frontier" program of President John Kennedy, on the other hand, offered no such ambiguity. Kennedy considered himself marshall of the frontier he created; his language clearly indicated that. As an associate has said,

JFK was "very conscious of his masculinity and virility," and liked to "shoot from the hip," as he did during the Cuban missile crisis.

In Lyndon Baines Johnson the real and imaginary West became one. The president himself could not tell them apart, as when he proudly boasted that his great-great-grandfather had fought at the Alamo and then had to be reminded that it was not quite true: His great-great-great grandfather had fought at San Jacinto. The curious difference is that the Texans won at San Jacinto but lost at the Alamo. They seemed to honor the defeat more than the victory.

So it was with the president. In *The Life and Times of Lyndon Johnson,* Ronnie Dugger described how LBJ "reared back in his rocking chair and bellowed" the schoolboy doggerel of his childhood:

> *Surrender or die! Men what*
> *will you do?*
> *And Travis, great Travis, drew*
> *sword quick and strong,*
> *Drew a line at his feet. "Will*
> *you come? Will you go?*
> *I die with my wounded in the*
> *Alamo."*

"The powerful story of the Alamo, structured in the President's character, was one cause of Vietnam," thought Dugger, for hadn't Johnson said to him, "Hell, Vietnam is just like the Alamo."

Scratching out a living on the plains of Texas and Kansas, the ancestors of LBJ were true cowhands. His grandfather knew Wild Bill Hickok up in Abilene and his great uncle was a cowhand on the great cattle drives. They "were living men," said Dugger, whose adventure, "filter [ed] through the fantasies of millions of people, through the decades, became the myth of the West." Lyndon Johnson inherited the legacy of those working cowhands; why then did he falsify the myth of the cowboy to demonstrate his manhood?

Ruefully commenting on this image, Aaron Latham has written apprehensively of our "new cowboy commander in chief—with his nuclear six-shooters strapped to his hips [who] may once again be tempted to replay old horse opera plots disguised as American foreign policy. By trying to reenact the way-the-West-was-won he could end up by acting out how-the-world-was-lost."

No one has more sharply and succinctly described why the image of the old cowhand is of no use to a modern politician, while the image of the new cowboy, six-gun in hand, fits so well, than did Henry Kissinger in an interview with Italian journalist Oriana Fallaci. And while Kissinger did not say whether his image of himself as an urban cowboy was influenced by the romantic German writer of Western fantasies, Karl Mai, whom he had read as a child, he did say: "The main point stems from the fact that I've always acted alone. Americans admire that enormously. Americans admire the cowboy leading the caravan alone [sic], astride his horse entering a village or city alone on his horse. Without even a pistol, maybe, because he doesn't go in for shooting.

"He acts, that's all; aiming at the right spot at the right time. A Wild West if you like. . . ."

And so the war in Vietnam became a fantasy "like the Wild West," fought by peacemakers "without a pistol, maybe." The myth of the new cowboy, and his transformation from the old cowhand, could not have been more complete; he had been turned into the mirror image of everything he had been, though he was disguised as himself. In a sense, the war in Vietnam was another frontier war, and President Johnson was more accurate than he knew.

The gun in the cowboy's hand was an essential piece of his new costume. And the twentieth century was the stage for the largest global wars in history. The bloody battles the cowboy fought were historically accurate—not for his time, but for ours. He was in a time warp.

As the writer George Fronval, who wrote no less than six hundred French Westerns, said, "The Frenchman wants the guns and the shoot'em-ups and the scalps." So did everyone else. Manhood had to be served—by death. The gun was a necessary part of the cowboy's disguise. For without his gun he might be mistaken for nothing more than a dirty old cowhand and no one would know he was a hero.

In a similar vein, some of the other disguises of the new cowboy were beyond recognition. He was not merely the president and secretary of state, he was Han Solo and Luke Skywalker, the heroes of the movie *Star Wars*; he was the test pilot with "the Right Stuff" as well as the long-haul truck driver, the Main Street low-rider and the professional football player, the German ecologist and the French intellectual, the Hungarian engineer and the Marlboro Man. The costume of the cowboy disguised the Israeli soldier, the Palestinian guerrilla, the young communist in his proud jeans and the capitalist who sold them.

The story is told of how Leonid Brezhnev and Richard Nixon, who were on their way to a summit conference in San Clemente in 1974 on Air Force One, were over the

113

Grand Canyon when the president pointed out the sight to the Soviet premier. Oh, I have already seen it, said Brezhnev, in the John Wayne movies in the Kremlin, whereupon the leaders of the two most powerful nations on earth stood face-to-face in the aisle of the plane, as in *High Noon*, drew their revolvers in the form of their fingers and shot each other dead.

Surely the manhood of these cowboys would have fascinated and intrigued men of other lands, because so many of their ideas of manhood came from other lands. The cowboy was not merely an Indian and Mexican *vaquero* with the blood of a European horseman; he was also a Persian, Arabian, Mongolian, Bedouin, Moorish and Spanish horseman. He was universal.

Accordingly, men no longer had to re-create their images to fit that of the new cowboy. His image was now their own, and they fitted into it without any effort at all.

The rebirth of the cowboy as an astronaut or space scientist was perhaps the most appropriate. In a study of the "Psychology of the Apollo Moon Scientists" that was funded by NASA, Ian Mitroff of the University of Pittsburgh's Graduate School of Business found that the "intense masculinity of the scientists [was] defined in the most traditional, and narrowest, senses of masculinity." They boasted of their "raw and even brutal aggressiveness," reported Mitroff, and were intensely masculine and *macho*. These spacemen were, he concluded, as they often have been called, the new "cosmic cowboys."

The legacy of the cowhands and cowboys had passed at last from men of the West. And, as expected, the heirs to that legacy did not ascend to the heavens but seemed to be suspended in space, between myth and reality, as legends should be.

Men of preceeding generations always said that the manhood of the West died every twenty years. The mountain men said it first in 1840, the covered wagon pioneers in 1860, the settlers in 1880, the Eastern writers in 1900, the cowmen in 1920, the cowhands in 1940, the old-timers in 1960, the newcomers in 1980. Manhood had died so often that it could not die. In the West, it was reborn with each new generation of dead men.

Not that its men were truly dead. The death of the unique manhood associated with the West would mean that the land had died, for that manhood was rooted deep in the earth that gave it form and shape and meaning. No, it was not dying. It was changing. And the "cosmic cowboy" affected and reflected these changes, but he no more created them than the astronauts had created space.

Old cowhands do not die. They do not even fade away. They have no place to hide. They get jobs in town and buy urban cowboy clothes and become weekend cowboys. Everywhere in the urban West one can see the phenomenon of rural men becoming their own myth, imitating themselves.

"The West is dead? Never! Long live the West!" intoned the Western historian Alvin Josephy, Jr., with the fervor of a true believer. "Myth and reality live on . . ."

The good old "doc" of the once-frontier town of Jackson Hole, Wyoming, Dr. C. W. "Buzz" Ely, Jr., came up with a practical way of preserving the manhood of the West. He had read about scientists who set up a sperm bank for the seeds of geniuses. So, he thought, why not preserve the seeds of "ranchers, cowboys, prospectors and gunfighters" in the same way? In his office he established a sperm bank where the seeds of the "real men" of the West could wait for willing women who desired "to keep the spirit and substance of the Old West alive. . . ."

Today, beneath the shadow of those Teton Rockies, where Shoshone once camped and mountain men dreamt and vast herds of cattle roamed, the sperm of the men of the "Old West" sit.

And wait.

SPACE COWBOYS: NOTES ON THE COSMIC COWBOYS

One morning in the Feed Bag Café up in Ashland, Montana, I heard this old cowboy story: It seems that a tourist lady had wandered into this saloon where an old cowboy was holding up the bar. She went up to him and asked, "Are you a cowboy?"

"Ma'am," he replied, "I guess so."

"Tell me why you cowboys wear cowboy hats," she asked. He told her.

"Tell me why you wear cowboy shirts," she asked. He told her.

"Tell me why you wear cowboy jeans," she asked. He told her.

"Then tell me why," she asked, "you are wearing tennis shoes."

117

"Ma'am"—the cowboy smiled—"that's to differentiate us real cowboys from the truck drivers."

The spirit of the daring, proud, individualistic old cowboy heroes of the West lives on in America, even if some of the modern would-be cowboys wear tennis shoes. One attempt to reinvoke this ideal of manhood in the early 1980s was *The Right Stuff*, both the book and movie, which portrayed the original seven Mercury astronauts as cosmic cowboys riding around the universe on NASA's bucking broncos. *The Right Stuff*, however, also revived all of the old conflicts over masculinity and patriotism in our culture without clarifying them.

In his book, Tom Wolfe described the Mercury astronauts as "pioneers of a New Frontier." On their jet-fueled steeds, they were astronautical Lone Rangers and John Waynes in space suits, the horseless "Knights of the Right Stuff," who looked down upon the earthbound citizen as a "mouseshit sheepherder from Shane," or so Wolfe said.

The film begins with test pilot Chuck Yeager, played by the actor Sam Shephard, riding out to Edwards Air Force Base on his horse. (He even looks like Gary Cooper, and the old airfield resembles a set on a Hollywood backlot.) Amid the cacti and Joshua trees sits a lil' old X-1 rocket plane in which Yeager is going to break the sound barrier. The cowboy test pilot circles the rocket plane like a cowhand eyeing a new, unbroken stallion. Then he gallops off to Pancho Barnes's Fly Inn to meet his cowgirl woman, who challenges him to a passionate mating race on horseback, and the two ride off into the sunset. Yeager falls off his horse and breaks a few ribs and his right arm—without a murmur of pain, of course. In the morning, he breaks the sound barrier with one hand—in good rodeo-cowboy style. In case anyone misses the symbolism, conversations between Yeager and his flight engineer drive it home. Yeager gets into his "saddle" (cockpit) before taking off to break the sound barrier. His "pardner" (engineer) encourages him by crying, "Put the spurs to her, Chuck!"

As we know, this particular "old-timer" did not become an astronaut. Nonetheless, it is the maverick Yeager who epitomizes the qualities summed up as "the Right Stuff" in both the book and the film; he is the real cowboy with the wildly impetuous courage and laid-back cool under fire of all good "fighter jocks." And though the Mercury astronauts may have had "the Right Stuff," too, theirs was confined to a metal container.

Neither the attitudes nor the language of that tumbleweed of a man, a free-willed and wandering cowboy, fit too well into the mechanized and collective world of space science. It is difficult to imagine Yeager, the old-time cowhand, strapped into one of NASA's space capsules like a chimpanzee. So, too, the conflicts were inevitable between the pilots, who saw themselves as cowboys, and NASA scientists, especially the German rocket experts led by Wernher Von Braun, who had designed the first capsule without a window or pilot controls, like a horse without reins. Dammit, we're pilots not monkeys, the Mercury astronauts insisted.

Not everyone is enamored of this cosmic-cowboy macho, of course. Those critical of *The Right Stuff* say it does not fulfill its heroic image. The *Christian Science Monitor*'s reviewer called it "a Class-C Western"; "it trivializes the notion of heroism," the reviewer said. His review was

119

entitled "Rhinestone Astronauts." Rhinestone who? Wasn't the reviewer confusing the astronauts with *Midnight Cowboy?*

It eventually dawned on NASA's psychologists that the astronauts' cowboy style might be a handicap on the team missions of the Apollo program. The psychological investigators of NASA wanted to find out what the conflicts would be when these rugged individualists worked in a corporate-like scientific collective. In other words: What happens when a cowboy programs the computers?

The men of the Mercury and Apollo space programs continued in the cowboy tradition established by the test pilots of the 1940s and '50s. Their programmed moon missions may have been controlled by computers, but at the heart of the systems were daring and adventurous pilots willing to risk their lives so they could sashay on the surface of the moon as if they were at a Western country dance.

The original macho astronaut, in the eyes of the media, was Alan Shepard, maybe because he was the first chosen to go into space. In the movie version of *The Right Stuff* he is played by Scott Glenn, no relation to John. Curiously, the actor earned his part with his performance in *Urban Cowboy*, in which he portrayed John Travolta's "macho nemesis." Glenn is known for his macho-type roles, says his agent. The "man with the sandpaper face," he looked like an astronaut ought to look; he *looked* like he had the Right Stuff.

In real life Scott Glenn is the role he so often performs. He lives not in Hollywood but in Idaho. The "rough life" appeals to him, he has said, and he prefers the cowboy world. Sometimes a man becomes the image of himself that is projected on the screen.

Although the astronauts, being private men, like the cowboys, bridled under the public acclaim that was their due as heroes, some of them gloried in the spotlight.

One evening while dozing before the television set, I was awakened by the sight of Wally Schirra in a space suit saying to me, "Can you imagine coughing in one of these?" Schirra was selling cough medicine. It was nevertheless a startling awakening to the realities of wearing Buck Rogers underwear. Suddenly I could think of a dozen other things one could not do in a space suit besides coughing—at least not on a satellite hookup and network television with the whole world watching.

At first glance the sight of an astronaut moonlighting as a salesman seemed a little unpatriotic. Should a man with the Right Stuff promote cough medicine? On second glance, why not? The media has reshaped these men, as it does all celebrities, into marketable products.

Even Yeager, who had the "purest" Right Stuff, was not too pure for a little advertising. One day, in *The New York Times*, there was Chuck Yeager selling whisky. The copywriter had written: "If there's anyone who has 'the Right Stuff,' it's Chuck Yeager. Especially when it comes to the Scotch he drinks, Cutty Sark." Of course, he wasn't drinking it while breaking the sound barrier—not at 86 proof. And who can blame Yeager, who was paid about $250 per month by the Air Force in the days he was breaking the sound barrier, for finally benefiting a little from his exploits. "One is punished for one's virtues," said Nietzsche.

Of course behind all the publicity that turned the astronauts into celebrities there were real heroes. They didn't need the media hype. They were old-fashioned men who were ahead of their time, as anachronistic as a cowboy in orbit. But the public, seeing what it was shown, confused the television pictures with life in a space capsule. A man in orbit is still a man, but the television cameras showed no pain, no fear, no sweat.

All of this reminded me of the years when "A-OK" swept the country in a euphoria of good cheer. In *The Right Stuff* what Alan Shepard actually said first was, "Please, dear God, don't let me fuck up." Shepard's second epochal announcement when he was asked if he was ready to blast off was, "I have to urinate"—which, after much scientific consultation, he was permitted to do in his space suit. It was a comment every cowboy would have appreciated. After all, did the cowboy not smell of cow manure? Or did he wear Ralph Lauren's Chaps cologne?

The memory of old-fashioned patriotism and bygone masculinity is what this story is all about. And that is its problem. Neither the moviemakers nor Tom Wolfe seems to know what this kind of patriotism and manhood really implies, and what they do know makes them uncomfortable. So they mimic it, mock it and parody it, but they do not know how to portray it.

Love of country is described as *"joie de combat"* by

Wolfe. That is not the same, however, as patriotism. In the book and movie, the men who believe in love of country are depicted as fools. So Lyndon Johnson, shown welcoming the NASA space program to Houston with a burst of patriotic rhetoric, is seen standing on an American flag, an unlikely stance for the President of the United States.

And yet, if manhood and patriotism are ridiculed, they are also glorified at the same time. It is as if the makers of *The Right Stuff* were embarrassed by the heroic themes and heroic men they had reluctantly created in the film, which John Glenn feared might become *Laurel and Hardy in Space*. In some ways *The Right Stuff* resembles the patriotic movies of the Second World War. But it is as if *Midway, Action in the North Atlantic* and *Destination Tokyo* were remade by Robert Altman into *M*A*S*H*, with Alan Alda cast in the role of General MacArthur.

Likewise, in the manner of a city slicker on a dude ranch attempting to comprehend Western life, Wolfe in his book seeks to understand why the astronauts "do it," why they are willing to go to "the edge of death." But he cannot. The heroism of these men must be a "Freudian death wish," he concludes, claiming that the Right Stuff/Death is a forbidden subject that no one at NASA will think or talk about. Smile when you see your psychiatrist, Wolfe suggests, was NASA's approach.

That, it seems to me, may be a misreading of the minds and psyches of the Mercury astronauts. When they went to "the edge," it was not to go over it but to challenge and overcome it. Death may hold a fascination for a Spanish matador in the bullring or a Shiite Moslem on a suicide mission, but it is not a very American idea of heroism.

More likely the astronauts thought of themselves as rodeo riders. They stared death in the face, winked and walked away; no cowboy wants to kill himself—he just wants to see how close he can come.

Similarly, if a man was a man, he had "it," according to Wolfe, but didn't flaunt it. For Wolfe, "it" seems to be "nothing less than manhood itself." "It" is "manliness, manhood, and manly courage," which a "man either had or he didn't"; "it" was "ancient, primordial, and even mystical."

Perhaps it was to Tom Wolfe. But don't tell that to a cowboy or an astronaut. They were just trying to stay in the saddle, for theirs was not the idea, but the deed, of manhood. They didn't have to *define* manhood; they *knew* they had the Right Stuff. It was a visceral feeling they did not have to—and could not—articulate in either locker-room words or academic terms.

Today, manhood is more difficult to define, and patriotism is almost un-American. "The Right Stuff," which is an expression of manhood, not its essence, is understandably popular.

The original test pilots were heroes because they were willing to push themselves beyond the limit of human endurance, Wolfe writes in a moment of admiration, but then he quickly reminds us that in our own age such virtue is "out of style." These men were really inspired, he continues, by the "infinite variety of goodies" they were offered, like the "juicy little girls" in the cocktail lounges of Cape Canaveral—as if any bar lush could be an astronaut if he were macho enough.

No, my guess would be that "it" was the astronauts' individualistic, ornery, obstreperous, independent, old-fashioned ideas of American manhood and patriotism.

After all, they were cosmic cowboys. Weren't they?

PART III

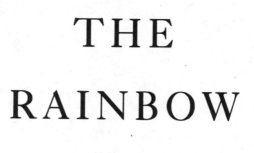

THE
RAINBOW
WEST

The essays included in The Rainbow West most profoundly represent Stan Steiner's life work. While some people think of the West in terms of cowboys, Stan always saw a rainbow of people when he looked at the West. He was deeply interested in the Chicanos, Native Americans, Chinese and others who contributed to the cultural diversity of the West. Stan never saw this cultural mix as a melting pot, but rather as a glorious rainbow with bands of color that frequently overlapped or blended, yet retained their beautiful, distinct colorations.

Much of his youth was spent growing up in a multi-cultural neighborhood on the Upper East Side of New York. Czechs, Hungarians and Germans were among those who settled in the area. He loved the cultural diversity, with a sense of community, that was a part of daily life there. He was therefore understandably saddened by the advent of high rises,

which led to the destruction of local bars and community houses.

Years later, the living presence of many cultures in his adopted Southwestern hometown of Santa Fe was significant to him. The Native Americans and Hispanics, who had deeply rooted traditions, in particular fascinated him, and he was fond of saying that the only other place in the United States that had the same degree of diversity and versatility of cultures was Hawaii.

His piece "None of Us Is Native" was written as part of a series of stories funded by a grant from the New Mexico Humanities Council, an affiliate of the National Endowment for the Humanities, for *New Mexico Magazine*'s "New Mexico's 75th Anniversary, Diamond Jubilee Year" project. The article was written to pay homage to the forgotten people who had settled the state—from Esteban, the black Moor who guided an expedition in search of the Seven Cities of Cíbola, to the Vietnamese boat people who have immigrated to the area in more recent years.

Stan's story "Jewish Conquistadors: America's First Cowboys?" was one of the most controversial to ever appear in *American West* magazine. Perhaps one reason why it caused such a stir was that it did not fit many people's preconceived notions of what the West was all about. Rather than becoming upset, however, Stan enjoyed the controversy. It excited him to realize he was able to get people to think about history in new ways. For him, that was part of the fun of being a writer, particularly a writer who was willing to take chances.

Of course, Stan had a strong personal interest in the impact of Jews on the West, since many of his ancestors were of Jewish extraction. And though he was raised in a home where Judaism was not practiced, his family's traditions were steeped in a vestigial central European culture that shaped its daily life. In addition, his wife, Vera, shared her knowledge of Judaism with him. Together they visited many of the places where victims of the Holocaust were honored, and over and over again they saw the name Steiner. Many of his aunts and uncles had been killed. Stan was profoundly touched by the experience and ever after identified with the history of genocide and oppression.

Stan always felt that the Chinese were another forgotten influence in the West. An excerpt from his book *Fusang: The Chinese Who Built America* is included in this section for that reason. The chapter "The Chinese Railroad Men" tells the story of the forgotten men who had such a powerful impact on the expansion of "civilization" into the West.

Several of Stan's most important works dealt with the strength of Native Americans in the West. His book *The New Indians* became a landmark piece about contemporary Indian leaders. He had a long association with Navajo leader Peterson Zah, who headed the Navajo legal council for many years. Theirs was a mutual respect for one another that developed over a long period of time.

Zah was, and is, the kind of person who represents most deeply the Native Americans portrayed in Stan's book. He's a Native American leader who remained powerfully connected to his elders but at the same time was able to mobilize and work with a broad range of people, from Harvard lawyers to Navajo sheepherders.

At the time of Stan's essay, Zah was recently elected chairman. Since that time, Peter MacDonald, who is also mentioned in the essay, was reelected as tribal chairman. At press time, MacDonald faced serious allegations by the Navajo administration that he had diverted funds.

Stan also conducted a personal inteview with Archbishop Roberto Sanchez for this book. Stan had admired the archbishop of Santa Fe for a long time, and was especially pleased and proud that someone who so deeply represented Southwestern traditions had become archbishop. In addition, Stan had always been profoundly attracted to and influenced by the great Catholic thinkers, especially to what he called their "integrated vision." He and the archbishop had many conversations over the years and would send one another notes and relevant articles. Stan was very taken with the archbishop and his clarity in seeing the relationship between family and the church. The piece, "The Church Is Family" is based on a personal interview with the Archbishop Sanchez.

Levi Strauss was a Jewish peddler whose most famous product—rugged denim pants—helped shape our image of the West. Over a number of years, Stan corresponded with and finally met Roy "Bud" Johns, who was then an executive at the Levi Strauss company. Stan was charmed and a bit surprised by Johns, a person who ended up in corporate America but had an earthy and wise approach to life. Fittingly, his testimonial concludes the section on the Rainbow West. For today, the Irish cowboy, Navajo lawyer, Hispanic rancher and Vietnamese boat person all find themselves at one time or another wearing Levi's.

NONE OF US
IS NATIVE

❖

"None of us is native to this land," Montezuma said to Hernando Cortés.

On that autumn day in 1519 when the Aztec emperor welcomed the *conquistador* of Spain to Mexico, he shook his head and greeted him with gifts of gold and "words of politeness." He thought the Spaniard was a god, a belief that Cortés considered "a joke." He told Montezuma, "My body is flesh and bones like your body," and added, "I come in peace."

The emperor and his Aztec subjects believed that everyone on earth was a stranger to the earth as well as to one another. Everyone was an eternal wanderer, they said.

It was so. The Aztecs once had been foreigners from the northern mountains and the Spaniards were foreigners from across the sea. Even the local Indians came from somewhere else. In their creation stories, they told of how their ancestors had emerged from the earth and wandered on long journeys until they found their home.

And to this day the mountains of New Mexico—like those of old Mexico—are home to wanderers and exiles from everywhere on earth. Refugees and adventurers still come to New Mexico, not only from Spain but from throughout Europe, Africa, Asia and South America.

Of the early Europeans to explore the New World, the first were led by Álvar Nuñez Cabeza de Vaca, who was shipwrecked in 1528 on the coast of Texas. For eight years he and three companions wandered across the Southwest, living like the area's Indians. The most famous of these reluctant explorers was the black Moor Estéban, who in 1539 was chosen by Don Antonio de Mendoza, viceroy of Mexico, to guide an expedition in search of the Seven Cities of Cíbola.

Not so honored were the black Moors who accompanied Cortés on his conquest of Mexico, said by some to number three hundred. History has forgotten them.

The Sephardic Jews from southern Spain were not quite as easy to ignore. By 1545, a quarter of the Spaniards in Mexico City were Jews, and some Spanish historians have estimated that by the 1600s half the population may have been Jewish. When the Inquisition came to Mexico, many of these exiles fled north to New Mexico.

From the beginning, the *entradas* (expeditions) of the *conquistadores* were made up of people from many nations. One of the most international was that of Francisco Vásquez de Coronado, who came to Nueva España, as New Mexico was called, in 1540. His company bugler was a German, and among the *conquistadores* who marched with him were two Italians, five Portuguese, a Frenchman and a Scot by the name of Thomas Blake who hispanicized his name to Tomás Blaque.

No less multinational were the armies of Catholic missionaries who journeyed north. These Jesuit fathers included Juan Bautista Grashofer, Ignax Pferferkorn, Juan Netvig, Ignacio Keller, Gaspar Stiger and Eusebio Stiger, who were no more Spanish than their surnames.

Through the centuries, the "Hispanic" or Spanish settlers of New Mexico were men and women of all nations, not merely from Spain. In Mexico, they were so diverse and varied in their origins that the Mexican philosopher José Vasconceles called them *La Raza Cósmica*, the Cosmic Race.

In New Mexico these settlers adopted the beliefs and customs of those who had come from Mexico and Spain. For example, the religious pageant called *"Los Moros y los Cristianos"* (The Moors and Christians) is performed to this day in the village of Chimayó, north of Santa Fe. And the Matachines Dance, which might have originated in Africa, was brought to New Mexico by the Spanish and still is performed in Hispanic villages, as well as in some of the Indian pueblos, where the dance has been adapted for their celebrations.

Not even the early *vaqueros* (cowboys) were wholly Spanish. In the beginning, in fact, they were mostly Indians. As a historian of Western cattle ranching, Arnold R. Rojas, wrote in his book *The Vaquero*: "I do not come from an 'Old Spanish family.' Old Spanish families are an invention of the *gringos*. They are a myth which *paisanos* have come to believe themselves, as Sancho [Panza] did his enchantment of Dulcinea in *Don Quixote*.

"The blood of *caballeros*, bullfighters, Jew, Moors, Basquez and Indian heroes ran in the *vaquero*'s veins," Rojas

133

said. "He was a strange mixture of races. He admired his Iberian fathers, but sided and sympathized with his raped Indian mothers."

Even the *vaquero*'s Western style of horsemanship was not Spanish. It was primarily African, Rojas wrote. The original "cowboy is indebted to the Negro for his culture. His way of riding, known as *La Gineta*, comes from that of the Arabs, Moors, Tartars and Cossacks," as did his horses, saddles and *macho* ideas.

In New Mexico, the *vaqueros* developed their own unique way of living and thinking. They were isolated from old Mexico and Spain—some by choice. And they were thought of by Europeans as *los bárbaros*, "the barbarians," a people with no home of their own, the wanderers.

The coming of the "Anglos" to New Mexico in the early nineteenth century did not change that legacy. Instead, the Easterners combined their way of life with the Westerners', re-creating their traditions to fit contemporary needs.

One of the first Anglos to come to New Mexico was Baptiste la Lande, a French Creole from Louisiana. A mountain man and trader, he settled in Santa Fe and married an Indian woman in 1804, the year of the Lewis and Clark expedition. Lande, however, was not the first Frenchman to see New Mexico. He had been preceded by Pierre Vial of Lyon and was followed by Jacques Clamorgan in 1807, who was followed in turn by Ceran St. Vrain, the Rubidoux brothers and dozens of others who became known as "squaw-men" because they lived as the Indians did.

Mountain men and fur trappers in New Mexico came from many nations. They were self-exiles who found peace among the Indians and Mexicans.

The best known of these mountain men was Kit Carson,

a hunter and U.S. Army scout who became a hero of the Anglo conquest of New Mexico. Carson protected himself from reprisals by having two wives, one Indian and one Spanish. In that way he personally mated opposing people by love.

Another symbol of these inter-cultural matings was the New Mexican mountain man Jim Beckwourth, who seemed for years to be all but invisible to historians. Maybe that was because he was a black man. In his time, Beckwourth was said to be the "most famous Indian fighter of his generation," and like Kit Carson, he had both an Indian and a Mexican wife. He was the Othello of the frontier.

In New Mexico the Indian, Spaniard and Anglo became part of one historical family. At the same time, on the old Santa Fe Trail, merchants and traders brought the East to the West. The *extranjeros*, or "strangers," paved the path for what Western historian Howard Lamar has called the "conquest by Merchants."

Later in the nineteenth century, railroads opened mountain villages to the commerce of the rest of the country. An influx of new immigrants was led first of all by the railroad builders themselves, Chinese workers whose influence lingered as they traded in their picks and axes to become merchants and restaurant owners after the railroad was built, and was reflected in the names of certain Indian leaders, including the tribal chairman of the Mescalero Apaches, Wendell Chino.

Today, we appreciate the fact that the religions and cultures of New Mexico always have been entwined and intermingled. Even though these cultures have often been antagonistic, they have, for the most part, existed side by side and often within each other's families and communities.

135

In the last hundred and fifty years New Mexico has seen Polish and Slovak miners settle near the coal fields around Gallup and Silver City. To the north, near the Colorado line, Japanese farmers have maintained vegetable farms for generations. To the south, in the cow towns and oil fields of Little Texas, Irish cowboys and German settlers who learned cowboying from the Mexicans became folk heroes, including Billy the Kid, the Irish boy born in Brooklyn who was protected by the Mexicans. From overseas came entrepreneurs to cash in on the territory's suddenly marketable wealth. There were German Jewish bankers in Santa Fe, Lebanese merchants in Albuquerque and English and Scottish ranchers working for the land and cattle companies of southeastern New Mexico.

Seeking a new life, refugees from around the world came to New Mexico. Nowadays they come not only from the East but from the Far East as well. In the old Hispanic *barrios* of the cities one can find Vietnamese, Cambodians, Laotians, Filipinos and numerous other peoples from Southeast Asia who have established communities of their own. In Albuquerque shopping malls there are stores carrying the foods and condiments of Asia. Spices of the Orient are sold beside the chiles and tortillas of New Mexico. Some of these foods are remarkably similar. It is only a matter of time before someone invents a Vietnamese burrito or a chile-and-curry salsa.

Many of these newcomers are exiles and refugees from our own Eastern cities. Some have come from the dying steel towns and bankrupt farms of the Midwest; others have left California's Rodeo Drive for the real rodeos of New Mexico. And then there are those who have come down the highways from the Panhandle and dry plains of Texas on their way to Los Angeles only to have their cars or campers break down in Albuquerque.

And they stay. . . .

They came and continue to come searching for the Enchanted Land, the Shangri-la of New Mexico promised them in tourist brochures. And so they seek not the gold of Coronado's Seven Cities of Cíbola but the reality of the dream, a home of their own, a place on earth.

To the Aztecs, people had no home on earth. And that may be why they were forever wandering in search of a home. So the Aztec poets sang:

> *And so we live on earth.*
> *Not forever, but a little.*
> *We came here to be born.*
> *Our home is elsewhere.*
> *All is like a dream.*
> *We live only in a dream.*

In the mountains and deserts of New Mexico, the dream seemed to be real. And it still does.

JEWISH CONQUISTADORS: AMERICA'S FIRST COWBOYS?

❖

On the eastern shore of Mexico where he landed with his armored soldiers and horsemen, Cortés unfurled the banners of the Spanish emperor and implanted the Holy Cross of Christ on the beach underneath the palm trees claiming all the land in the name of Charles V, his Sacred Majesty, the Potent Prince, the Most High and Excellent Emperor of the Realm, and the King of Spain. By his side stood his friend and fellow *conquistador*, Hernando Alonso, a Jew.

Of those who came with Cortés there were six known Jewish *conquistadores*. There were undoubtedly many more, but these six were known by name to the Holy Inquisition.

Less than a decade after they had charged across the land with swords drawn and conquered Mexico in the name of Spain, two of these Jewish *conquistadores* had been burned at the stake, fallen heroes.

One of those who was burned alive was Hernando Alonso. He died on October 17, 1528.

In spite of his fame and wealth, no one could save him. His brother-in-law, Diego de Ordaz, was not only a fellow *conquistador* and a rancher second only to Cortés, but was the representative of Governor Velasquez of Cuba; he was therefore a man of great power at the court. In spite of his efforts on Alonso's behalf, a heroic Jew was nonetheless a Jew, and so he died.

The Jewish *conquistador* who marched beside Cortés was more than a *conquistador*. He was not just a conqueror, he was also a settler on the land—a horse rancher. And he was, perhaps, the first Jewish cowboy in America.

Eighty miles north of Mexico City, at the town of Actopan, Hernando Alonso established a cattle ranch, one of the first in Mexico, and there he raised cattle and supplied meats to the city. There, too, he bred what may have been the first foals born in the Americas. He was one of the earliest known ranchers in the New World, and his ranch grew large and prosperous.

Many of the first European ranchers, cattle growers and horse breeders in Mexico were Jews. The raising of livestock was not unfamiliar to the Spanish Jews, and since most of the *conquistadores* in the Cortés expedition were not interested in ranching—Cortés said disdainfully that he had not come to America "to work with his hands"—it fell to others to raise the livestock. And for the Jews who were in the land illegally—the Spanish laws prohibited any Jews

139

traveling to the Americas—it may have seemed a safe and inconspicuous way of living. They came to hide from the laws. And once in America they disguised themselves as ranchers, something the Spaniards tolerated, at first, since they needed meat and grain as they themselves searched for treasure.

Even if the Jewish *conquistadores* had found gold, they could not have taken it out of the land. They could not return to Spain. And so ranching became a quiet refuge for these exiled Jews, who were the first cattlemen of Mexico and helped introduce cattle ranching into the American West.

They are the most forgotten and ignored of the dark and dashing horsemen, which is unfortunate, for their saga is one of the most exciting and significant in the history of horsemanship.

One of the largest of the cattle ranches in Mexico, Nuevo León, was established by Jewish *conquistadores* near Pánuco on the Gulf coast in late 1579. In that forsaken region, two hundred miles from Mexico City, twice as far north as the Alonso ranch had been, more than one hundred Jewish families settled and founded a vast ranching operation.

Far from those intrigues and conflicts in Mexico City, these settlers probably thought they would be beyond the reach of the Holy Inquisition. That may have been one of the reasons Philip II of Spain granted them the land called Nuevo León—to isolate these Jewish exiles away from the Mexican capital.

Nuevo León was one of the largest royal land grants ever given by the king. It ran from the Pánuco River northward across the Rio Grande, known then as the River of the Palms, onto the plains of west Texas, to the site of the present-day city of San Antonio—six hundred miles!

On May 31, 1579, the royal charter for Nuevo León was drawn up by Antonio Pérez, the secretary to the king. Pérez at that time served as the alter ego and, some said, the Machiavelli of courtly Philip, who signed it in the name of "God and me," as he liked to say.

The "empire within an empire" was given to the *hidalgo* don Luis de Carvajal y de la Cueva, who was to be its governor-general. He came from an old and distinguished family. One of his maternal uncles, Francisco Jorge de Andrada, had been a captain-general in the court of the King of Portugal and one of his brothers was an influential monk in the Jesuit order. The Carvajals were a family of some prominence and stature in Spain as well. It was a Carvajal, Dr. Luis Galindez de Carvajal, a noted jurist, who was appointed correo mayor, or postmaster general, of the Indies. And it was a Carvajal who was the director of the Casa de Contratacion, the omnipotent House of Trade in Seville that regulated all commerce to and from the Americas. These were gentlemen of comfort, and they lived an opulent and extravagant life.

In the Americas, the world of the Renaissance palaces and courtly trading houses seemed as distant as the stars. The lizards slid up and down the walls of their mud houses, and snakes lay coiled beneath their beds. And to a certain degree these wealthy Jews were going to have to live like Indians.

Pánuco was no promised land. It, too, had its terrors. The forest beyond the beach was dark with real and imagined dangers. Not only were there the small sleek cats, the ocelots and lynxs, but also the frightening jaguars and pumas.

In the dense growth of vines and ferns the darkness was almost impenetrable, even in broad day. And in that subterranean world there lurked poisonous snakes and vampire bats that awaited an unwary traveler. The forest was treacherous and deceptive; it enticed the romantic with a display of incredible beauty and then entrapped him like an animal. So, the land conquered its conquerors.

Life was hard in paradise; it was "an uncomfortable and hot place," one settler wrote. And it was "full of mosquitos." The disillusioned Jews even had to walk "barefoot."

None of this was very new to don Carvajal, though; he came to the Indies in 1566 and gained some small reputation as a naval captain who had "fought against the Indians," though there is no record of his having done so. In any event, he had the proper credentials for a *conquistador*.

A man of dignity and courage, don Carvajal personally led the settlers to their royally promised land. He had, after all, financed the expedition largely by himself, as was the common practice of those given royal grants. The generous king gave them a beautiful piece of paper saying a part of the earth was theirs, but the rest was up to them.

The north country had been explored before by don Carvajal. He had led several expeditions as far north as the Rio Grande in the 1570s. On these journeys, it was said, his soldiers had captured eight hundred to one thousand Indians, "for all the world as if he had gone hunting rabbits or deer," and had sold them in Mexico City as slaves, though don Carvajal of course denied that he had engaged in the slave trade.

In any event, don Carvajal was as much an explorer as a *conquistador*. He may have been one of the first "Spaniards" to have crossed the Rio Grande and entered what is today the United States. If he did, he was surely the first Jew.

The strange and daring expedition of don Carvajal was unique in the conquest of the Americas. It resembled a quixotic "Ship of Fools." For among the *conquistadores* who sailed with him were such men as the son of the viceroy of New Spain, don Diego Enriquez; Manuel de Morales, a Hebrew scholar whose father-in-law had been Grand Rabbi of Portugal before he was burned at the stake; Antonio Machado, whose house was used as a synagogue by the settlers and whom they called the *Gran Rabino*; Antonio de Morales, a Jewish doctor; and the families of Rodriguez, de León, Martinez, Hernandez, Marquez, Lopez, Espinosa, Nava and Juarez, all bearing Sephardic Jewish names; as well as almost the entire family of Don Carvajal, who were later to be burned at the stake or banished as "secret" Jews.

By that time there had been a great number of "secret" Jewish emigrants to Mexico. There were *hebreo cristianos* (Hebrew Christians), *nuevo cristianos* (New Christians), *conversos* (converted Jews) and those who were called the *marranos* (the swine).

By 1545 one-quarter of the Spaniards in Mexico City were Jewish. The royal census of that year counted a European population of 1,358, of whom, according to the survey made by the Marquis de Guadalcazar, 300 were openly admitted Jews. And that would not include the "secret" Jews. From these figures Francisco Fernandez de

Castillo concludes, in *Libros y liberos del siglo XVI*, that in Mexico City "there were more Jews than Catholics."

. In 1506 the Bishop of Puerto Rico complained that Portuguese boats arriving in the New World were bringing "mostly Hebrews." While in 1510 the Bishop of Cuba complained that every new boat from Spain "was full" of Jews, *conversos* and "secret" heretics.

Even the father of the church and chronicler of the conquest, Bernardino de Sahagun, a Franciscan monk, was born of Jewish parents, according to Father Angel Maria Garibay, Canon of the Basilica of Guadalupe in Mexico City. And so, too, was Francisco de Vitoria, the Archbishop of Mexico, and the church historian Father Diego de Duran, who was born the "natural son" of a *mestiza*, a half-Indian woman, and a Jewish *conquistador*.

So many Jews had come to Mexico that by the 1650s, one hundred and fifty years after the beginning of the Holy Inquisition, there were fifteen synagogues in Mexico City. And there were, as well, three synagogues in Puebla, two each in Veracruz and Guadalajara, and one each in Zacatecas, Campeche, Merida and Monterrey.

And Jewish representation among the conquistadors in the colonies of South America was no less numerous. A sixteenth-century Peruvian writer, Pinto de Lima, estimated that sevent-five percent of the Spaniards in Peru were or had been Jews, while Laerte de Ferreira said that "Jewish blood" was common among all the *conquistadores*. In this vein the Spanish historian Salvador de Madariaga wrote that when the Inquisition exiled the Spanish Jews they "left behind a deeply judaized Spain and they went abroad no less hispanified."

Many, if not most, of the families of those *conquistadores* who came with don Carvajal were publicly and openly Jewish. They were "unrepentant," as the historian Leslie Bird Simpson writes, and the Holy Inquisition was to confirm this. For they were a people obstinate in their beliefs as well as in their pioneering spirit of survival.

Some of these reluctant Jewish *conquistadores* may have been swordsmen and horsemen in Europe. In Mexico they all had to be—they had to defend themselves against their fellow *conquistadores* as well as the Indians.

Ever since the Spaniards had come to Pánuco they had fought one another for its possession. The town was no more than a few mud huts, but its harbor was one of the finest on the Gulf coast. The remnants of the de Soto expedition had sought refuge there, as had the expedition of Grijalva in 1517, whose report of Indian gold inspired Cortés to sail in search of treasure, a voyage that began the conquest of Mexico. One of the first lands that Cortés claimed as his own was Pánuco.

Of all the slave estates that Cortés founded, few produced greater revenue in gold and cloth than Pánuco. The tributes seized from the Indian tribes of the area alone amounted to five thousand gold pesos a year. These tribes also became the source of the slaves who were forced to work on Cortés's estates.

No sooner had Cortés announced the creation of his personal empire than he was challenged by Governor Francisco de Garay of Jamaica, who landed at Pánuco with an army of more than six hundred men and three hundred horses. They surrendered almost at once in a battle unremarkable except for one thing: In his chronicle of the battle, Peter Martyr, for the first time, mentioned the great plains that ranged north from Pánuco to Texas.

And then there were the Indians . . .

When the Spanish came to Pánuco they decided to Christianize the native people. Somewhat overenthusiastically Cortés named the settlement Santiestivan, Saint Steven, and ordered the building of churches. But the tribes did not look reverently upon his endeavor. They burned the churches to the ground.

In the royal charter given to don Carvajal the resistance of these Indians was unhappily noted. The new settlers were ordered by the king to pacify these rebellious natives—or lose their charter:

> ". . . *On the confines of Panuco territory . . . are people [Indians] . . . formerly Christianized but for five years they have been in rebellion, destroying churches and doing other damage. The Viceroy has dispatched his captains and soldiers to subdue them, but though they have tried hard they have been unable to pacify them. . . ."*

The settlers were thus ordered to do what the soldiers could not. "You are obligated to bring the Indians to peace and Christianity," the royal charter decreed. And this was to be done "within eight years."

If the secretary to Phillip II saw any humor in ordering converted and crypto Jews to Christianize Indians the solemn wording of the royal charter offered no hint of it. Nor did the Holy Inquisition comment on the irony of this document.

Not many conversions of Indians to Christianity took place in Pánuco, though don Carvajal did order the building of a church for them in Cueva. Whether any of these Indians were converted to Judaism was not recorded.

Some of the settlers were understandably dissatisfied with life at Pánuco. The unrelenting heat and unending tropical rain of the river delta made them restless and disconsolate; they felt the atmosphere was oppressive.

And so the bolder of the Jews decided to abandon Pánuco. They headed north into the mountains of Zacatecas and across the arid lands of Coahuila. In the Tarahumara Indian country they founded the ranching settlement of Monclova, south of the Rio Grande; it was the first ranch in the territory that was to become a breeding ground for the long-horned cattle and mustangs of northern Mexico and southwestern Texas.

Pioneers on the frontiers of Nuevo León in the 1590s, these ranchers who headed north then disappeared into history. Even their names are now forgotten. They left no memoirs. They kept few records.

Nothing is known of their explorations. If some may have reached the Rio Grande, as was likely, and crossed over into present-day Texas, there is evidence neither to confirm nor deny it. All that is known is that some adventurous Jews on horseback from the colony of Pánuco rode north at the end of the sixteenth century, settled in Monclova, set up a cattle ranch and then vanished from known history.

"Brave, daring, high-spirited" men and women, the Mexican historian Alfonso Toro calls them, belonging to "the hidalgo class"—somewhat of a romantic view. And yet, these Jewish *conquistadores* did live by "force of arms" in much the same manner as any settler in the Mexico of the day; they were scholarly soldiers and Hebraic horsemen. "They were half merchants and half men-at-arms, who conquered the Indians in order to despoil them of their goods and to enslave them, who developed mines, and founded cattle ranches," Toro writes.

On the coasts and the plains of northeast Mexico a new era had begun. And the cattle ranches of the Jewish *conquistadores* and cowboys in the expedition of don Carvajal were harbingers of a new way of life in what would become the American West. The "conquest of Nuevo Leon was the most successful ever undertaken by New Spain," Simpson writes; "it transformed that remote corner of the kingdom into an orderly and prosperous community."

In spite of, or perhaps because of, his success, Governor Carvajal was arrested by the Inquisition. He was accused of being a "secret Jew."

The secretary to the king, Antonio Pérez, had himself been accused of being a Jew. He had fled from the court of Spain and gone into hiding. Philip II ordered an investigation to find proof of Pérez's heresy, and the royal charter to don Carvajal was presented as evidence.

Carvajal was then charged with "observing the Law of Moses." His grandmother, his mother, his wife, his sister and her entire family were "apostates of the Holy Catholic faith," said the Inquisitor, Dr. Lobo (Spanish for *wolf*) Guerrero, and don Carvajal had been their "aider, abetter, harborer and concealer." If he did not confess it was recommended that he be "put to torture."

One of the reluctant *conquistadoras* who had refused to sail with him had been his wife, doña Guiomar de Ribera. She was "a Jewess, but never had revealed that fact to her husband." If don Carvajal was naive about his wife's religious faith, he could not have been as ignorant about his sister's. She had been given in marriage at the age of twelve to a devout Portuguese Jew, Rodriguez de Matos. And when tortured on the rack by the fourth turn of the wheels—"Naked, covered with blood, defeated, she kneeled on the floor" and confessed; she was a Jew, so was her sister, the governor's wife and all of her family.

> *I believe and adore the Law of Moses, and not Jesus Christ. Have mercy on me, for I have told you the whole truth. I die! Oh, I die!*

On the wooden scaffolding of the Inquisition, with a burning green candle in his hands, don Carvajal denied the accusations. "They tell me that my mother died in the Jewish faith," he said. "If that is so then she is not my mother, nor I her son." Nonetheless, he was imprisoned. He died within the year.

His sister, Francisca de Carvajal, was burned at the stake on December 8, 1596, in Mexico City. So was his nephew and namesake, Luis de Carvajal, and his two nieces, Lenor and Cataliva de Leon y de la Cueva. In all, nine Jews were burned alive, ten were burned in effigy and twenty-five were imprisoned, some for life.

On the collapse of the Carvajal family fortunes, the royal persecutor sold their palatial "haciendas containing mares, mules and other animals." But there is no record of what happened to their Indian slaves. Nor is there any mention of the mestizo children, half-Jewish and half-Indian, of the Carvajal men.

Not all of the Carvajals fell victim to the Inquisition at that time. Some not only escaped, but set out on a new expedition.

One of the Carvajals, Juan de Vitoria, joined the Oñate expedition that brought the first Spanish settlers to Nueva España, New Mexico, in 1598, two years after the auto-da-fé of the Holy Inquisition. He was a soldier—an *alferez*, or ensign. But, in later years, he ironically became the standard-bearer of the Office of the Holy Inquisition in Nueva España. Even so, his wife was accused of heresy, of using "magic roots" like an Indian, but there is no record of what happened to her or to her three sons.

The Catholic church historian Father Angelico Chavez writes that the reasons were "obscure," but no one seemed to know what had happened to "the remnants of a once great family." In Santa Fe, New Mexico, there is now not a single Carvajal.

And yet, I do not believe the pioneering Jewish ranchers and horsemen vanished completely into history, as had the Jewish *conquistador*, Hernando Alonso, before them. They remain with us as ghostly ancestors of the founders of our Western history.

No one heretofore has thought them significant enough to write about in any serious way. But the influence of their style of living and beliefs cannot be ignored; their memory persists in many of the traits of Western ranching and horsemanship. These Jews were the first to bring the *gineta* riding style, the high-horned Persian—now Western—saddle, the tossed lasso and the Andalusian ancestors of the quarter horse into the deserts of the Southwest. And they did it in their particular and peculiar way—as Jewish ranchers.

One of the qualities that has characterized the rancher is his taciturn and laconic nature. It is a quality that suggests a sense of privacy, the manner of a man who is closemouthed about himself and who does not wish a public display of his thoughts. That is not a quality rooted in the flamboyant verbosity of the *conquistadores*. But may it not have originated with the early Western ranchers who had to hide their beliefs and hide themselves—the *conversos*, the hidden Spanish Jews?

These ranchers, of necessity, had to be unobtrusive and low-key in order to hide from the Inquisition. And yet the influence of their diffidence and reticence of the Jewish ranchers on the modern lifestyle of the cowboy ethic is little known. The roots of the ranching mystique have been traced to every possible influence, in my opinion, but to where they originated. Those Jewish *conquistadores* who moved north and became ranchers may be the historical missing link that illuminates the coming of the dark and dashing horsemen to America.

That may well be the most significant and influential contribution of the Jewish *conquistadores*, for whatever is consciously suppressed and hidden can never be forgotten; it becomes a powerful and eternal unconscious force no matter what disguises and distortions clothe it.

THE CHINESE RAILROAD MEN

M*en of China (the Chinese railroad foreman
said) were skilled at work like the big
job. . . . Their ancestors had built fortresses in
the Yangtze gorges, carved and laid the stones
for the Great Wall [of China].*
—The Great Iron Trail

*There was no train to Jerusalem, and the Lord
of Life rode into the city in the humblest
guise, upon a donkey.*
—The World on Wheels, *Chicago, 1874*

And then the day came when the final spike, the "Golden Spike," was to be hammered down to hold the last length of track. The iron rails had spanned a continent. In celebration of the occasion, the dignitaries came—bankers and railroad tycoons, politicians and railroad men—to be photographed at the uniting of the nation. Of the hundreds of people in that memorable photograph taken at Promontory Point in Utah on May 10, 1869, there was one large group who were wholly invisible.

The Chinese . . .

Nowhere to be seen were the thirteen thousand railroad men from China who had dug the tunnels, built the roadbeds and laid the track for half of the transcontinental line—that of the Central Pacific Railroad—crossing the most precipitous mountains and torturous deserts of the West. These Chinese workingmen had become faceless. They had disappeared.

One oil painting of the event later symbolically depicted three railroad men crouching beside the tracks as they drove in the Golden Spike. Two of the three were Chinese.

That famous painting was reprinted in hundreds of thousands of copies; it proudly hung in saloons and brothels throughout the West for years. And yet, in the reproduction of the painting a curious thing had happened. Beneath the painting there was a drawing in which the people who had gathered for the joining of the tracks were outlined, each face numbered, so the viewers might identify who was who. But there was no drawing of the three railroad men.

Once again, the Chinese railroad men had been rendered faceless. They had vanished from history.

Men of China not only built the western half of the first transcontinental railroad, they built the whole or part of nearly every railroad line in the West. In spite of that, or perhaps because of it, their labors were belittled and their heroism disparaged for a century afterward; the white workers on the Western railroads were resentful of the skill and strength of the "little yellow men" whom they contemptuously compared to midgets and monkeys.

From the beginning, the white railroad men had ridiculed the young men of China as too "effeminate" to do a "real man's work," such as laying iron rails. They were too "delicate." They had "too small hands." They were much too small. A railroad historian reflected the popular prejudice of the time when he described how "the Chinese marched through the white camps like a weird procession of midgets."

So convinced were the white railroad men that these "celestial monkeys" could not do the work of white men that when James Strobridge, the tough-minded Irish work boss of the Central Pacific, was ordered to hire Chinese men he exploded with rage: "I will not boss Chinese. I will not be responsible for work done on the road by Chinese labor. From what I've seen of them, they're not fit laborers anyway. I don't think they can build a railroad."

His contempt was a commonplace. When Leland Stanford, one of the owners of the Central Pacific, was elected governor of California, he condemned the Chinese emigrants as a "degraded" people who were the "dregs of Asia." They were unfit for honest labor.

The "lack of manhood" of the men from Kwangtung was evident not only in their diminutive size, but in the ways they dressed and bathed. In the rugged frontier camps, after work they religiously washed in hot bathtubs made from empty whiskey kegs. Every man soaped and rinsed himself "like a woman," in "flower water," and emerged "smelling of perfume." Surely to the Yankees from the puritan East who were roughing it in the wilderness, and to the peasants from Europe to whom bathing was an aristocratic vice, these habits were suspiciously feminine.

Stranger still, and more suspect, were the odd ways they ate. It was said "the Celestials devoured mice and rats." In their work camps their cuisine was even more exotic. They refused to eat the manly diet of beans and beef that the white men consumed. Instead they imported their food from China: dried oysters, dried fish, dried abalone, dried fruits, dried mushrooms, dried seaweed, dried crackers and candies, and an endless variety of roasted, sweet and sour, and dried meats, poultry and pork, rices and teas. Each group of twelve to twenty Chinese workmen had its own cook, who prepared dishes to fit the local palate. And each cook had the duty not only of preparing these feasts of "Un-Christian foods," but of brewing the barrels of tea that had to be served all day long in tiny cups such as "ladies see fit to use."

In these customs of the Chinese the Yankees imagined dark, mysterious rituals. These men from China were not merely "heathens," they turned ordinary things into "heathen" and somehow "feminine" practices that were deeply disturbing to the men of the frontier.

And yet the dreams of conquest of the railroad owners were more powerful than their workmen's prejudices. Though the Central Pacific had been founded in 1861 to construct the western section of the dreamed-of transcontinental railroad by 1865, it had succeeded in laying only thirty-one miles of track. Not only were the owners humiliated by the lack of progress, but the work was frustrated by the lack of responsible workmen. Strobridge needed five thousand men, he said, but his work crews rarely numbered eight hundred. Even these were untrustworthy and worse: The *Sacramento Union* sarcastically referred to these white workers as the "enterprising cutthroats" who either ran off to the gold camps or preferred to work at "robbing Sacramentans at the alley corners." Those who did stay on the job were more trouble than those who did not, for they tended to be "drunken and wayward."

"Hire Chinese!" was the order of the railroad's general superintendent, Charles Crocker.

Strobridge, a stubborn Vermont man, unwillingly hired fifty Chinese workmen; he assigned them to menial jobs such as filling dump carts. They were too "frail" to swing a jack hammer, he insisted.

On the day these men were at last permitted to work at grading the roadbed for the tracks, it was reported that "the coolies' right of way was longer and was smoother than any white crew's." It was embarrassing, for the Chinese were so inexperienced that many had never been on a railroad or even seen one.

Enraged, the white crews vowed to avenge their shame. In the days that followed, they not only worked at top speed, but voluntarily halved their lunch break. Still, at the end of a week the roadbeds of the Chinese workmen were the longest of "any gang on the line." The white railroad men "who wouldn't work within a hundred rods of them" threatened to strike or quit, and many did.

An observer wrote that this was surely "the cruelest blow of all to the ego of the whites."

The muscular young men from China were given the jobs that the whites had abandoned. "Wherever we put them, we found them good," said the delighted Crocker. "And they worked themselves into our favor to such an extent, we found if we were in a hurry for a job of work, it was better to put Chinese on it at once." Even the stubborn Strobridge barked, "Send up more coolies."

And they came as the gold miners had come before them, from the same regions of Kwangtung province on the Canton delta, mostly from the sea-swept maritime districts of Sunwui and Toishan, in the area known as Sze Yup. They came by the thousands and tens of thousands. So many young men wished to come that the ships of the Pacific Mail Line, which brought most of them, were often overloaded by their captains with a third too many passengers. At the inevitable congressional investigation of this lawlessness, the captains were redundantly accused of greed, though no one asked the young men of Kwangtung to testify as to why *they* were so eager to come to America that they crowded onto obviously overloaded ships.

Of these men it is said that most were the sons of farmers, but on the land of their fathers, near the coast, the traditions of the sea were as alive as the sea's winds. These were the lands where the seamen and adventurers of China had come from for centuries, and these young men were aggressive and pugnacious. Even more than the gold miners, they seemed to enjoy, to relish, to seek after the challenge of unknown and exotic foreign lands and the adventures they offered. And working on the railroad they found them.

On the undulating hills of those ridges of rock that form the spines of the Sierra Nevada foothills, the serpentine

157

iron rails climbed in winding arcs. The ravines and valleys in between had to be filled by untold tons of dirt or be bridged by great trestles. Some of these trestles, such as the one at Deep Gulch, rose one hundred feet high and were five hundred feet long. They were built of logs, felled and tied by hand, for there were no steam or power tools; even the tons of dirt had to be moved entirely by hand. In awe of the strength and skill of the men from China who did this work, Albert Richardson of the *New York Tribune*, who had been Horace Greeley's most distinguished correspondent during the Civil War, attempted to describe the epic scene:

"They [the Chinese] were a great army laying siege to Nature in her strongest citadel. The rugged mountains looked like stupendous ant-hills. They swarmed with Celestials, shoveling, wheeling, carting, drilling and blasting rocks and earth. . . ."

Soon the "great army" was to face even greater mountains. On a high, sheer cliff towering above the gorge of the American River, the roadbed of the railroad was to climb fourteen hundred feet up the sides of the precipitous rock face. There were no ledges. There was not even a goat trail. The blasting crews chipped away at the seventy-five-degree incline for days. Inch by inch, they advanced less than a foot on some days.

The tale is told of how one day a Chinese work foreman came to see Strobridge. He politely waited, hat in hand, until he could speak. "Maybe we can be of some help," he supposedly said. "My people, you know, built the Great Wall of China! Of stones."

The carving of roads that clung to cliffsides, like bird nests on inaccessible ledges, was a very ancient art to Chinese

158

engineers. One spectacular reminder of their skill was depicted in the famous painting of Emperor Hsuan tsung's retreat from his Tang dynasty capital, in 775 A.D. Upon a mountain in the painting there is a winding road that is supported by logs and dug into the side of a sheer rock face; it is perched on the mountain as though suspended in air.

Feats of road construction such as this had been commonplace in China for thousands of years. If the ability of the men from Kwangtung to hang from cliffs at dizzying heights and to blast a road out of midair seemed amazing to their Yankee bosses, who "sneered in disbelief" at the thought, it was not new to Chinese technology.

Skeptical as ever, Strobridge gave his begrudging approval. He had nothing to lose.

The men wove great baskets, large enough to hold several workmen, of tall reeds and vines. On the waist-high baskets they knotted four eyelets, in the directions of the Four Winds, and inscribed them with the proper prayers. Ropes were tied to the eyelets, and the baskets, each holding two or three men, were slowly lowered from the edge of the cliff down to the site of the marked roadbed hundreds of feet below. In the swaying wind, the Chinese workmen set dynamite blasts in the rock face and swung away for their lives with all their might. Many fell below. Many died. But in a few weeks the roadbed had been blasted from the rock. They were "becoming expert in drilling, blasting and other rock work," said the railroad's engineer, Sam Montague.

The summit lay ahead.

In the icy winds that whistled through the infamous Donner Pass, which rose to 7,042 feet in the High Sierras, the crews were snowed under during the winter of 1865.

The engineers had planned a tunnel that was to be dug beneath the summit exactly 1,659 feet long and wide enough for two tracks. But the rock was so hard the "blasting powder merely shot back out of the holes." And the Chinese tunnelers were forced to camp, in thin canvas tents, under ten- to twenty-foot snowdrifts. For month after month, they lived like seals, huddled together in padded cotton clothes. Several of their camps were swept away by avalanches in the arctic oblivion of those mountains, and the dead were not recovered until the snow thawed.

Spring brought a renewal of work on the tunnels. There was not one but fifteen tunnels to be dug and hundreds of ravines to be crossed before the railroad could go through. And by the winter of 1866 the tracks still had not reached the summit. Not willing to wait for another spring, the railroad owners ordered that three locomotives be pulled over the mountains by hand. It seemed an impossible task.

In the snow that was higher than a man, hundreds of young men from Kwangtung hitched themselves to mule teams that were to attempt this feat. The men cleared a path two hundred feet wide through the forests on the mountainsides. "Not Yankee trees" is the way an official described the giant trees. And yet "the tiny lumbermen" cut a roadway in the snow that was miles long. On log sleighs that they greased with pork lard, they pulled the locomotives and an entire wagon train of highly volatile nitroglycerin and supplies up the mountainside.

Said a historian of the railroad: "The yellow man had proven his superiority by hard labor."

In their desperation to span the mountains before their rival railroad builders did, the owners of the Central Pacific forced the Chinese crews to work from dawn to dark, seven days a week. Still, the Irish crews of the Union Pacific had the advantage of easier terrain and wealthier owners. That meant better wages and entertainments.

On the dry flats of the deserts of Utah, the Chinese crews of the Central Pacific, coming from the West, and the Irish crews of the Union Pacific, coming from the East, met head on. They literally blew each other up. In the race of the railroads to lay the most track (the government subsidized each mile at $16,000 to $42,000, plus hundreds of millions of acres of right-of-way), the rivals ordered their crews to lay parallel roadbeds for hundreds of miles. In grading their roadbed, the "Irishmen were in the habit of firing their blasts without giving warning to the Chinamen," reported a surveyor for the Union Pacific, Grenville Dodge, and "from this cause several Chinamen were severely hurt." The Chinese crews, "appreciating the situation," responded in kind. One day they set off a dynamite charge right above the Irish crews, and several Irishmen were buried alive.

"From that time the Irish laborers showed more respect for the Chinamen, and there was no further trouble," said Dodge.

In the race of the railroads to outdo one another, these Chinese crews were to distinguish themselves in more productive ways. Crocker, in bravado and some say on a bet, announced that on a single day, April 28, the Chinese crews would lay ten miles of track; the "Ten Mile Day" he named it. Together with eight Irish rail handlers, they did just that, laying ten miles and fifty-six feet of new track, spiking 3,520 rail lengths to 25,800 wooden ties.

The feat was a fitting finale to the completion of the great transcontinental track less than two weeks later. On Promontory Point, where the nation was joined together by the "iron nerves" of the iron rails and orators proclaimed "This way to India!" the historic event that created a truly United States was symbolized to a contemporary writer by the image of "the Anglo Saxon and the Celt [meeting] in friendly greeting [with] the tawny Asiatic"—a fantasy that was more real than fact.

Years later, in his testimony before the Joint Special Subcommittee of the Congress, in 1876–77, which was deciding whether the Chinese had the "right" to remain in the West they had pioneered and built, one of the railroad builders, West Evans, declared forthrightly: "I do not see how we could do the work we have done here without them; at least I have done the work [on the railroads] that would not have been done if it had not been for the Chinamen . . . work that I could not have done without them."

On the prairies and in the mountains of the West there were few railroads that these young men of Kwangtung did not build, in whole or in part. They helped build the Southern Pacific in the deserts of the Southwest and the Northern Pacific in the forests of the Northwest. They worked by the thousands upon the Canadian Pacific as well. They built the roadbeds and laid the track of almost every railroad from Texas to Alaska: the Atlantic and Pacific; the California Central and California Southern; Nevada's Virginia and Truckee, Eureka & Palisades, Carson and Colorado, and Nevada; the California and Oregon; the Oregon Central; the Seattle and Walla Walla; the Texas Pacific and the Houston and Texas Central; the Alabama and Chattanooga; and numerous smaller lines.

And thousands of these young men gave their lives in the building of the railroads. The dead were never counted, nor have they been memorialized. Some twenty thousand pounds of bones were gathered from shallow graves along the roadbeds and rights-of-way, according to a newspaper of 1870 quoted in *The History of the Chinese in America*, by Philip Choy and H. Mark Lai. These bones of the about twelve hundred Chinese who died in the building of the transcontinental line were eventually shipped home. But many others lie to this day in unmarked graves in every Western state.

The ghosts of these Chinese railroad men hovered over the mountains and lingered beside the roadbeds and haunted the whistle-stop depots long after they had gone. On the prairies, where there was "not a tree nor living thing in sight," one early traveler on the transcontinental trains recalled coming upon a bowl decorated with "some quaint pattern for Chinese ware," like a specter of the past; and at Omaha one day, he was surprised by the sight of a "steam caravan come in from what used to be 'forty years in the wilderness' region, direct from the Golden Gate." That, he said, was "a tea train from the Celestial Kingdom." Surely "the Iron Horse" was the "Angel of Abundance" and the "arm of Christendom," for "its mountain-eagle elocution" would carry civilization into the wilderness and "whistle [the] barbarism of the Orient down the wind." By 1874, the year this was written, the travelers on the transcontinental railroads had already forgotten that those Chinese men who were buried beside the roadbeds had laid many of the tracks they traveled on.

And it remained for a stranger from Europe to perceive the blindness of those white men who could not see the Chinese as humans. On his tour of America in 1879, the Scottish novelist Robert Louis Stevenson traveled to California in a third-class "immigrant car" on the Union

163

Pacific Railroad. He grew troubled by the segregation of the Chinese railroad men in a separate car; but even more disturbing to him was the attitude of the white passengers toward those who had helped build the railroad they were traveling upon—"the stupid ill-feeling," he called it.

Of these white Americans' conceptions of the Chinese railroad men, Stevenson wrote: "They seemed never to have looked at them, listened to them, or thought of them, but hated them *a priori*." They did not see them at all.

Still, there were quiet nights along the rails when the ghosts emerged. On those nights, in the darkness, the history of the railroad men from China reappeared as an apparition, a folktale, a fantastic legend.

One of these folktales was reported in the *Daily New Mexican* of Santa Fe, New Mexico, on the twenty-seventh of March, in the year 1880.

At Galisteo Junction, the terminus of the Atchison, Topeka and Santa Fe Railroad, south of the territorial capital of New Mexico, the specter appeared. Soon after the arrival of the evening train from Santa Fe, the station operator and a few friends had taken a stroll along the tracks. Coming "from above them" in the sky they heard loud voices and, looking up, they were startled to see a "large balloon coming from the West!" Whoever was in the gondola of the balloon was talking in a strange language, "entirely unintelligible" to the people on earth.

The marvelous balloon was "monsterous in size," the newspaper said. More wondrous than its hugeness, though, was its design, for "it was in the shape of a fish." Painted on its sides were "very elegant" and "fanciful characters" of an unknown but obviously Asian language, which added to its mystery.

As the fish-balloon sailed overhead, its mysterious oc-cupants dropped two objects onto the desert below. One was a "magnificent flower" made from a "fine, silk-like paper," and the other was an earthen cup, perhaps a teacup, with a blue design.

Sounds of music and of laughter drifted down from the fish-balloon. In the cool of the evening air it fluttered there, like a cloud, for a moment. Then, as silently as it had appeared over the Sierra Colorado mountains, it dis-appeared. It simply sailed away.

On the evening of the following day a "collector of curiosities" on horseback happened to ride by the isolated depot in the desert. He bought the silklike flower and the cup for a large sum of money. Being a connoisseur of curiosities, he was asked where, in his learned opinion, he though the fish-balloon might have come from, and he answered at once, without hesitation, that the "balloon must have come from Asia."

MOTHER EARTH
AND
FATHER ENERGY

A Navajo medicine man, resplendent in a beautiful head-band, sprinkled sacred corn pollen on the wall-to-wall carpeting of the executive offices of Atlanic Richfield's new Office of Indian Affairs. Some of the corn pollen blew onto the lens of a television news camera. In his prayer he chanted to the spirits of the East, West, North and South.

"I'm blessing our Mother Earth," said the smiling medicine man. "Even though it's three floors below us."

The ceremony that afternoon in the fall of 1982, in Albuquerque, New Mexico, had brought together two hundred corporate officers and Indian leaders in a cultural time warp, suspended between the centuries. Eskimos had flown in from the North Slope of Alaska on jets fueled with petroleum from their land. No one wore native dress, other than for a cocktail party—except the old medicine man. All the rest seemed to be wearing pin-striped suits made by the same tailor. It was difficult to tell the corporate officers from the Indians. And both groups seemed to have come to the ceremony with the same mixture of curiosity and self-interest. They were uneasy, a bit suspicious, and too polite —like men from distant planets meeting in outer space.

My thirty-five years in Indian country had not prepared me for the combination of a cocktail party and a medicine man. A few years back it would have been impossible to imagine such a scene. These corporate officers and Indian leaders had been drawn together by something that was "sacred," in different ways, to both of them: energy resources.

The Indian lands in the West, which were once thought barren and worthless, are, in fact, the site of what *Fortune* dubbed "the Persian Gulf of coal." It has been estimated that from 25 to 50 percent of the retrievable coal in the West lies under Indian land. In addition, 10 to 15 percent of the nation's oil and gas and 75 to 90 percent of its uranium lies under land belonging to these Indians.

An old Pima Indian leader from Arizona told me with a smile: "The white man gave to us his worst land, but God has given to us His best lands."

So vast are these coal deposits that President Ford, during the energy crisis of 1975, proposed 250 "major new coal mines" and 150 "major coal-fired power plants," using primarily Western coal. The coal mine at Black Mesa, the sacred "Female Mountain" of the Navajo, was alone worth three-quarters of a billion dollars, said an executive officer of Peabody Coal. It was, he thought, the richest strip mine in the world.

Now, the guests at this Blessing Ceremony of the old Navajo medicine man eyed one another uncertainly. And quietly sipped their cocktails. Onto the podium strode Robert O. Anderson, then the chairman of the board of Atlantic Richfield. He thanked the medicine man and welcomed the guests by saying his company had established its Office of Indian Affairs to overcome suspicions and misunderstandings between the energy owners and producers. "If we understand Native Americans better," Anderson said, "we would understand the Third World better."

The modest but elegant boardroom of the Office of Indian Affairs was not merely miles away from any Indian reservation. It was centuries away. Its meetings did not open with prayers. Its roof did not leak. Its windows were not broken. Its unemployment rate was not 70 percent. And those few who worked in it earned more than the average of $2,000 a year earned by Indians living on reservations.

And so I asked Jerry Bathke, the director, how he hoped to bridge the gap between the boardroom and the reservation. Was it really possible for an executive officer of his corporation to understand what Indians thought and felt? Was it really fair to ask that of someone?

"Education of company people" is essential, Bathke replied. He saw it primarily as an "internal rather than external" problem. The company employees had to become "more aware of Indian sensitivities." One way to do that was simple enough: Listen to the Indians. "A lot of Indian leaders know firsthand, from their own experience, what we are doing. So, over a period of time, we ought to rely upon the Indian community for their opinion of what the company is doing," Bathke said. "Ask the Indians for their opinion of us. . . ."

Bathke, a University of Chicago graduate, had worked for years in the remote desert settlements of the back-country Navajo. He married a Navajo woman. Later on, in Washington, D.C., at the request of President Carter, he worked on Indian energy development in the Department of Energy, where he helped create the Council of Energy Resource Tribes (CERT), which has been called "the domestic OPEC."

To Bathke, the culture and beliefs of the Indians have to be respected for any energy policy to succeed. If this was done, a more "cooperative, smoother, better-understood relationship" could be achieved, he said. Most important is the understanding that Indians believe in the sacredness of the earth, sky, air and water. And the energy companies would help themselves immeasurably if they appreciated what that meant.

Nor was this only a practical matter; it was a moral one, said Bathke. It reflected the policy of "corporate social responsibility" that Robert O. Anderson advocated, and it ought to be practiced in the self-interest of the "entire business community."

But there had to be a balance. The Indians had to elect a "qualified, capable leadership with an understanding of how business operated." Our country simply "isn't going to have successful natural resource development on Indian lands unless tribes have qualified leadership experienced in the energy business," Bathke said.

The Navajo Nation has since elected a new chairman, Peterson Zah; whether he will turn out to be that "qualified capable leadership" remains to be seen. Some people have expressed concern, to me, that Zah lacks experience in national energy politics, while certain government officials worry that Zah's "adversary" role as a tribal lawyer may carry over into his attitudes as a leader. But most of the Navajo people I have spoken to are more concerned about what politics will do to Zah than what Zah will do to politics. This attitude is similar to the one an old Hopi elder voiced at the time our first Mercury astronaut was launched into the heavens: The white man does not undestand, he told me, that if he goes into space, then space will go into him.

Not many of the Navajo would speak critically, in public, of the new tribal chairman. It is not considered proper to "bad mouth" someone to outsiders. Whites often take this silence for approval, which it is not.

On a wintry day in early January, 1983, 8,000 Navajo came from across the reservation to listen to the inaugural address of their newly elected tribal chairman, Peterson Zah. They came from Lukachukai, Greasewood, Cow Springs, Rattlesnake, Shonto, Canyon de Chelly, Two Grey Hills, Mexican Water and Mexican Hat. And their pickup trucks stretched as far as the eye could see.

The rugged-faced and thoughtful-eyed Peterson Zah did not disappoint them. Some said he represented a "new mood" among the Navajo. He certainly looked the part. On his dark leather jacket there was a spray of wild flowers, and around his neck he wore a simple turquoise necklace. He was not dressed in a business suit.

And he spoke forcefully, like a tribal elder, not a young man. To the Navajo, eloquence in oratory is one sign of a leader.

"For too long we have been on the defensive and they have been on the offensive," Zah said. It was time "for the roles to be switched." From now on the Indian people would attempt to control their own destiny and their own energy resources, "with all due respect to our Mother Earth." And they, the white men, had better start listening to the Indian, Zah said.

"To give our people the key to determining our own destiny we must decentralize our government," Zah was later to tell the Tribal Council. Politicians and bureaucrats run the government the white men had established for the Indians; it was not democratic. "As in the days of our traditional government," he said, "we must give them [the local people] authority through government decentraliza-tion."

Who was this young man who was asking for a modern tribal government based on the old traditions? "Man from Low Mountain," he was called by some. In that old, tra ditional community in the heart of the reservation he was born, in 1937. His family still lives in Low Mountain.

In the years when he was growing up, the settlement was little more than an enclave of hogans, the traditional Navajo houses made of logs and mud. Neither a school nor a trading post existed there in his youth. Though he was sent away to the Indian boarding school in Phoenix, in a sense Zah has never left Low Mountain. Even now, he tends his flocks of sheep when he finishes his day's work as tribal chairman. He believes in combining the traditional and modern ways of tribal life. "Today, after work, I have to go to the mountains," he says, "and give my sheep hay. That's the traditional life. I still have to do that." Being elected chairman has not changed that. "I don't feel any

171

different, I'm wearing the same clothes, drive the same truck and act the same."

One of Zah's first orders after his election was that tribal officials give their Lincoln Continentals back to the tribe. It isn't right, he said, for a leader to ride in a Lincoln if no one else can afford one. The truck that Zah drives is an International, vintage 1969. After all, it isn't easy to transport sheep to market in a Lincoln.

An Indian politician who, like most, had learned to wear the three-piece suit, belittled him as "a man running around in Levis." But that was before he was elected.

The Gandhi-like image that Zah seeks to project is symbolized by his house. He built it himself. "I pounded in every nail," he says proudly. "I like the concept of building things," he says. Besides, "to contract out work to an off-reservation company just creates a [Navajo] money drain."

Zah is not without enemies, however. He founded the Navajo Tribal Legal Services, and during the twelve years he headed it (he's not trained in U.S. law), he brought hundreds of cases against Indian traders, loan sharks and the like. Thus, when the house he had built burned to the ground, arson was suspected. True to character, he built another one.

Most newspapers reported that the election of Zah was a triumph of "the youth vote" and a mandate for change. That may be so. But none of them seems to understand how traditional a Navajo Zah is.

Though Zah's overwhelming defeat of longtime Navajo chairman Peter MacDonald was seen as an upset by outside observers, it was no surprise to the Navajo. MacDonald, who ruled the tribe for a dozen years, had lost popularity because of his high style of living and what his opponents said was the high-handed manner in which he negotiated energy leases. He repeatedly ignored the vote of local Navajo chapter houses against the leases he signed. Many Navajo communities feared the energy development permitted by these leases would end their traditional way of life; to the Navajo, the earth was sacred and the leases blasphemous.

Zah, as head of the Navajo Tribal Legal Services, often defended the local people in these cases. In addition, opposition to MacDonald may have been underestimated because it came from the grass-roots and back-country Navajo. One Indian leader said to me: "MacDonald made all the decisions by himself. That isn't done the Navajo way. Leaders don't decide for people, people decide for leaders." [McDonald was ousted due to scandal in early 1989.]

As is the case with many Indian tribes, the Navajo do not have a political party system. The candidates for election are, in a sense, chosen before the elections by a consensus of the people, by word of mouth, by family ties, by clans and by communities. So it was that Peterson Zah began "running" for the chairmanship of the tribe fifteen years ago. He waited until the time was right and then he was chosen, almost in a biblical sense.

"The will of the heavenly powers," as much as the "mandate of the people," was responsible for his election, Zah says. "It is not by chance," he believes, that he was chosen; it is a "sacred trust."

Zah is a deeply religious man, in the Indian way. "I am traditional in many ways," he says, "and my religion has a role in that. I believe people should live up to their religious commitment every day. In the white world, a day

173

is set aside to worship. To me, that's not living the full commitment to your religion."

Still, he is a modern young man with a university degree in education. He has lived in both worlds, on and off the reservation. A Yale graduate and Santa Fe attorney, Robert Hilgendorf, who worked for Zah in the Navajo Tribal Legal Services says of him: "I've never met anyone with that unique combination. He is in both the Anglo and Navajo worlds effectively, at the same time."

It remains to be seen what effect the world of national politics in Washington and elsewhere will have on this man from Low Mountain. He doesn't seem to be awed by it. Though he is a quiet man, better known as a listener than a talker, he is not modest about his charisma. "I have the ability to excite people," he says matter-of-factly. And he has a flair for eloquence that has reminded some people of John Kennedy, as when, in his inaugural address, Zah said, "Our tasks ahead are great. But our abilities are greater. Let us forget the oppressive policies of the past. Your suffering will become my suffering. Your strength will become my strength. Let us begin."

On the road to the Navajo capital of Window Rock there is a sign greeting the tourists and Indians with the words WELCOME TO THE NAVAJO NATION. Not the tribe, not the reservation, but the nation. By international treaties with the United States, the Navajo are recognized as a nation within a nation. More important perhaps, that is how they see themselves in their hearts. These words, *Navajo Nation*, are not understood by the white man.

The Navajo Nation covers parts of four states—Utah,

Colorado, New Mexico and Arizona. Its area of 25,000 square miles is larger than that of Israel and Belgium combined. Its 150,000 inhabitants make it the largest tribe in the United States.

In the long-ago past the Navajo were a nomadic people composed of bands of families. They have been called the Jews of the Southwest, eternal wanderers; they turn adversity to their advantage and make do with what they have.

Today, to the Navajo, the ideas of sovereignty and self-determination have become the touchstones of modern tribal life, as they have to other tribes across the land. That status was implicitly recognized by President Reagan in his "Statement on Indian Policy" in January 1983, when he spoke of federal relations to Indians being on a "government-to-government basis." The president said, "This Administration is determined to turn these goals [of Indian self-government] into a reality. Our policy is to reaffirm dealing with Indian tribes on a government-to-government basis and to pursue self-government for Indian tribes *without threatening termination* [emphasis by the president]."

One of the great fears of the Navajo and other Indian tribes is not economic change, or even corporate investment. It is that the federal government will terminate its treaty obligations and protection of Indian lands. Though sometimes ridiculed as politically antique, the treaties have been recognized by the U.S. Supreme Court as the highest law of the land, as all international treaties are under the Constitution.

Nonetheless, the government did briefly establish a "Termination Policy" in the 1950s that resulted in the termination of the treaties of eleven tribes. From time to time since then termination has again been advocated. In 1977, a bill was introduced in Congress that enabled the U.S. government to sell the reservations for a "fee simple" to individual Indians, who could then sell the land to whites.

That same year the Western Conference of the Council of State Governments, meeting in Santa Fe, almost unanimously passed a resolution calling for the elimination of Indian reservations entirely. Indians, they said, "are not sovereign in their own sphere," and "ultimate authority over Indian land use" should be with the "state planning agencies." Recently, the American Farm Bureau Federation called for the "abolition of the Bureau of Indian Affairs and termination of special treaty rights."

Then-Secretary of Interior James G. Watt heightened Indians' fears when he wondered aloud whether the reservation system ought not to be finally ended. It represented a "failure of socialism," said the secretary, unleashing cries of anguish that brought every major Indian leader to Washington, D.C., in dismay as much as anger. One young Indian leader quipped to me, "The only socialists we've got on the reservations are those employees of Mr. Watt, unless the energy companies, like Exxon and Gulf, are socialists."

Peterson Zah was more diplomatic. After meeting with Watt, Zah told the press, "The secretary is being pressured by groups who'd like to use Navajo natural resources." To Zah, termination was merely one more attempt to "steal our land." In his quiet manner Zah said, "We said we'd be willing to sit down and consider their programs, but it's up to the Navajo people themselves as to what they see and think."

The statement by Zah was an astute echoing of President Reagan's own pledge to Indians: "This administration affirms the right of the tribes to determine the best way to meet the needs of their members, and to run programs which best meet those needs . . . encouraging self-government with a minimum of Federal interference."

And to that assurance, Zah added that from now on, "The Navajo Nation will control its destiny."

On a summer evening some twenty years ago, John McPhee, the administrative assistant to then-chairman of the Navajo Paul Jones, had invited the head of the Santa Fe Railroad and me to dinner. McPhee was not a Navajo. He came from the Arizona Mining Association, and he was trying to convince the cagey old railroad man to build a spur line onto the reservation so that its coal deposits could be mined. "I would not touch that coal," said the railroad man. "No one would touch it with a ten-foot pole."

As a young man wandering about the Navajo reservation I remember how we would break off chunks of coal from surface outcroppings and use it in our campfires. The coal was so soft it crumbled in your hand. One old saying was: "No one can tell if it's cheap coal or rich dirt."

Back then most people believed the coal was of too low a grade to be profitable. The Hopi had mined it for generations, but only for their personal use. So unfamiliar were the Navajo with coal mining that they thought it was like drilling for oil. Old-timers tell me that they never imagined that a strip mine would be miles long. "If we knew what a strip mine was we would not have agreed to the mining," a sheepherder on Black Mesa said. Black Mesa was where the first strip mine was begun. Because it is the sacred Female Mountain, to the Navajo its choice was especially symbolic.

The enormous coal deposits on Navajo land were discovered by accident. In the winter of 1949 a bitter blizzard buried the reservation, endangering thousands of families. Congress passed a relief act that offered the Indians $88 million in aid, including $550,000 for a survey of natural resources. Some of the Navajo leaders were startled to learn, as one said at the time: "They say we have more coal than the state of Pennsylvania."

Even so, the Tribal Council voted 26 to 19 not to accept the government money, fearing it might be a scheme to take their land. One councilman said, "We were hungry, but not that hungry." (At that time, none of the Navajo leaders had had much experience in negotiating coal leases, and their first royalty payments per ton on previously signed leases were literally in pennies.)

In the old days elected Tribal Councils and chiefs did not exist in Indian tribes. But after large oil and gas fields were discovered on Navajo lands in the early 1920s, the Interior Department's Bureau of Indian Affairs constituted a Tribal Council to sign the leases. The Navajo Treaty of 1868 had decreed that no tribal lands could be leased without the approval of three-fourths of the male members of the tribe, but the government never enforced the voting provision.

The energy leases were originally written and negotiated for the tribes by the government. Even now, the secretary of interior must approve the terms of all leases. Many observers feel that if the tribes could negotiate directly with the energy companies, without the government as intermediary, communications would improve and the Indians could get a better deal.

An economist for the Navajo, Philip Reno, cites these

figures in his *Navajo Resources and Economic Development*: The Navajo have leased 2.6 billion tons of coal and have reserves of 1.4 billion tons. In the years from 1959 to 1975 the royalties they received on this coal totaled approximately $8.3 million, or as little as 15 cents a ton on some leases.

Petroleum leases were more and less profitable at the same time. In the years from 1955 to 1975, according to Reno, more than 300 million barrels were taken out of Navajo land and sold for $2 billion in crude and $100 billion in refined products; for this the Indians received about $300 million in royalties, bonuses and rents from the energy companies.

If the Indians did not understand energy production in those days, the energy producers did not understand the Indians. One executive officer of Peabody Coal expressed surprise at the protests by the Navajo at the company's Black Mesa mine by saying, It never occurred to us "that there were Indians out there." After all, one coal industry journal had assured the energy companies that in the desolate deserts of the Southwest there were merely "a few sheep, coyotes and Indians," while another well-meaning executive had tried to calm the protests by explaining that "natural lakes" for boating and fishing would form in the desert coal pits.

No doubt the most wonderfully incongruous example of cultural misunderstanding was the proposal made by Westinghouse, at the request of the Four Corners Commission, to build an ultramodern city of 250,000—"a model city for Indians"—in the Farmington region of New Mexico. All the Indians in the region would be resettled in this city, which was described as "a novel approach to urban problems" in bringing "the twentieth century to the Indians."

179

In commenting on this "novel approach," *U.S. News & World Report* wryly noted: "Most Indians, it is believed, would prefer to live on the reservation and commute. . . ." The city was never built.

And yet, if the corporations and Indians alike were confused by changes brought by new energy production, the government was more so. If leases on Indian land were limited by statute to 2,650 acres, as Rogers Morton, secretary of interior in the Nixon Administration, had pointed out, then many of the government-negotiated leases of over 2,650 acres were in violation of the law and invalid. Morton even went so far as to grant the Cheyenne Indians of Montana the right to cancel their coal leases. Government actions contradicted government regulations, and, as usual, the Indians had been caught in the middle.

So it was not surprising that upon his election as chairman, Peterson Zah announced, "Existing leases will be reviewed immediately." And, he added, "Where necessary we must rescind previous actions in order to protect our assets. We cannot afford to give away our precious resources through unfair leases to outside multinational corporations. We must renegotiate, once and for all, all unfair mineral leases, which have plagued us for so long.

"All due respect for our Mother Earth" must be paid, Zah said.

Not so many years ago I happened to be in Window Rock on the day when Peter MacDonald, the newly elected tribal chairman whom Peterson Zah was later to defeat, was moving into his office. MacDonald had bought a huge desk and thronelike chair. And both he and his assistant, Marshall Tome, were struggling to move the massive furniture to its proper place.

I offered them a hand. Back and forth for almost an hour we pulled and pushed that desk and chair until MacDonald was satisfied with their position. Then he sat in his thronelike chair and playfully put his feet on the desk. "That's perfect," he said. Exhausted from our effort, the chairman and I collapsed on a settee in the reception area to rest.

"Peter?" I asked him. "Why on earth do you need to have a desk as big as that?" MacDonald smiled at me. "When my people come to see me I want them to think they are in a bank." And he laughed. It was just a joke, he said.

Peter MacDonald was an engineer who had come from California to be elected chairman. He was an urban man with an urban life-style. In his years as chairman some said he was responsible for the modernization of the tribe and the signing of the energy-fuel leases that had made the Navajo the largest energy producers of all the tribes. He was hailed as "the most powerful Indian in the country" by *Time* magazine and *The New York Times*. "I came from the private sector," he said, "and I knew how to deal with them."

After his electoral defeat, MacDonald emptied his huge desk and his filing cabinets into a van and drove away. The tribal police seized the van, but as the new chairman, Peterson Zah, said, "We do not know what records are missing." Or why? MacDonald replied, "They are mine!"

The mysterious case of those missing files reflected the difference between these two men and what they represent. Peterson Zah emphasized that difference in a statement about the desk and chair MacDonald and I had so laboriously installed. Zah said, "I will not sit at the same desk. I will not sit in the same chair."

A publication put out by the National Indian Youth Council, *Americans Before Columbus*, has already found evidence in Zah's administration of "the precursor of a new age in Indian politics." As an example of Zah's style, the publication cites the way he is seeking to resolve the century-old land dispute between the Navajo and the neighboring Hopi tribe. Zah and the Hopi leader, Ivan Sidney, even met face-to-face to try to solve the bitter battle. And government lawyers were barred from the meeting.

"We want them to stay out of whatever we are talking about," Zah said. "One hundred years ago the government put the reservations on top of each other. They gave money to the Hopi and said, 'Sue the Navajo in court.' Then Congress gave the Navajo money to fight in court. So we're saying now, 'We'll talk and we're going to ask you to pay the bill for this mess you created.' "

To that the Hopi tribal leader nodded. "When you get two lawyers together it is a difficult thing." Then he quietly added, "I think the Great Spirit intended things to happen the way they are happening now."

Not even the government lawyers could argue with that.

THE CHURCH
IS FAMILY

TESTIMONIAL BY
ARCHBISHOP
ROBERTO SANCHEZ

I*n the mountains of the Southwest there is a saying: God is still in His heaven only in the sky of New Mexico.*

There is a holiness that people feel in these mountains. It makes them humble. And that may be why the Franciscan fathers, who first came here in the sixteenth century, were at peace in these mountains they named the Sangre de Cristo, the holy mountains of the Blood of Christ.

The archbishop was born in the desert town of Socorro, New Mexico. It was almost a ghost town, all but abandoned to the tumbleweed and sagebrush. He grew up a poor country boy beneath the shadow of the mountains, which looked as stark as the face of the moon.

Years later, in the Vatican, his youthful poverty gave him the strength he needed when the pope appointed him the first native Mexican-American archbishop in the United States. He had been a poor parish priest whose congregations had always included native people, the Indians and Hispanos. After being consecrated, one of his first pastoral acts was to offer a Mass at the Cathedral of Santa Fe in Spanish, English and Tewa, the Pueblo language of the local Indians. To be the archbishop "of all the people," he said, was his goal, and he set forth to make the Catholic Church of the Southwest the "moral conscience" of America.

"In my heart I am still a poor parish priest," Sanchez said. "And if I can no longer serve the people I will resign."

Sanchez, "the Man of the People," the media proclaimed. The archbishop politely ignored the media hype. He was simply a man of the Southwest.

The holy mountains of the Blood of Christ, the Sangre de Cristo, were a spiritual place to the archbishop. He was the son of his family, of the history of his people, of the land. "Father loves the mountains," said a friend of the archbishop. "On a free day he takes off into the mountains, by himself, or with his brother. To think. To be by himself. When the piñon trees are full he loves it especially. Maybe he feels renewed by the mountains. There is something in the mountains and in the sky that cleans our souls."

A friend in the hierarchy of the church said, "He is not like the other bishops."

ARCHBISHOP ROBERTO SANCHEZ:

A sense of family. The church developed a sense of family out here. The church was family.

The sacraments are not received for the benefit of the

individual. But, rather, so that the individual might share his spiritual enrichment with the entire community. I should not be eating just for my personal pleasure, but so that I have energy to serve my entire community. The church regards this as a gift of grace.

The cities of our country have experienced a sense of individualism, especially with the advent of the suburbs. Many people in the large cities have lost their sense of community and have become isolated. They've adopted a new stance: My religion is an expression of my personal faith in God and what He means to me. And I really don't have to be concerned about others.

In theology these people became more Protestant than Catholic. The Protestant theology and ethic stresses the individual's relationship to God. The vertical. Not the communitarian, the Body of Christ. The horizontal.

Our Catholic theology has stressed the Body of Christ, the "we" rather than the "I." The Catholic Church in the Southwest, I think, can restore to America the sense of the communal. We have to create a community again. If we don't, we are not going to create for America a sense of belonging.

Those in the cities who have become isolated begin to build walls of separation between themselves, and they feel fear; that is what is happening to our country. It's a sense of selfishness, it's a feeling that I have to protect myself. We, in the Church, have to break down these walls. At the Vatican Council II we talked about going forth with a communitarian concept of the Church as opposed to an individualistic approach to faith.

Our Church in the Southwest can do this. I have advocated in my diocese and in the national Church that we do this. And I have brought people from the Bishops' Conference here to experience our sense of the Church. Where did you come from? they ask! They can't believe it! This can't be the American Church, they say! This warmth!

In our Catholicism of the Southwest we have a faith in God that comes from the heart, not just from the head. It's not a rational faith in God. It's a heartfelt faith.

God is our father and all people are sisters and brothers. Then we have to let our heart reach out so we have intermarriage, as there has been, and faith can be shared and our blood can be shared and our traditions can be shared and food can be shared and people can learn to live together, as many people—Indian people and Hispanos—have done and have mixed blood in themselves, because of intermarriage.

There is something to be learned here. I feel that it is God's will, a mission given to us in the Catholic Church of the Southwest.

In the Second World War so many of our young men went out from our little villages and were exposed to the knowledge of good and evil. They decided: "I don't have to live on a farm in a village." They became attracted to wealth and all that is involved. I am afraid of that. They go out and flirt with it. And then they'll ask: "What's left? There has got to be more to life than this."

Our country has ceased to have a philosophy—a faith—to guide it. We have replaced the philosophy of "In God We Trust" with "In Me I Trust." It is all around us. The country is already suffering enormously from this.

The values we are glorifying today, aren't they strange? They are the opposite, I would say, of those values that have made the civilized world. The values I hear proposed today are subtly and overtly not true. We are going to have to pay attention to a philosophy of life that is truly Christian in order to sustain ourselves.

It can't just be the "me" and "I." It has to be the "we."

Never can I say, "God blesses me, Robert, and that's why I do this." I say, "God blesses me, Robert, so that I can go and share my blessing with the people." That is being Christian.

The myth of America as it once was versus the America of today is not just an historical problem. It is a religious problem.

For many years I went from town to town and village to village preaching sermons on cultural traditions, on our heritage, telling people they were Christians and to be proud of who they were. That's the important thing to be, to recognize yourself as a child of God, because God creates only first-class citizens. He does not make second-class citizens. Men create second-class citizens because we try to lord it over others.

The mystery of the incarnation of God becoming man is key to our Catholic faith—especially to the Catholicism of the Southwest. Because it is so human an event. It is a credible event. God taking flesh. If God has become man, He has ennobled us. So that being human with all of its imperfections is okay, because even God decided it was okay. We do not have to be puritanical. The only command of God was that we love and respect one another.

Man can say, "Nothing is of real value to me but myself, and I don't have any respect for myself, I just have respect for my comfort, for my pleasures, for my freedom."

But evil is present if people become so self-centered they begin to make gods of themselves; for by doing that they are denying God.

Evil exists!

Our Church should be a prophetic voice in this country. It has to be a public conscience calling the country back to the consciousness of fidelity to its roots. And I feel that the Church, the Catholic Church, can do that. Even at the price of being unpopular.

If building bombs is wrong because it's denying food to the world and is taking the world to the brink of a nuclear holocaust, then we in the Church have to call this country, and all the countries in the world back, to sanity. No other voice is going to do that. No president is going to do that. It has to be a power apart from political power.

The prophets were not very popular. They were stoned.

And if we speak out in this way we may be stoned, too. But I think that we have to continue to be the conscience of our country.

THE PANTS
THAT WON
THE WEST

TESTIMONIAL BY

ROY "BUD" JOHNS

A *wandering Jew by the name of Levi Strauss sailed around the Horn to San Francisco more than a hundred years ago with no thought of making pants. He was a peddler who sold dry goods. And he established a wholesale dry goods store. It was mostly by accident that he began to make the jeans that came to be known as "Levi's." In fact, old man Strauss disliked the word* jeans *and he wouldn't let anyone use that word in his presence. Because of his aversion to the word, Levi's were advertised as "the Pants That Won the West." Not as jeans.*

In time, of course, Levi's became one of the most enduring

symbols of the West, and were called "the garments of inde-
pendence of the independent man."

Not only were they rugged, they were made with rivets
and stitched as strongly as though laced with rawhide. In ap-
pearance as well as fit, they popularized the image of the down-
to-earth, plain, no-nonsense cowboy, the Marlboro Man.

The wearing of cowboys' clothes is more than a fad. It is
like donning a mask of masculinity. Aaron Latham, in an article
titled "The Ballad of the Urban Cowboy," has written: "When
a city cowboy dons his cowboy clothes he dons cowboy values."
And when he puts on his cowboy hat he "drives from his head
thoughts of his job."

Maybe so. Maybe not.

In any event the changing image of Levi's is part of the
history of the West. And it is told below in detail by Roy "Bud"
Johns, a former executive of Levi Strauss.

ROY "BUD" JOHNS:

The Arizona Lumber Company up in Flagstaff operated a logging train that ran from its sawmill to its logging
camp thirteen miles away. One day the engine was pulling
seven heavily loaded cars piled mountain high with immense
logs when two miles out of camp the coupling link that
connected the tender with the train broke. No other links
were available and, owing to the strain of those heavily
loaded cars, none could be safely disconnected.

Our engineer, wearing copper-riveted Levi's, took off
his pants, soaked them in water, twisted them into a rope
and tied them into a link connecting the engine with the
train and proceeded on the journey to Flagstaff, negotiating
several heavy grades along the way.

That is from a letter a Los Angeles attorney wrote the company in 1956 about an event he had experienced fifty-seven years before in 1899. It was a piece of Western history.

We duplicated the feat in 1972 with a train on a narrow-gauge railroad to use in an advertisement. That may be why legends persist and become more real as the legend fades. That may be why a pair of pants has become legendary.

During the 1970s there were a couple of stories where kids duplicated the experiment. A magazine called *Rags*, an offshoot of *Rolling Stone*, duplicated the test with two Volkswagons. It became part of people's legends.

Levi Strauss was a real man, of course. But he begat a legend.

Dick Cronin was at least a midwife of the legend. He was the advertising manager of the company before, during and after the Second World War. He was a little man who always wore a derby or a homburg in the office, not a cowboy hat. Even if he didn't originate the slogan "the Pants That Won the West," he did decide that the way to popularize Levi's was through the cowboy images of the West.

The early Levi's didn't look any different than the farmers' overalls that they wore back East. Levi Strauss hated the word *jeans*, and his product only took on that name after his death. Before that, they were always known as the "Two Horse Brand Waist Overalls."

In a Montana store, on an Indian reservation in Arizona, wherever they sold Levi's, they became their quality jeans. Somewhere I have tucked away old letters. One of them was from a cowboy in Wyoming who wrote that when he was young you wore Levi's unless you were down-and-out. It was a sign that you were prosperous, doing all right. There weren't any others in the small towns but those from Sears Roebuck or Montgomery Ward catalogues. And the supposedly free-spirited Westerners looked down on mail-order jeans. They were all right for sodbusters.

The story goes that an early prospector who saw the first pair of pants made by Levi Strauss came to San Francisco and wanted a pair "of Levi's pants." Ever afterward they were called "Levi's," but Levi didn't call them that. He was just a peddler who began by selling dry goods. But a name, a phrase, becomes important to a myth, a legend.

Then Levi's became the cowboy product. It was the garment of independence, of the independent man. An Indian guide by the name of Wahoo Charlie who led wealthy Easterners—including Theodore Roosevelt—on hunting trips in the West said, "Where we go we need just five things." And he checked them off on his fingers: "Guns. Bullets. Salt. Blankets. Levi's."

On the dude ranches that people came to from the East, the first thing they were fitted with was Levi's. Back East, they became part of their image of the West. They took on the aura of the free-spirited fearless Western characters. It was a hype. But it was a very real, natural hype. Here was a product sold all over the West. And a cowboy in New Mexico would wear them and a cowboy in Montana would wear them. Many of the cowboys in those days were real cowboys. Some still are.

It was the first purchase that a divorcée made when she went to Reno to get divorced. Not to look like an outsider. She knew that it was a real garment of the West.

After the Second World War the Levi's boom began because fellows came through the West in the services. They found Levi's were a comfortable and inexpensive garment that were identified with the free-spirited life of the West. Levi's became known as the garment of young people, of independent young people.

Then Marlon Brando and James Dean wore them in their movies. They became the garment of the Beats and hippies. It became a uniform. Some people in the company weren't happy with that image. But they had the good sense not to "tamper" with it.

One of the reasons for the success of Levi's was that the company didn't take itself too seriously in those days. We knew there were more important things in the world than making a pair of pants.

Back in 1969 we did an early television commercial showing an old prospector on the desert, his horse standing by, as he dug a grave. And he said that after a man has the same pair of Levi's eight, ten years, he sort of gets attached to them. Once he got the grave dug he opened his saddlebag and took out a worn pair of Levi's and laid them down gently and covered the grave with dirt. Better to have had Levi's and loved them, he said, than not to have had Levi's at all.

The people understood the feeling. We need things we can believe in. And it helps if we can believe in something as simple as a pair of pants. It is not a legend. It's not a myth. It's real.

Myths become legends and legends become myths. And they become real to people.

PART IV

❖

THE

NEW WEST

W hile the sun sets on the Old West, the dawn breaks on a New West. Stan greatly lamented the passing of the Old West, but always harbored the hope of rebirth in its successor.

Ironically, he recognized that the emergence of the New West was dependent on the acceptance of the West by the East. The Old West, while recognized for its fierce independence, was often virtually ignored by Eastern politicians and the Eastern press. The New West, with its rapid population and industrial growth, has become a strong political force. Stan recognized this potential long before futurists and politicians began taking a serious look at the West.

This section of the book examines how the Old West's ideology and values have shaped the New West. Many of the issues raised in the following pages were the issues that Stan grappled with the most in the last years of his life. It is also the section that perhaps

needs the least explanation. It is filled with grief commingled with passion, for Stan powerfully juxtaposes the loss of rural life with the emergence of a political fervor and force unknown in those bygone days.

In his chapter "When the Bomb Fell on New Mexico," Stan talks about the militarization of his adopted homeland, where missile ranges have replaced many of the Old West's cattle ranges. Today, talk of Star Wars, not gunfights, dominates many Westerners' conversations. Stan was deeply interested in and concerned with the impact the military has had on the New West.

Stan's chapter on the cowboy politicians was quite prophetic. Written well before the end of President Ronald Reagan's administration, it is a telling analysis of the president's popularity and style of administration (which was clearly Western).

Two testimonials are included in this section. When Stan spoke with Rex Myers, Myers was the Montana State Historical Society librarian. Myers's observations about the interpretation of history and how Westerners see themselves fascinated Stan. Today, Myers works as the Dean of Arts and Sciences at South Dakota State University.

Stan met cultural historian Frederick Turner after Turner had written a review of Stan's book *The Vanishing White Man* for *The Nation*. Both men were deeply immersed in their respective work and had strong, but often divergent, opinions. Yet, they shared a kinship in their experiences as writers. These two men—who shared a preference for shaping their thoughts with pens and typewriters—corresponded frequently. For several years, in fact, even though they lived near one another in Santa Fe, they enjoyed a lively and stimulating correspondence.

Writing this section on the New West was a painful, yet gratifying, task for Stan. Examining the New West was traumatic because it meant he had to accept the waning of the Old West. But there was hope in the West's rebirth. Sadly, Stan died while working on this section of this book.

WHAT IS THE
NEW WEST?

The American West has always been our dream of freedom. It is still the land of that dream.

From the beginning of our history men and women from the East did not go West to conquer the continent and advance Manifest Destiny, or to Christianize the Indians and civilize the wilderness. The pioneers went West, as old Daniel Boone simply said, "to be free." In the past, as in the present, the dream of freedom did not always become the reality, but the reality did become the dream, and, thanks to this legacy of the Old West, the New West may not be quite what it seems.

The politics of the West is the politics of the elements—of the earth, the sun, the sky, the water. It arises from the nature of the land and is defined by it.

"Eastward I go only by force; but westward I go free. . . ." wrote Henry Thoreau. "I must walk to Oregon, and not toward Europe. And that way the nation is moving and I may say mankind progresses from east to west. . . . Every sunset which I witness inspires me to go West."

And yet, Henry Thoreau never in his life went west of the Hudson River. It did not matter. To him the West was "a country of the mind."

Today we find that once more the country is moving West. There has been a vast migration for the past generation, as millions of people have left the older cities and industrial centers of the East to seek the Promised Land of our ancestors.

And once more the dream has become so entwined with the reality that it is as difficult as it was for Henry Thoreau to distinguish between the two. There is a new West arising from the Old West that is much discussed and little understood. Even the new Westerners sometimes confuse "the country of their mind" with reality, for in a sense the nation has launched upon a "vision quest."

The politics of the New West is the politics of that American dream revisited.

One has to look beyond the stereotypes of the Old West and the ideologies of the New West to be able to distinguish between the dream and the reality. To understand what is happening to the West, and to the country, it is necessary to see beneath the labels of "conservative" and "liberal," "Democrat" and "Republican," "Easterner and Westerner." The meaning of the very words themselves are changing. And sometimes they not only mean something different than they did in the past, but define things that are the opposite of what they seem to be.

199

It is one of the ironies of our history that the New West was created from the Old West. What is this New West? That is a question I have spent most of a lifetime trying to answer. On the roads crossing the prairies and in the mountains of the West I have wandered for forty years, traveling hundreds of thousands of miles, exploring this New West.

In those many decades I have seen the rural countryside and small towns change from childhood memories to adult nostalgia. The laments for the death of the Old West and the passing of the old Westerners have become a chorus of funeral elegies so wistful and sorrowful that they have captured the heart of the nation, for the dream of freedom in the New West is alive in these lamentations.

The death of the Old West has been exaggerated, as Mark Twain once said of a report of his own death. A New West is being born that is becoming—if it has not already become—the future of the nation.

In our generation the center of gravity of the country has been moving West, quietly and imperceptibly, but inexorably. The demographic center of America is now somewhere near Manhattan, Kansas, not Manhattan, New York. Not merely does this represent a shift in the population of the country, but, more importantly, it means the economic, political, cultural and psychological power of the nation is moving West.

"Land, water, energy and people moving West are going to be the main issues, for at least ten years. This could be the battle of the decade," as the late political columnist Richard Reeves once said.

Why have these changes not been recognized by the East? These fundamental changes in the nature of the nation are more difficult to understand and accept than superficial ones that are easily visible.

No longer is the country divided into North and South at the Mason Dixon Line, as it was for generations by the Civil War. The country is divided into East and West at the hundredth meridian.

In many ways the country has become two nations within one country. The conflicts between East and West have been more subtle because they have not been marked by bloodshed. Nonetheless, the two halves of the country are polarized not merely by physical geography but also by an historical and political geography—the "landscape of the mind," as one rancher's son in Montana has said to me.

For years that difference had little national significance. It was taken for granted, as if it were a relic or landmark of the West that one visited on a vacation and forgot about the rest of the year. If the New West begins to assume the political and industrial leadership of the country however, this difference in the "landscape of the mind" increasingly acquires a national importance. The decline of the older cities and manufacturing industries in the East as sources of influence and power is occuring simultaneously with the rise of the energy and high-tech industries of the New West. And this change in the power structure is more than just one of economics. Increasingly, it reflects the rise of a new kind of politics and politicians, not just a change in style from the East to the West.

No one has intuited and taken advantage of these changes more astutely than did Ronald Reagan, who swept the West in two elections and extended his popularity across the country from that solid Western base.

At the same time, there is no longer any clear line of ideological demarcation separating traditional liberals from conservatives. Westerners still vote by gut instinct. How else could the citizens of Arizona vote for Barry Goldwater and Morris Udall in the same year?

No, something more fundamental to the nature of the West is being expressed. It is not merely the necessities of contemporary politics, but the historic character of the West itself that guides the voters, and it has begun to influence voting patterns elsewhere in the country.

It is no wonder that the pundits of traditional political wisdom had difficulty in assessing the landslide victory of Ronald Reagan. His strength was based on a new image of politics offering "new ideas" that are essentially old ideas presented in a new way.

One of the greatest changes taking place in the New West is the political rise of Hispanos. In fact, by the turn of the century they are likely to be the largest minority in the country, surpassing blacks in total population, if not in influence. Obviously, the potential of their political power, from Texas to California, could have an unforeseen effect on the West, as well as the nation, and could change the balance of power.

None of this can be explained adequately by the growth of the Sunbelt. It is a change that is more fundamental and unpredictable.

All of this does not mean the ascendancy of the West is inevitable. The reigns of political power are still held in the East, in Washington, D.C., and in New York. Politics is almost always behind the times, and in conflict with reality—especially when it is changing profoundly.

The politics of the New West is confusing to the politicians themselves. It is not clearly defined or understood —even by them. It is a new phenomenon. But it has its roots deep in American history, going back to the democratic philosophy of Thomas Jefferson, the backwoods politics of Andrew Jackson, the frontier beliefs of Abraham Lincoln, the agrarian populism of the Old West and the New Deal of Franklin Roosevelt. Maybe it's a contradiction in terms. In our technological and corporate age, it may well be an anachronism. Whether it is or not remains to be seen. In the meantime, it may have a powerful effect on our lives —if not on our national and international policies, then on our illusions.

One thing is certain. The politics of the New West has touched the dreams and hopes of the American people in ways that no one could have predicted just a few years ago.

And so, the origins of the New West and its politics should be explored sympathetically as well as critically. Where did it come from? Why has it arisen at this time? What are its human dimensions? Who are its spokesmen and women? What is its history? What is its future?

To me there is no better way to do this than to go directly to the people involved, the new Westerners, and let them speak for themselves.

THE END OF
RURAL LIFE

❖

On the dry and windy plains of the Texas Panhandle is the shadow of a town named Shamrock.

Years ago, it was a quiet country town on old Highway 66, home to ranchers and oil riggers, except on Saturday nights when the truckers stopped to eat and dance in a café and then sleep in one of the ma-and-pa motels along Main Street. On those noisy nights the town was alive.

The cafés have long since been boarded up and the ma-and-pa motels closed down, and the grass has grown through the cracks of the sidewalks on Main Street. Ever since the new interstate passed the town by, Shamrock has become a ghost town.

"The worst kind of a ghost town," says an old resident, a retired rancher, "'cause the town is dead and nobody's given it a decent burial. Maybe they should've run that damned highway right down Main Street and got it over with.

"And we wouldn't have to be a sittin' here waiting to be dead."

In the old days, on the Fourth of July, the townspeople halted traffic going through town on Main Street and gave the travelers a free slice of watermelon. There would be a Western band, and the townspeople and strangers would dance together on Main Street.

No one dances in the streets, anymore.

The quiet of the small towns has become quieter than ever.

On Main Street there are few people, even at noon. Most of the stores are closed. What used to be the bank is now the Church of the Soldiers of Christ. The Grange Hall is a boutique. And the movie house is boarded up; the last picture show it showed was probably *The Last Picture Show*.

A silence has fallen on the small towns. There is little sign of life, merely a calm that comes before the summer storms. It almost seems as if the towns are abandoned sets on old movie lots. There is an eerie peace.

In the nearly deserted mountain and prairie towns, tumbleweeds blow down the middle of Main Street. There are few cars. The tumbleweeds cling to the parking meters and frolic in the parking lots. On the horizon church steeples and grain elevators look like giant tombstones. The sky is pure blue, as blue as it has ever been. But the buildings have turned gray.

No one knows how many small towns have died, be-cause small towns do not die like people. They cannot be pronounced dead, for there is life in the ruins. And there are no statistics that can measure how dead a town is.

In the small towns many of the townspeople have left for the cities. Long ago. They have left because when the family farms failed, so did the towns. But in every small town there are people who have stayed on. They have no-where to go. And if these people are asked why they stay, they say, "I was born here. I grew up here. And I will die here." It is estimated that today the population of small towns is half of what it was before the Second World War, and it is declining every year.

Across the land these small towns and family farms are dying, if they are not already dead: It is hard to say which is worse.

"One out of every five ranchers will be out of business a year from now," says Peter Decker, a cattle rancher on the Western Slope of the Colorado Rockies. Soon many of the farms will be bankrupt and abandoned, and the small towns with them.

"If you asked me, I would say it's like having a family member who you hope and pray for, but you know is terminal," says a Baptist preacher in rural Oklahoma. "And so I would say, let's not fool ourselves with false hopes. Pull the plug and let the sinner die.

"God said to have faith in Him," the preacher adds. "Not in some politician's citified farm bill."

The death of the small towns and family farms is not something rural people easily accept. In the eternal opti-mism that Westerners believe in as if it were gospel, the

206

idea of defeat has no place within their faith—to suggest such a possibility is nothing less than blasphemy.

"Dead!" an angered rancher in a Utah café exclaims in disbelief. "Do I look dead?!"

"Hell, you won't know if you was or wasn't," scoffs a companion. "We're all good as dead."

"Maybe we are on death row economically," says a farm wife in the Dakotas, "but I know the Good Lord, and He is going to deliver us. Because the only sins I see that we have committed was to work hard.

"And I don't see where it says in the Bible that hard work is a sin. That's not Christian."

In the fondly cherished ethic of the family farm and small town, decency and hard work are rewarded. Not punished. That belief in the American dream persists even in the face of a harsh reality that denies it.

"Our trouble was we believed in free enterprise," a wheat farmer up in North Dakota says bitterly. "And what made it worse was that we've been naive enough to try to practice it in a time that don't.

"Sometimes I wonder if there's any free enterprise left in this here free enterprise system."

The *Gazette* in Billings, Montana, dourly editorializes on the approaching disaster in rural life: "Well, the old West has returned. It [has] returned in its true light. Dirt, hard living and death." For the pastoral idyll of the old West was just that, nothing but a romantic dream, the *Gazette* writes. It is now as it has always been, a time of hardship.

In a motel bar in Sheridan, Wyoming, the man squeezes his beer glass in his hands. He squeezes it as hard

207

as he can. Earlier that spring he lost his ranch when the bank foreclosed on it. Now he raises his glass of beer to toast his banker.

"Oh! bury me on the lone interstate highway," the rancher says. "I'm good as dead."

"Rest in peace," the banker mumbles. He is drunk.

On Sunday, after the church service, the rancher drives home. He goes into his hay barn and picks up his hunting rifle, loads it and shoots himself in the head. He dies at once. He is buried in the lower pasture, down by the creek, a favorite place of his on the land he lost.

The suicide of bankrupt ranchers and farmers "has become an epidemic," says a rural doctor. No matter how hard they work, there is no way out of their debts. Farm debts in the 1980s owed by American farmers exceed that of Mexico, Brazil and Argentina combined. The interest on these debts is larger than the indebted farmers' net income. And so there is no way that farmers can ever repay their debts. They face the death of their way of life and, though their hearts deny it, in their heads they know it is the truth.

A Montana rancher smiles to himself. "Why would a reasonable man stay in ranching? Either we are dumb or perverse. Or both.

"No one in their mind ought to stay in ranching. It's a dead horse. It has no future. These days only the fool wants to be a shit shoveler if he can be a land developer," the rancher says in bemusement.

"Hell! Then why on earth do I do it?" he asks himself.

"They can mortgage the place but they can't mortgage me. I'm not for sale," he says finally. "They can't auction my memories."

A housewife in southern Colorado bitterly says, "Darn near lost every memory we had at auction. My things. My mother's things. My grandmother's things. There's not enough left to fill the trunk of the car.

"It's like as if we're back in the covered wagon days with just the clothes on our back." Then she curses quietly.

These farmers "are pretty much the salt of the earth," said Secretary of Agriculture Clinton B. Anderson after the Second World War, but they "contribute little to feeding the urban population." And so they became obsolete.

On the high plains the richest farm and river bottom land is disappearing as fast as the family farms. The land is rapidly being turned into suburban developments and shopping malls. By the year 2000, one magazine estimates, sixty million acres of choice farm land and three hundred million acres of grazing land will be urbanized. To which *Fortune* magazine comments cynically, but accurately, "The land might have to be written off."

In the past, our presidents, from Franklin D. Roosevelt to Richard Nixon, have called for a balance between rural and urban life. Lyndon Johnson, in his various messages to Congress, evoked the need "to restore the balance," even as his under-secretary of agriculture called for its end.

Small town and rural people seem slow to recognize what is happening. If they do, they do not believe it is possible. After all, rural America has been the backbone of Western life for generations.

It wasn't until the farm crisis of the 1980s that people began to realize what was happening. At first they were too stunned to think or act. But to practical rural people, it soon became evident that the death of the family farm was as inevitable as the spring rains. Even then they were reluctant to anger.

In *The Plains Truth*, a grass roots Montana ranchers and farmers publication put out by the Northern Plains Resource Council, a writer put it bluntly: "The sudden death playoff of rural America" meant "the farm crisis 'has turned' into a rural economic emergency. Record farm foreclosures and small business failures [are] causing epidemic suicide, depression, and personal violence."

The fabric of rural life, woven through the generations, was beginning to come apart. It was too late, or so it seemed, to preserve it, for farming has become an urban industry, with its corporate farms, feedlots, huge farm machinery and factories-in-the-fields that no small farmer could hope to compete with.

Laughed an Oregon rancher, "Why do I work in the fields? Damned if I know. I guess it's a habit. On some of these days when I'm broke down I just figure there's something wrong in my head.

"Foolishness. We may be dumb, but we're not that dumb."

One of the leading exponents of modern mechanized farming and the citifying of rural life was Harry Truman's first secretary of agriculture, Clinton Anderson, who later became the "father of NASA" as chairman of the U.S. Senate Committee on Space. In the Department of *Agriculture Yearbook* of 1949, Anderson heralded the blessing of the new technology: "On my farm in New Mexico and on farms the country over, I have watched and marveled on [*sic*] the onward surge of science in farming. Now [we]

210

have tractors that pull heavy equipment, grade roads, clean barnyards, lift loads, grind feed. We can buy a kind of chemical to kill weeds. Insecticides make our houses and barns more sanitary and comfortable." Anderson was talking about DDT.

"These are the results of years of agricultural research. More are coming," exulted Anderson. He did not suggest what might happen to the family farmer who could not afford this expensive machinery.

"If God gave Adam a tractor he wouldn't of left Eden," one farm equipment dealer in Sioux Falls, South Dakota, said. "And if Eve had some pesticide perfume she wouldn't of had no troubles with that snake."

In the years of the Great Depression, less than half of the farms and ranches in the West had pickup trucks. Or trucks of any kind. Even after the war, little more than half the farmers and ranchers owned tractors. In the Southwest, barely one-third had any modern farm machinery at all. No wonder they were awed by the new technology.

It has been forgotten that rural electrification, begun before the war, did not reach many Western communities at first. It was not until the 1950s, in fact, that electricity was installed on many of these farms. The fact that these changes irrevocably ended the independence of rural life in the West is also usually forgotten.

By the early 1980s, farming had become "secondary use" of land. It was time to forget the "agrarian myth" of the family farmer, said the National Water Commissioners of land usage in the West. Many family farmers and small towns reluctantly began to suspect that there were those in Washington who had decided their way of life was no longer

211

"needed" by the economy. There were farmers, as Peter Decker said, who "will not survive [because] presumably shrinkage of the number of working farmers is what is needed if we are to cut the federal deficit."

The family farmer and the small town had become expendable. No longer was the family farm an economic necessity. It was being eliminated as a government priority. This opinion was voiced by OMB director David Stockman before a congressional committee hearing in which he advocated the end of federal aid to farmers.

(Later, David Stockman was admonished by his mother, who said that her son should know better. He had grown up on the family farm in Michigan. He was a farmboy.)

Stockman, as a congressman from Michigan, had contemptuously argued against rural life. "After you spread the taxpayers' and consumers' gravy on the russets, where will you strike next? Broccoli? Turnips? Peppermint? It is about time that the Department of Agriculture stop playing nursemaid to the proliferating array of crybaby communities in this country."

"Crybaby farmers?" the *Progressive Farmer* magazine asked.

If the family farmer was to be driven from his land, his federal aid cut, "Who will then farm the land?" asked Helen Walker, herself a farmer in McCone County, Montana. Her answer: agribusiness. "Farming has been manipulated by outside influence to the point of economic collapse," she said.

So, the family farm was pronounced dead. Like the small towns, it had no economic reason to exist. Both were sacrificed to the needs of our modern society. They were ignored, forgotten, written off and discarded, not only by history but by the conscious design of those who govern our society. It was not a farm crisis that we faced, nor the demise of the family farm, nor the death of the small town, but the result of deliberate and purposeful policies that would forever change the American dream.

The family farm and small town have always existed on the edge of survival. Even in the heyday of rural America, in the 1890s, some counties in the West reported that as many as 75 to 90 percent of the farms were mortgaged.

It is true that there are some homesteaded farms that have been in the hands of the same family for two, three, even four generations. But most farms change hands as fast as they go bankrupt. In the fifty years from 1920 to 1970, the number of family farms decreased from 6,500,000 to 2,900,000; from 1970 to 1985, the number dropped from 2,900,000 to 1,500,000. Today, it is estimated that a hundred thousand farm families leave their farms every year. The farm crisis has always been with us, but it has become an exodus. By the year 2000 there will be few left. There is no way in the foreseeable future that the family farm will be profitable again. It simply cannot support a modern family.

This melancholy passing of the family farm and small towns everywhere has been called "the depopulation of rural America." Before the Second World War, a quarter of the country's population lived on the farm, and together with the small towns, these country folks made up half of our population. But by 1970 the farm population had been reduced by 73 percent, and 22 million people had left their farms for the cities.

And who did they leave behind? Fourteen million people who were 40 percent of the nation's poor, ill-housed and aged.

If the migration continues, by the year 2000 sixty percent of the people in the United States will live in four metropolitan areas. Barely twelve percent will live in cities of less than 100,000. Even today seventy-four percent of the people in this country live on little more than one percent of the land. The famous *New Yorker* magazine cover showing America as an empty, anonymous space between New York and Los Angeles may no longer be a fantasy.

Not surprisingly, the sorrow of farmers has resulted in a black rural humor. In small farm towns across the West, hardware salesmen, farm machinery dealers, local bankers and cattlemen find little to laugh about. The down-home comedienne, Mrs. Pat Leimbach, is often called upon to lighten the gloom with funny but bitter country jokes.

Joke:

"How do you get a banker out of a tree?"

"Cut the rope."

Joke:

"What's the difference between a farmer and a pigeon?"

"A pigeon's the one that can still afford to place a small deposit on a piece of machinery."

Joke:

"How do you tell the difference between a dead banker and a dead skunk?"

"The skunk's the one with the skid marks."

And yet the small-town way of thinking of the family farmer persists, even if, ultimately, his rural way of life will not. He is as tenacious and stubborn as his land. He hides his sorrows as well as he can. The clothing of country people may change in the city, but beneath the clothing their rural beliefs live on.

Many city people come from the country, and they bring their memory of the country with them. It may be a romantic memory, or an embittered one, but it does not matter how distorted the memory is. To city people from the country, rural life lies somewhere between the dream and the reality. No longer the pastoral idyll it was for generations, it nonetheless provides the nostalgia for a passing world of rural innocence.

"Even if you know that it wasn't like that," an urban cowboy in Las Vegas says, "on looking back you like to remember the good old days."

The small town has become its own historical theme park. Today, it is enshrined as a romantic monument to itself in movies and on television, where the foreclosed family farmer is portrayed as an heroic and courageous relic of the past—an honor he was denied while he struggled to survive.

One by one small towns are abandoned and the townspeople leave for the sprawling cities of the West, and beyond. The young people go first and their families follow, until small towns like Shamrock, Texas, become living ghost towns. It is a sad and unwilling exodus of people who desert their rural way of life because they have nowhere else to go. So, they leave their family homesteads and small towns and travel on down the interstate highways to the suburbs of Los Angeles and Dallas and Houston and Phoenix and Denver.

They, whose ancestors came West with the covered wagon trains to escape from the city now journey back to the city. In so doing, they leave behind the memories of the generations who created the American dream of rural life.

One hundred years ago farmers in the West sang in sorrow, lamenting the end of their way of life:

Where, oh, where will the farmer be . . .
Drowned by the combine and
Drowned by the bank trust
Sank by his interest or usury
Where, oh, where will the farmer be . . .

In the cities the sorrow and the anger they brought with them seems out of place. They are strangers in their own land, and they are met with indifference and ignorance. Even their religion is ridiculed, labeled as fundamentalist or evangelical; it is a faith that the established churches often say is as fanatical as it is archaic. And the country-style old-time politics they believed in, with its suspicion and distrust of political machines, seems equally threatening. It is a face-to-face, personal politics of small towns, and it has given birth to the new politics of the West, which favors the individual rather than the political party.

The quiet anger and unspoken rage they harbor is at first hidden by their easygoing, laid-back country manner.

But it smolders like smoke that hides a fire. In their souls they feel a bitter hatred for those they accuse of destroying not only their way of life, but the values of the American West.

And it will, in time, ignite and burst forth with an anguish that will change the West.

LIKE THE GUNS
WE CARRY IN
OUR PICKUPS

❖

TESTIMONIAL BY

REX MYERS

In some places the covered wagon trails are still visible. Along the superhighways that often follow these old trails, the ruts of the wagon wheels cannot be detected by unknowing eyes. No, to see the imprint of history, like the footprint of a dinosaur, the traveler has to go as slowly as those who made their mark on history, and be as close to the earth.

The history of the West is just beneath the grass, Rex Myers, a former Montana State Historical Society librarian and now the dean of Arts and Sciences at South Dakota State University, once told me.

This is a living history, Myers said. That means that those who created that history are often still alive, or personally remember those who have died. Because of this, Western history is a personal story that changes from teller to teller. It is a reminiscence, a newly found diary, a suitcase filled with old, yellowing letters and documents under someone's bed.

In the Montana State Historical Society reside thousands of such personal papers gathered by family historians. In the state archives in Helena, Montana, shelves are heavy with additional documents.

In the West, the duties of state historians and state librarians are peculiar to the region. They are the arbitrators of old family deeds and land grants, as well as the boundaries of Indian reservations and government land. And they are constantly called upon to define and redefine history, separating myth from history and memories from reality.

If, that is, myth can ever be separated from history. Myers, for one, believes it cannot.

REX MYERS:

Now, the concept of the frontier, of individualism, still exists. A lot of the changes that we call progress didn't come to Montana until very late. If you are talking about paved roads, well, look at the state highway maps for the 1950s; a lot of the roads were dirt. So, people who are not very old can talk of gumbo roads and being isolated. And in some areas, electricity, the REA [Rural Electrification Act], did not come until the late 1950s or early 1960s.

So there are people who can talk of their frontier experiences, and they were only fifteen or twenty years ago.

219

It is part of their life experience. And they are frontier experiences that are quite real to them.

You can talk to a rancher who knows about using horses to feed. Maybe he does it himself in the winter, or knows somebody who does or has. Even if he's never held the reins himself, he can talk about it with some kind of authority, because he has almost the same feeling as a man who *has* done it.

Concepts of the West are as important as what actually happened there. If people thought Indians were a threat, then Indians were a threat. Even though there may have been only one murder, one feather on a hill, you have to deal both with what *actually* happened and what people *think* happened. It is foolish to try to deal with just one or the other. It is equally foolish to try to make the two of them coincide. They are not going to. When you deal with people, the facts are not necessarily going to fit their memories.

Both are worth preserving. I don't see it as a problem. Fortunately, or unfortunately, history deals with people, and when you are talking about people, you are talking about inconsistency, you are talking about the memory of history, and it is very fragile.

Now, historically, the individualism of the frontier did not exist. But people think it did. They jump on it and hold onto it. But if you go back in history you discover that very early on the government provided aid to the settlers, and the settlers *asked* for federal aid—to clear rivers, to encourage railroads, to build U.S. Army forts in their territory—not necessarily because they were worried about Indians, but because it would pump money into their local economy. It goes way back, this problem of the conceptualization of the frontier.

It's like these guns we carry in the back of our pickups. Now, we don't use them from day to day. Oh, we may go hunting, but we don't really need them. They are just there. Sometimes I think we perpetuate our image of ourselves with those guns in the back of our pickups.

And having the gun is part of the tradition. It's part of the concept of the West. It's valid. The West is a place you have a gun, and you can use it as you need to. But the fellow who is here, he doesn't need to exhibit it, while the fellow from outside has to exhibit it to show he *is* part of the West.

Maybe it's the difference between a dream and the reality of that dream. I don't know.

Or maybe it's a conflict between economic reality and philosophical self-conception: "I came out here to the West to make it on my own," someone will say. "And one of the ways I'm going to make it on my own is to get a government contract, but I don't want the government to tell me what to do."

Individualism here is nurtured by the land. In Montana and South Dakota, plains and mountains surround you; you cannot live without feeling the vastness of the terrain. That feeling is a consistent thread in the pioneer letters and diaries that historical societies have saved. It has modern equivalents—like interstate highways or land use, for example. Westerners like interstates, they like paved highways. But they don't like the federal government to set the speed limit and tend not to obey it.

People see themselves in relationship to the land. In South Dakota, residents live "East River" or "West River," using the Missouri as a dividing line. Residents describe themselves accordingly—"I'm from West River."

Throughout the West, features of the land provide identity: Westerners live in "the Hills," in "the Milk River County" or "the Big Hole," on "the Western Slope." It's their land, and while they're willing to take federal dollars to build highways or subsidize lumber and crop prices, they don't want "outside" interference on how fast they drive, where they cut trees or what they grow.

It is a concept of individualism that's been in the West for a long time. And it continues to be there. And it will be, in one form or another.

WHEN THE BOMB
FELL ON
NEW MEXICO

On the sunny morning of May 22, 1957, a hydrogen bomb was dropped on the city of Albuquerque, New Mexico.

The bomb fell out of the belly of the B-36 that was carrying it. "By accident," it was reported. It landed about five miles from the main streets of the city. Miraculously, the detonation explosives in the bomb went off but the bomb itself did not, for the 42,000-pound Mark 17 hydrogen bomb was 625 times more powerful than the Hiroshima atomic bomb.

It was a "beautiful, clear, smooth May morning," said a pilot who watched the bomb fall from the plane that day. He was flying a patient to the Veterans' Hospital in Albuquerque in his single-engine Cessna and was about a mile from the B-36 when he saw the parachute attached to the bomb open as it drifted to earth.

Not long after, the conventional explosives in the bomb exploded upon impact and sent a cloud of smoke at least 1,500 feet into the morning sky.

On his Cessna radio he heard the traffic controllers at the Kirtland Air Force Base ask the pilot of the B-36 if he had dropped something. The bomber pilot replied innocently, "Who me?"

"What just fell out of your aircraft?" the controllers persisted.

"Ah, nothing," the pilot said the bomber pilot told them.

The pilot then told his passenger to look out the window at the explosion below them. He remembers that the war veteran said, "Gee, that's pretty. I wonder if they're going to do it again."

The tower at the base then asked the bomber pilot if he had a "hot cargo" of nuclear bombs on his plane. When the B-36 pilot replied that he did have a "hot cargo," the pilot decided "to get out of the area" and forget the whole thing.

The black lava flow darkened the desert. It was quiet and ominous where the lava had spread across the barren hills and dry river beds of New Mexico from a place that was called "the Valley of Fire." Hundreds of years before the *conquistadores* of Spain had passed this way through the deadly desert and called it *El Jornado de Muerte*, the Journey of Death. It was now deadlier than ever.

In the unearthly quiet of this desert, the first atomic bomb had been exploded at Trinity Site near Alamogordo.

On the roadside beside a cattle fence there was now a small sign that said NO TRESPASSING. DANGER. No reasons were given. There was no monumental monument to commemorate the event that marked the beginning of the nuclear age. There was no monument at all.

A side road led to the site where the blast had occurred. Few of the tourists driving past stopped to take a photograph. It was too desolate and eerie a place.

No one lived along the road anymore. Abandoned ranches and decaying barns stood silent sentry for mile after mile, adding to the unreality of the scenery. It seemed like a landscape of the moon after a nuclear interplanetary war. All the buildings were in ruins. There was no sign of human life. A few birds flew overhead. They seemed to be outnumbered by the jets flying above them.

The land at the Trinity site had been condemned by the government during the Second World War. Not only was the first atom bomb exploded here, but the deserted desert was surrounded by the White Sands Missile Range.

Four hundred years had passed since the *conquistadores* had come this way. After all that time, the Journey of Death had not changed.

And yet the ranchers had not abandoned their ranches. They were forced to move away and were promised that one day they could return. They were patriots. And so they reluctantly obeyed.

Many of their families had homesteaded on this godforsaken land. Their grandparents were buried in it. For generations they had cultivated the desert and grown grasses and livestock and, year by year, created a way of life on the parched earth. They created life out of death.

Now their rural way of life was gone, replaced by nuclear missiles and a space shuttle landing field. The frontier of the Old West had died in an atomic holocaust.

One of the few recognizable buildings that remained was what seemed to be an old café. Its crumbling walls were grayed by the relentless sun and its roof had fallen in. But, in the evening, young lovers came from nearby small towns to make hidden love in its ruins. On the walls they memorialized the dates of their triumphant amours and proudly signed their names.

It was the only sign of life amid the ruins.

Down the road at the site of Trinity, the government had erected a column of volcanic rocks in the shape of a huge phallus. The plaque on that pillar of black stones merely said TRINITY SITE WHERE THE WORLD'S FIRST NUCLEAR DEVICE WAS EXPLODED ON JULY 16, 1945.

On the day the first atomic bomb was exploded the Old West ended and the New West began. The age of innocence ended in a ball of fire. No one knew it at the time, but that moment marked the beginning of the end of rural life. The West entered the nuclear age of post-industrial America without ever having to suffer the strife and conflicts of industrialization as the East had before it. The fallout was to affect every aspect of life in the West.

In the Promised Land the New West's prophecies were to be fulfilled in ways no one could have imagined. Not even prophets like William Makepeace Thayer, who in 1888 wrote in his *Marvels of the New West*, ". . . the New West will decide the destiny of our land." In the West, Thayer continued, men "have seen an empire rise and grow rich and make such strides of progress that usually exist only in dreams." It was "God's will," he said.

Maybe it was fitting that the scientists and bureaucrats who developed the Manhattan Project sent their creation from New York to New Mexico. As the resources of the American empire moved from East to West, so too did its power and military might.

Ironically, the atomic bomb was created in the sacred Jemez Mountains of the Jemez Pueblo Indians. The laboratories in the town of Los Alamos were built on the sites of ancient Indian shrines. Neither the scientists nor the government was aware that their laboratories had been built on holy ground. If they had, it probably would have made little difference to them, for the beliefs of the Indians were merely thought to be superstitions.

To the Indians, on the other hand, the creation of the atom bomb may have seemed the fulfillment of a prophecy. In the religion of the Indians it was often said that the white man would destroy himself. Now the prophecy was becoming a reality. The white man had committed the ultimate blasphemy. He had attempted to usurp the power of the gods.

Robert Oppenheimer later recalled that when he watched that first nuclear explosion he thought of a line from the *Bhagavad Gita*: "I am become Death, the destroyer of worlds."

The federal government owned and operated Los Alamos as a company town. Everything was built and belonged to the government: barracks, houses, stores, laboratories, schools, streets, even the sidewalks. In the day-to-day life of the town, the government supplied everything, ran everything, did everything for the scientists. It even washed the diapers of the scientists' babies.

It was like a frontier town. The scientists' rugged individualism and freedom for experimental thinking were financed and protected by the government bureaucracy. Similarly the exploration and settlement of the West had been fostered by the government in the nineteenth century.

Los Alamos was indeed a modern recreation of the paradox of the frontier. The untrammeled individualism of settlers in the wilderness had also been made possible by the federal government, which financed the clearing of rivers, the building of railroads and the protection of settlements by the U.S. Army.

The pioneering scientists in Los Alamos were in some ways like frontiersmen. Los Alamos itself was not so much a city as a settlement; its barrack-like buildings and makeshift laboratories gave it the look of a transitory army camp that at any moment could be dismantled and moved elsewhere. There was no sense of permanence. None of its buildings had the ivy-covered walls and cloistered look of the Eastern and European universities that many of the scientists had come from; nor did the remote community on the mountain have the comforts of urban life. In some ways it was more like a frontier fort than a town. Not only was it fortified and guarded, it was also isolated and insular. The need for secrecy had separated it from the outside world and separated the outside world from it. The mountain roads from Santa Fe to the town were not merely physically but also mentally closed by secrecy. Not even its name was spoken in public. The Santa Fe newspaper cryptically called it "the Hill." It was not on the maps. It did not exist.

It was a rustic place. Before the scientists came it had been a dude ranch for wealthy and wayward boys who did not fit into the atmosphere of the proper prep schools back East. One of those brilliant, troubled boys who was sent to the Boys' Ranch before the war was Robert Oppenheimer.

For reasons that may have been as sentimental as they were scientifically sound, it was Oppenheimer who helped choose the mountain site for the laboratories. The West, he seemed to feel, was the right place for the atomic bomb to be built. He even began to dress like a Westerner.

Most of the other scientists, however, remained Easterners in manner and dress. The environment of Los Alamos seemed to be a distant foreign country to them, a place some compared to Thomas Mann's Sanitarium in *The Magic Mountain*. Many of them—Enrico Fermi from Italy, John von Neumann and Hans Bethe from Germany, Niels Bohr from Denmark, Leo Szilard and Edward Teller from Hungary, Stan Ulam from Poland—were refugees from the Nazis and shared a sense of unreality about the West.

As refugees and exiles from Europe, they became refugees and exiles in America as well. They were strangers to the Western land. Even so, though they were ill at ease in (if not oblivious to) the surrounding environment, they were not unaffected by the majesty of the mountains, the grandeur of the deserts and the awesomeness of the nearby *Valle Grande*. The largest volcanic crater in the world, it served as a reminder of the destructive power of the universe while mocking their endeavors to create its man-made equivalent. In their more reflective moments they may have even thought that there was no setting more fitting to the building of atomic bombs. It was a perfect place for men to imitate the gods.

It may have been with that thought in mind that Oppenheimer named the site of the first atomic explosion Trinity—some said for the Father, Son and Holy Ghost. But it was said by others that he had chosen the name from the lines of a poem by John Donne:

Batter my heart, three person'd God; for you
As yet but knock, breathe, shine and seek to mend

On the old frontier, death was always on the mind of the pioneers. They had no choice, really. The confrontation with it was a daily occurrence. Most of the time it was barely more than one false step away.

Maybe that was why the preachers of death and damnation were so popular in the frontier settlements—and still are. The elemental nature of the Western landscape seems to affect the thinking of most people, causing them to see things in absolutes like life and death, sin and salvation.

For generations the history of the American West was a story of survival and conquest. It was not merely a military history. It was a cyclical history. The conquerors were conquered by those whom they had conquered, who were in turn conquered by others.

No one should confuse the settlement of the West with the comic-book history of the gun-fighting cowboys of the movies. It was, instead, a very real drama for the men and women who fought to survive, whether they were Indians or Mexicans or Europeans or Asians. The battles were not only against one another, but the land itself, its lonely horizons, its vast distances, its violent storms, its beautiful and brutal mountain peaks and desert sands.

The nature of the West was both a temptation and an

obstacle that challenged human society. At times, it seemed fit only for wild animals. And so the raw, elemental life in the West required the might of military arms to conquer it, whether by bow and arrow or the atom bomb.

The military relocation from East to West began during the Second World War. Before that time, the military had gone West as a conqueror, not to make the mountains and deserts the center of operations. During the war, however, the government saw a need to disperse its bases in inconspicuous places for security reasons. The open expanses of the West, most of which were owned by the federal government, offered the desired locations. Besides, there were huge deposits of energy resources such as uranium that could be hidden from public view, and there was also a seemingly endless supply of water needed by the war industries. Few realized how limited water was in the West.

During the years of the Second World War, the rural states of the West "underwent a rapid transition which is not yet understood by much of America," wrote Neil Morgan in *The Westward Tilt*. It was an "unprecedented migration" that resulted from the building of a new "industrial complex."

And so it was that the Sunbelt was born and the Rocky Mountain boom began, two major demographic trends not recognized at the time, partly due to the requirements of military secrecy. Millions of people began to depend on the military, directly or indirectly. The military and its corporate suppliers became the largest employers in the West, and this "military-industrial complex" became the region's most powerful political force.

The Army's influence was, of course, already dominant in the West as early as the mid-nineteenth century, however.

Simply put, without the help of the Army, the settlement of the West by whites would have been impossible. It was the Army and its armaments rather than the Colt revolver that "won the West." As the distinguished historian William Goetzmann wrote in the *Army Exploration of the American West*, the Army not only conquered the West, it opened the wilderness to exploration and settlement. The Army was "a central institution of Manifest Destiny," wrote Goetzmann.

The military dominated and determined the history of the West from its beginning. It not only conquered the indigenous people but prepared the path for "the settlers who would take full possession of the Continent."

In time its influence was to reach far beyond the borders of the country. The foreign policies of the United States were a continuation of the military conquest of the West; it was no historical accident that old Indian fighters like General Nelson Miles were to lead the American expeditionary forces overseas in the conquest of Spain's last colonies during the Spanish American War. Not only did the West supply the officers for that conflict, it also supplied the soldiers and the tactics. Nor was it coincidence that Theodore Roosevelt recruited the majority of his Rough Riders in the same conflict from among the ranks of cowboys and ranchers, sheriffs and outlaws, in New Mexico and Arizona.

And, though it may seem implausible to some, the methods used a hundred years later by the American military in Vietnam were a direct extension of those used in the conquest of the West. The relocation of Vietnamese peasants to enclosed villages, like the relocation of Indians onto reservations; the defoliation of rice crops with Agent Orange, like the slaughter of the buffalo, whose meat the Indians depended on; and the frustration of fighting guerillas on their own terms, like the elusiveness of Indian leaders such as Geronimo and Sitting Bull—all seemed to echo the wars against the Indians. If they escaped the rest of the country, newspapers in the West recognized the similarities. As one Colorado newspaper commented wryly, Vietnam was just "another Indian war."

Even so, the military mystique has always been powerful and popular in the West. It had to be. For many settlers, it was a simple question of economic necessity. For many merchants and farmers, the supplying of Army forts and troops with goods and grains was one of their major sources of income. Several great family fortunes, like Senator Barry Goldwater's, were built on the shipments of government-subsidized wheat for the Army. The rugged individualism that characterized free enterprise on the frontiers often was paid for by the bureaucracy in Washington. One of the most startling examples of this paradox was the Apache Wars.

After the Civil War, in an attempt to end the warfare in the Southwest, the Army dispatched a General Ord to study the Apache situation. The general recommended at first that the Army annihilate the Indians: "capture and root out the Apaches by every means and hunt them as they would wild animals," he advised. But his military fervor was quickly tempered by economic reality.

The general discovered to his amazement that the war was an economic necessity for the white settlers in the region. He reported to his superiors in Washington that "Almost the only paying business of the white inhabitants of the territory is supplying the troops . . . and I am informed

233

that if the quartermasters and paymasters of the U.S. Army were to stop payment in Arizona the great majority of white settlers must be compelled to quit.

"Hostilities were therefore kept up with a view of supporting the [white] inhabitants," the startled general concluded in disbelief.

The historian Donald Worcestor of Texas Christian University commented in *The Apaches* that this might be "why the Apache hostilities were kept up [by the government] when the Indians were tired of fighting and wanted peace at any price." Not only was the military a way of life in the West, it was a livelihood. To maintain the fragile economy of the region there had to be a military enemy, real or imagined. If not the Apaches, it would have had to have been someone else.

The irony of this reality appealed to Westerners' sense of paradox in the nineteenth century, as it still does today. Montana is a good example. "Federal expenditures have kept the Montana economy going," wrote Senator Lee Metcalf. "The Defense Department has spent hundreds of millions of dollars in Montana at the Malstrom Air Force Base and the Minuteman [missile] complex in central Montana. Montana is thirty percent federally owned. In other Western states an even higher proportion of the land is federal. Growth of the West depends on federal investment."

Senator Metcalf then added in true, laid-back Western style: "This year's bustling missile site may again be prairie within a decade," while "the development of wood and water is likely to be growing still at the end of the century." His was an old faith in the earth's power to renew itself.

Naively, Westerners widely believed that military bases and silos holding nuclear warheads could do little damage to the countryside. They did not visibly darken the sky with smog as steel mills and auto plants did, and though the radioactive fallout from bomb tests might be deadly, it was invisible. It was a case of out of sight, out of mind.

"Few people know what the Atomic Energy Commission is doing here, or even that we are here," an official of the AEC recalled. The revelation in recent years that the mountains east of Albuquerque were a vast storage area for nuclear bombs shocked the city's inhabitants, who used the mountains for picnics and recreation. And yet there was no public outcry or inquiry.

Not even the accidental dropping of a hydrogen bomb on the outskirts of the city was met with public protest or alarm. It was soon forgotten.

There prevailed, instead, a nervous silence. Either people did not know or did not want to know that nuclear warheads were stored a few miles from their front doorsteps. One observer commented on these "schizophrenic aspects of the nuclear invasion" upon the West, as though people could not comprehend the enormity of what the military mystique of the Old West meant in the era of nuclear weaponry. Nothing in their past had prepared these Westerners for their frightening present, or for the awesome power that now lay beneath their feet.

For years there has been a saying in the West that the three greatest nuclear powers in the world are the United States, the Soviet Union and Montana. It is meant to be a joke. There are now four or five. New Mexico and Wyoming, it is said, have their own stockpiles of nuclear bombs that rival those of most foreign nations.

On the remote ranches and farms in the hills of New Mexico and Wyoming, on the prairies of Nebraska and the Dakotas and in the mountains of Montana and Nevada there are believed to be many hundreds, perhaps thousands, of these nuclear bombs. They wait in their silos like sleeping giants.

The ranchers and farmers, if asked, simply say these missiles are the "bombs out back," as if they were nothing more than old outhouses. In the past few rural people opposed these weapons. Most pretended in their laid-back manner that they really didn't disturb or worry them.

If the people in the "Missile Belt" complained of anything, it was about personal things. The Air Force crews, they said, did not always treat them with respect. Sometimes these crews left the cattle gates open and let their livestock stray onto the roads. Or crews lay in their wheat fields and threw beer cans into their pastures. Or they drove down the middle of narrow country roads at high speeds with boyish bravado, ignoring the customs of rural courtesy. No one in the beginning, however, questioned the bombs.

Then, near the state line of southeastern Wyoming and western Nebraska, the complaints finally gave rise to protests against the bombs in the late 1960s. At first the targets were the "hometown" missile silos on their land, and later the MX missile system. But even then their attitudes were hardly political. They spoke out reluctantly against the military they admired. And they remained philosophical about it.

"Yeah, I opposed it," said local cattleman Rod Kirkbride, "but it doesn't look to me that the opposition's going to get anywhere. It's going to go on, life is. As long as they don't blow 'em up. If they blow 'em up, that'll be the end."

"I don't like being on the liberals' side," said another local rancher.

Ranchers and farmers in Utah and Nevada, where the MX missiles were to be placed, were equally alarmed. The construction of each part of the system would require 30,000 acre-feet of water yearly. A small ocean. In the dry farmland of the desert, the earth would turn to dust. In addition, it was estimated that cities housing 100,000 people would be built and rural life would all but disappear.

It wasn't merely the ecology and peace groups in the West that opposed the MX missiles. That was to be expected. But so did the Cattlemen's Associations, the sheep growers and the Bankers' Associations and the Mormon Church. Conservative little towns, mostly Mormons began a campaign to stop the MX, enlisting the help of their equally conservative church and political leaders. Never before had they opposed a military installation. Even the tests of nuclear weapons had been unopposed.

Ranchers and farmers, bankers and merchants in small towns across the West successfully halted and limited the MX missile system. They did so not because of their political differences with U.S. military policies or for the sake of arms reduction. They did so because they wanted to preserve their small towns and rural way of life, their grazing lands and water resources, their Western heritage.

"In the past the feds gave us subsidies. Now they give us MX missiles," said an old rancher in Idaho. "I prefer the subsidies."

The determined and stubborn opposition of these conservative and patriotic Westerners must have come as a surprise to the military planners in the Pentagon, in Congress and in the White House. Presidents Carter and Reagan both seemed to be startled by the outcry against the MX, which crossed political lines all across the West. It was a movement without an organization. It was a political movement without politics. It was a lost cause that won.

After all, President Reagan had once compared the MX missile to the "Peacemaker," the Colt revolver—"the gun that won the West," he called it. (In truth, the Peacemaker had been manufactured by Colt in 1903, after the West was already lost.) Even so, Westerners were a stubborn, ornery breed of men and women. They would not give in easily.

Not far from Trinity Site, where the first nuclear bomb had been exploded, the ranchers became even bolder. They reclaimed their land. On the deserts of the White Sands Missile and Bombing Range in New Mexico, the grassroots movement took hold in the sand in a surprising way.

The ranchers who had been forced off the land during the war returned to their condemned and abandoned ranches and barns. An old rancher by the name of MacDonald put up a sign on the road to his ranch that read WARNING. U.S. ARMY. NO TRESPASSING. Despite repeated advice from the military that his ranch was unsafe because it was in the middle of the bombing range, the old man refused to leave.

"I want my land back," he politely said. "I want to die on my own land."

The flowers that are growing in the bomb crater blow in the desert wind.

On the site where a hydrogen bomb accidentally fell on Albuquerque in 1957, radiation levels are tested from time to time. The Geiger counters register no greater radiation than what is normally found on earth or in the skies. The site is neither unusual nor dangerous say the officials of the city's Radiation Protection Bureau. And to the unsuspecting eye, the bomb crater does indeed look like any small sand pit in the desert.

At the edges of the crater there is a thick growth of sagebrush. The crater itself is filled by a sparse cover of desert grasses and patches of yellow chamisa.

There is no other sign that a hydrogen bomb fell to earth. And did not explode.

THE COWBOY
POLITICIANS

❖

The dead man had "a darn good chance of winning,"
they said.

On the borders of Texas there was a local election.
But the candidate for district judge had died too late to have
his name removed from the ballot. Though "some people
may not want to vote for a man who is dead," admitted an
old-line political boss, "a lot of people think he was a good
man and should go through life—and death—undefeated."

One of the candidates for county attorney in the same
election was indicted on a felony charge—for the possession
of cocaine. He posted a $5,000 bond and resumed cam-
paigning for county attorney.

Then there was the candidate for county commission
who was arrested for hitting his campaign manager on the
head. The candidate accused the campaign manager of re-
fusing to return a refrigerator, stove, washer and dryer and

television set. And he, too, posted a $5,000 bond and was released from jail in time to vote in the election.

And then there was the candidate for county judge who was known as "Hoss." His mother asked that he be committed for psychiatric evaluation after her son had allegedly thrown two bowling balls through the window of a neighbor's house. At his competency hearing he reportedly attacked the judge and county prosecutor. The judge demanded that the candidate undergo psychiatric examination. So the would-be judicial candidate moved his campaign headquarters to the county hospital psychiatric ward, although he acknowledged that his address would not help his chances of election. Still, he remained optimistic and soon requested that he be sent to jail instead. A prison cell was a better address for a politician than a psychiatric ward, he said, because in jail, at least, "they know I am an honorable man."

It was a good old-time election held in that old fashioned, free-for-all "West Texas style," a local newspaper said. No one objected too much. They were used to it. Besides, it was the last act of the down-home country politics that soon would be replaced by the new politics of the West.

In the meantime . . .

The dead judge was reelected as he lay in his coffin.

The politics of the future is in the West.

The late columnist Richard Reeves thought that "East vs. West" conflicts "could be the [political] battles of the decade." And to this prediction fellow columnist Joseph Kraft agreed that the "revolution in the Rockies" was causing a political shift in the "national energy base," whereby more stodgy Eastern political domination was yielding to a more animated Western spirit.

. Even the West was moving West. The frontier was not dead, as had been said, just crowded. By the turn of the century the Census Bureau estimated that California would be home to some 30,600,000 people and Texas to an additional 20,700,000. At the same time, it reported that the cities of the West had doubled and tripled in size in just one decade, and that the populations of Alaska, Arizona, Colorado, Idaho, New Mexico, Oregon, Utah, Wyoming and Washington had grown exponentially in the same decade.

The migration to the West continued. No longer simply a matter of statistics, the migration foretold the future direction of the country.

The change had actually begun in the 1960s, but few old-line politicians recognized what was happening at the time. Signs of the change were ignored, as were Western political writers like Neil Morgan, who wrote in *Westward Tilt*, in 1961, that "the move West is one of the least understood wonders of the modern world." Political observers were unaware of this change because they viewed the West through the "malignant stereotypes created by Eastern editors."

The Rocky Mountains in particular were politically unimportant in national politics. A few noteworthy men had come from the region, but no political programs or ideas of any importance to the East. "Less is written about it than is written about Disneyland," he said.

"Despite the regional unity of the New West, its surface pattern is one of a marvel of diversity," Morgan continued. That made it all the more difficult for the old politicians in the East to understand the new politics of the West. "Its party politics were unpredictable," he said, a situation that did not lend itself to building Eastern-style political machines. "Whatever his party, the Westerner is a political paradox," wrote Morgan. But these Westerners merely were voicing the old frontier tradition of voting for the man, not the political party.

There are still towns in the West where the mayor and city council run for election as individuals. And the voters tend not to cross party lines as much as they ignore them. It has been traditional for voters in most states in the West to elect Republicans and Democrats in the same election. If the governor comes from one party the legislature might come from another.

"Folks out here like to cover their bets," said a legislator.

From Montana to New Mexico the political picture was the same. In Texas the maverick *Texas Observer* laconically noted that "not all races break down in simple liberal-conservative lines." Many candidates, it wrote, prefer to take "a populist stand" and not be confined by the policies of either political party or by old-time party ties. No wonder the *Christian Science Monitor* once commented on Western politics with the headline OUT WEST, A POLITICAL RODEO. "The races will be controlled to a great extent by local factors," the newspaper wrote, in 1982, and not by "party alignment."

Even Richard Nixon was nonplussed by Easterners' failure to comprehend the Western style of politics: "I wonder if they'll understand it. That's the point. They may resent it. I don't know. To me this is one of the most [politically] exciting places in the world."

A generation earlier the novelist James Michener had predicted that "after the census of 1970 we [will] witness the transfer of political power from the East to the West." This would create a new center and style of politics that would be "purely American power" native to the land and people of the West, Michener believed. It would be uniquely American.

In turn, this new politics bred, and was bred by, "a new type of man," Michener wrote. Himself an Easterner who had become a new Westerner, the novelist was fascinated by this new type of man who was "being reared" by and in the West, a born-again American.

Who was this "new man"?

"He was taller, ate more salad, had fewer intellectual interests of a speculative nature and had a rough-and-ready acceptance of new ideas," Michener enthused.

These traits of the new Westerner somehow gave him "a vitality that stood out," the novelist continued. "I view with envy the West's freedom, its wild joy of living." It was as romantic a portrait as any that had appeared in the nineteenth century.

Not everyone was as enthusiastic about these new Westerners as Michener. To the critical eye of H.L. Mencken, the Western man had been "intensely and cocksuredly moral, but his morality and his self-interest is crudely identical. He is a violent nationalist and patriot, but he admires rogues in office and always beats the tax collector if he can. He exists in all countries, but here alone [in America] he rules."

Most likely both Michener and Mencken were accurate in their portrayals. They had merely seen two sides of the same man—a man who was more complex than he pretended to be and more of a paradox than he appeared to be.

At the same time, many politicians were viewed with a skepticism and distrust in the West. Never vote for anyone whom you don't personally know and wouldn't invite for dinner, the saying went. A man's political beliefs were not as important as the kind of man he was; he could change his ideology or rhetoric more easily than he could change his nature. There was also a saying that held while politics might not be the last refuge of the scoundrel, it wasn't the first either.

As Eugene V. Debs, the old-time prairie socialist leader, once said: "The trouble with voting for someone is that the person who you vote for might be elected."

This distrust of politicians was as old as the Old West itself. Politicians were portrayed as entertaining fools and buffoons, and their political campaigns compared to religious camp meetings and medicine shows at the county fair. No one took a politician too seriously in the era before the media elevated politics to television drama.

In *The Devil's Dictionary* the nineteenth-century satirist Ambrose Bierce described a politician of the day as "an eel in the fundamental mud." That is, he mistook his tail for his head. But then had he not defined politics as "a strife of interest masquerading as a contest of principles." The government, he complained, was the "seat of misgovernment" and the president was a "greased pig in the field game of American politics. . . ."

About the politicians of the Old West, however, no one wrote as critically and contemptuously as did Mark Twain. "If a man be rich he is greatly honored and can become a legislator, a governor, a general, a senator, no matter how

ignorant an ass he is." To these politicians, he declared,
"Money is God," for they were "wealthy made by all manner of cheating and rascality" of the "infernalest wickedest"
of Easterners. The men who ran the political parties had
"small minds, the selfishest souls and cowardest hearts God
makes," he fumed. He could not tell if they were inspired
by greed or corruption.

In his fury Twain echoed Western independents'
hatred of Eastern political parties. Political machines in-
sulted the free spirit of the West. "No one holds the priv-
ilege of dictating to me how I shall vote," Twain thundered.
The East's "atrocious doctrine of allegiances" to party loy-
alties also infuriated Mark Twain. In the physical freedom
and open spaces of the West, the organized and controlled
political parties of the East seemed out of place.

Not even Abraham Lincoln escaped the scorn of Westerners, even though he nurtured his political career on the
Illinois frontier. It was almost as if the country lawyer had
forsaken "the common man" once he was elected president
merely by the act of getting elected. He had become an
Easterner and, worse, a politician. There was even a song
they sang in the West about what had happened:

> *Old Honest Abe, you are obeyed*
> *For military glory;*
> *An arrant fool, a party tool,*
> *A traitor and a Tory,*
> *You are a boss, a mighty hoss,*
> *A snortin' in the stable.*
> *A racer too, a kangeroo,*
> *Whip us if you're able.*

The East was fascinated by the country lawyer from the West who became President. But, the West was no longer convinced he represented them. Lincoln himself often reflected about his misgivings about politics in the East, but he eased his feelings of discomfort by telling jokes.

Nonetheless these independent-minded citizens defied the established parties at their own perils. "The surest way for a man to make himself a target for universal scorn, obloquy, slander and insult," said Twain, "is to stop twaddling (about) these priceless independences and to attempt to exercise them."

"I always did hate politics," he melancholily wrote.

That melancholy might explain why Westerners like Mark Twain didn't support the new politics of the populists that Ambrose Bierce once mocked as that of a "fossil patriot of the early agricultural period." He didn't believe the new politics of the West could defeat the East.

In many ways the grassroots showmanship of the populist movement was the answer of the rural and small towns of the West to the party politicians of the East. Most populist politicians performed as though they were actors and politics was a stage. And they did so with a melodramatic style and rhetoric that Constance Rourke in *The Roots of American Culture* called "the theatricals" of the "Puritan and anti-Puritan." These were enacted with "a romantic passion for the exploratory" of rural Populists such as "Sockless" Jerry Simpson, the "Socrates of the prairie farmers"; Ignatius Donnelly, the gargantuan Falstaff of populist politics; and "Cassandra Mary" Lease, who coined the dramatic battle cry "Raise less corn and more hell!" charged their oratory with, as Rourke put it, "a romantic passion for the exploratory. They lampooned not only their opponents but themselves. It was the "bond of humor" that became the populists' "weapon of satire," for they were rural jokers.

More often than not, when rural populists fought the representatives of urban life, especially the banks and railroads, the battle was waged with down-home humor. It was often scatalogical. The grand old man of Oklahoma populism, Governor "Alfalfa Bill" Murray, was typical of that rural tradition when he quipped, tongue-in-cheek, "Running a government was like running a farm" because "there was so much manure that you had to shovel." Will Rogers, another Oklahoman, served up his own brand of caustic humor: "We have the best Congress that money can buy."

Not everyone laughed. "Most politicians in the West are stand-up comics," said a newspaper man in New Mexico. "But they don't see that the joke is on them. They think that they can solve a problem by telling a joke, but all that does is to postpone it so that they don't have to do anything. Telling a joke is their way of playing dumb."

This populist style of politics gradually spread to the salons and back rooms of the cities. It proved especially useful on television debates and talk shows, and the informality of the new politics of the West was soon being imitated by the politicians of the East. Even presidential candidates began to appear in their shirt sleeves and old sweaters, and drama coaches were hired to teach them how to act "natural" on their new media stage. The down side, according to Frank Mankiewicz, who managed George McGovern's campaign for president, was that "the format . . . worked against candidates who take issues and ideas seriously." The new politics, he said, was based on "electronic coverage" that favored candidates' appearance and not their programs.

"Politics," thought Mankiewicz, "is like what Earl Weaver (Baltimore Orioles manager) said about baseball. It ain't football."

The old populism had moved from its rural political stage to the television studios of the city. The paradox was bittersweet: For generations the family farms and small towns had been dependent upon the modern machinery and economic resources of the East; in turn, they had exported their produce and children to the cities. *The Farm Journal* had often said that people were the farmers' "biggest export." Now, the rural West had even begun exporting its political "theatricals" back East. The irony was wonderful.

Political populism can no longer preserve the rural way of life. It is too late. And yet its most profound influence may no longer be on the countryside but on the political machines of the cities, where its effect has not immediately been recognized in its urban disguise. The popular demand for the decentralization of the federal bureaucracy is not only based upon rural democracy but upon an urban democracy. It is a revival of the tradition of independence that rural people gradually lost over the decades.

After all, if the new politics can elect a president, as it has, twice, its future cannot be as easily dismissed as it once was. The new politics might just become the politics of the future.

One of President Reagan's senior advisors in the White House told *The New York Times* that the president had confided in him, saying, "By God! What am I doing in politics? The kind of things I've done are so far away from this. But I thought that a substantial part of politics is acting and role playing. And I know how to do that."

Here was a new kind of politics and a new kind of president. He came from the New West.

None of his predecessors in the White House were quite like him. He was not a Westerner, but a New Westerner, not a real cowboy, but a cowboy actor. He was all the more fitting for the part.

On the stages of television studios he performed his "role playing" with ease and acted his part well. In his retirement from acting he ran for president; the audience applauded and he won handily. To them he was the quintessence of the Western hero they had seen in movies and on television; he was friendly but determined, soft-spoken but outspoken, easygoing but unbending, light-hearted but righteous. He seemed to embody all the traits of a Westerner. Even if he was acting.

The President was not born as a New Westerner. He had to study the new politics of the West. He learned his part well.

Of all his roles, he was best known as the small-town boy next door, in the White House. He was a living reminder of the bygone American dream of independence and individualism. In an era of sprawling cities and suburbs, increasingly centralized government, vast international corporations and military bureaucracies, he presented himself as the David of the New West who could turn the rural populism of the Old West into an urban expression of the freedom of the individual.

He was a modern populist. He was a born-again American.

The grassy roots of populism had long ago been bulldozed and paved over for the parking lots of suburban
shopping malls. It was ironic, therefore, that one hundred
years after the populist parties had been abandoned and the
populist causes all but forgotten, the "role playing" of a
cowboy actor won him election as president in one of the
greatest landslides in U.S. electoral history.

One disdainful columnist ruefully commented, "The
Lone Ranger rides again." He was appalled by the thought
of a "cowboy President," who he feared would be portrayed
around the world as an occasionally comic stereotype out of
the American West.

And he was right. . . .

But the new politics of the West had created a new
Westerner. He was neither a stereotype of the past nor a
rural populist. He was an urban cowboy in a business suit
and cowboy boots and hat.

The "cowboy President" had an easygoing, hometown
manner that was comforting and reassuring—even when
he acted the role of the gunfighter. He had a fondness for
the heroic old days of the West that were legendary, halfway
between nostalgia and history. He may have dreamed of
being Shane or the Duke, but he had to settle for Rambo.
As he once said, "I saw the movie *Rambo* last night. And
now I know how I should have dealt with the hostage crisis."

On the stage of world politics, a new image of the
country was emerging from the past. The new populism of
the West was re-creating an older form of Americanism,
which had survived history disguised as an urban cowboy.

"America is back!" the president said.

THE MEANING
OF AMERICA

TESTIMONIAL BY
FREDERICK TURNER

Easterners dream of the West. It is still a dream to them.

In his cabin in the woods on the shore of Walden Pond, not more than a few miles' walk from Main Street in Concord, Massachusetts, Henry Thoreau dreamed of going West. "Eastward I go only by force," he wrote. "I must walk to Oregon and not to Europe. And that way the nation is moving and I may say mankind progresses from East to West. Every sunset which I witness inspires me to go West."

But he never did.

"The island of Atlantis and the islands and gardens of the Hesperides, a sort of terrestial paradise, appear to have been the Great West of the ancients," said Thoreau. It was the dream *of a new Garden of Eden, a Shangri-la, on the far shores of the Missouri that he never reached.*

One of Thoreau's spiritual descendants is Frederick Turner. But, unlike the sage of Walden Pond, Turner has traveled West through myth and the reality of fast-food restaurants and gas stations into the world of the modern emigrants who have been cast out of Eden into Los Angeles and Las Vegas. For all that, and despite his sorrow as a cultural historian on the American West, he has not lost his faith in the grandeur and wonder of our land.

Fittingly perhaps, Turner now lives at the end of the old Santa Fe Trail. He does not drive a pickup truck and he does not wear cowboy boots. He cherishes the West in his heart.

FREDERICK TURNER:

The meaning of America still resides, somehow, in the West. From the beginning it is clear that the spaces west of where you are always seem to contain the essence of America.

It seems to me that the West has always been something that receded before Americans—that wherever they were, that was the West, that was the frontier. Beyond that was a kind of future that receded before them as they hacked and cut and blasted their way westward.

From the origins of our Republic there has been the notion that the West contained whatever America really was. And essentially that seemed to be a kind of freedom, a kind of expansiveness, of space. It may well be that the West does contain the essence of what America is. But I am not sure that the realities of Western life have justified those hopes, that dream.

253

Rugged individualism is an important theme of the West. The ability to do things with your own hands. Born in the city, as I was, and having almost no manual skills, I can't tell you how I admire people who can work with their hands. Who can build fences and corrals. Who can build houses, to last. Who can fix an engine. Who know how to wire, to plumb. Who know how to work with animals, to brand, to slaughter.

So I think that's a great thing. And I do think it encourages the habits of the mind and attitudes of the heart. And this does occur in the West. And it encourages a pride and a hostility; a pride that you are able to do these things, and a hostility because the outsiders who can't do what you do can buy almost everything they need in a store.

And yet in some ways, rugged individualism is an historical lie. From the beginning of settlement the pioneers expected government help and they got it.

The settlers of the West didn't come into an empty land, they didn't make that land, they didn't originate it. They came into a land that was peopled. And they took that land from the Indians and Mexicans and they could only have taken it with government help. And I mean government help as in military assistance.

So when one talks of rugged individualism, of how we built this with our own hands, carved this ranch out of dirt and rock and built up our herds, fenced our fences, all of that is true. But I think a lot of people forget this other dimension, this other aspect, the beginning of the Western mode that seems so precarious now and therefore so precious. From the very beginning this rugged individual was subsidized by the government. And it seems this is something people chose to ignore.

The people who stay on a piece of land have an attachment to it that is in some sense historical. And yet our sense of history has always struck me as terribly impoverished, as terribly narrow. It includes those things that we chose to dwell on, on our own hardships, but it has a tendency to exclude the hardships of others. So we drop out of the box of memory those things that made rugged individualism possible. And we forget the people on whose backs the prosperity of the West has been built. I am speaking of the Indians and Mexicans. That's something that the rugged individualism of the West often chooses to ignore.

For the West to be the West, I'd like to hope you will not have to drive your pickup full speed down the highway with a couple of thirty-thirties in the back and a sticker on the bumper that says, in effect, "Fuck the Rest of You. I'm Being Me." I'd like to think it isn't necessary to hate outsiders—the Reds, the niggers, the Jews, the Easterners. I'd like to think it isn't necessary to be suspicious of anything different.

But it may be necessary. It's just that it's not going to be enough to maintain the spirit of the West. It's not an effective weapon against the hucksters, against the real-estate developers, against the fossil-fuel speculators. The spirit of rugged individualism is not enough to save the West.

The time has come for a Western ethic to emerge. Not out of the social programs. Not out of the academies. But out of the West and Westerners, out of a truer sense of the people and places that are already here.

PART V

EPILOGUE

I first met Stan when I interviewed him for a
newspaper story about the Western Writers Conference
he was helping to organize with author Elliott Barker
in 1982. We met in his library/writing studio in a
guest house on the grounds of his home in Santa Fe,
New Mexcio. It was a wonderful place chock-full of
old and new books that filled towering shelves.
Horseshoes, feathers, pottery shards and other
fragments of the West filled this environment. Outside
the windows of the old adobe studio were the pinõn,
junipers and chamisa that dot the Santa Fe landscape.
Everything about Stan and his studio seemed Western
to me.

He was a soft-spoken man who chose his words
carefully after long puffs on his pipe. Often quiet in
his demeanor, he spoke with passion about his
interests. I found his love and enthusiasm for the West
infectious and was even more impressed by his
advocacy for Western writers. The day my story

appeared, my telephone rang at 8:00 A.M. I cringed, because that usually meant someone was unhappy. But he had called to say how much he'd enjoyed the story. It touched me because he was so encouraging. I later found out that he frequently sent notes of encouragement to writers.

Over the next couple of years I'd see him off and on, at writers' conferences and meetings of the Santa Fe Writers' Co-op, which he had founded. After I became editor of *New Mexico Magazine*, he wrote two stories for me—one on Elliott Barker, who was celebrating his 100th birthday, and another called "None of Us Is Native," which appears in this book.

The last time I saw him was on his birthday, January 1, 1987, at a social gathering of the Santa Fe Writers' Co-op. Stan served mouth-watering ribs that he had made. (He loved to cook and enjoyed sharing food and conversation.) It was also one of the first times I really had an opportunity to meet with his wife, Vera John-Steiner. I knew that Stan did not look well that day, but I was unaware he was suffering from Parkinson's disease. I later learned that his writing and daily chores had become a struggle for him. We lost Stan shortly after that, on January 12, when he died of a heart attack while working on this book at his typewriter.

His dear friend, writer and educator Joseph Dispenza, organized a memorial service for Stan, and it was fitting that it was held one day before the opening of the new Santa Fe library in the library's meeting room. There, he was honored amidst many of the great Western books by some of the West's finest writers. In addition, many prominent authors spoke eloquently of Stan and his

legacy, including John Nichols, San Juan Pueblo author
Alfonso Ortiz, Chinese-American poet Arthur Sze,
Navajo writer Rain Parrish, architect and author William
Lumpkins, his close friend and writing colleague Richard
Erdoes and many others.

Not long after that, Vera requested that I review
this manuscript and help determine if there was enough
material to publish a book. Suddenly, I found myself
back in that writing studio surrounded by Stan's books
and mementos of the West. And there, Vera and I
discovered that Stan had indeed left the world one more
book about the West.

We thought it would be fitting to conclude the book
with an interview and excerpts from an interview with
Stan. The first one was conducted by László Borsányi, in
February 1981, when he was a graduate exchange student
from Hungary studying cultural anthropology at the
University of New Mexico and doing field work among
the Navajos. In Hungary, László is an historian whose
main field of study is the American West and the history
and ethnology of American studies. His interview with
Stan first appeared in *El Palacio* magazine, published by
the Museum of New Mexico.

The final piece included in this book is from Stan's
last interview, conducted just a month before he died.
The interviewer, Dr. David K. Dunaway, is a professor
in the Department of English Language and Literature at
the University of New Mexico. The tape-recorded
interview was part of a radio series titled "Writing the
Southwest."

CHALLENGE AND GUSTO: A LIFE-LONG AND FERTILE LOVE AFFAIR WITH THE AMERICAN WEST

INTERVIEW WITH
STAN STEINER
BY LÁSZLÓ BORSÁNYI

LB: *Nearly all of your twenty books are important contemporary surveys of minority and occupational groups of the American West—Indians, Chicanos, Puerto Ricans,*

Chinese, ranchers, cowboys. Why do you think that these unique groups are important?

SS: I know it's old-fashioned, but I feel patriotic about this country. I'm interested in what is unique, what is special, about it. My books are really a series about America as a "nation of nations."

LB: *Mostly your approach to America as a "nation of nations" concerns the American West. As an expert, you are considered to be an important spokesman for this part of the country. . . .*

SS: I'm not an expert. I am a writer. I always like to say a journalist writes about something, an academic studies it. A writer doesn't write about something and he doesn't study it; he becomes what he writes about, he becomes what he studies, he becomes the person. It is an act of re-creating yourself into the person you're writing about.

When I am writing, I will sometimes say to someone, "You have to believe that I am a member of your family, that I am your brother." When I wrote *La Raza*, I said to [Cesar] Chavez and people like that, "I'm your brother, and if you can't believe that, I can't write about you. And if I don't feel it, I can't write about you either." I spoke to a group of ranchers last year, and when I finished speaking they started to talk about cattle prices . . . they were sure I was a rancher.

LB: *You are known for your interviews. Could you tell me more about using this personal technique?*

261

SS: I don't like to do interviews. I try to avoid them because I think an interview is a formal communication between two people and I try to get a more informal, direct communication. There are some people who are institutions, like governors, and you have to have a tape recorder because they don't believe the interview is real unless the recorder is plugged in. But with normal human beings who are used to talking to another human being, I try not to have a tape recorder and I try not to do an interview, just talk. And that can take a couple of hours, or it can take a couple of years, or it can take a lifetime. My method is no method. My method is not to have a method. It's not to conduct an interview.

LB: *Can you give me an example of this non-method?*

SS: I was told when I was writing *The New Indians* that there was a man I had to see named Dan Raincloud at a Chippewa reservation in Minnesota. He was a medicine man; he was vice-chairman of the tribe; he was also the local carpenter and plumber. And he lived in an old village. When I went to see him he wasn't home, so I waited all day. It was hot there; it was the middle of the summer; there were lots of mosquitos. Terrible. And, finally, around six o'clock he came. He said people had told him I was there, and he said "I'm gonna eat." And I was sitting on a rock, sitting for five or six hours by now.

He finally comes out maybe a half an hour later—he's picking his teeth, he sits down on the rock with his back to me and he says, "What do you want?" So I say, "Mr. Raincloud, I'd like to ask a question—What's the meaning of life?" So he turns around and he says, "The anthropologists always come, I give them my words in feet—a dollar seventy-five a foot. But no one ever asked me a question like that. . . . Yeah, in a lifetime I can tell you the meaning of life." And we became good friends. That's my non-method. I didn't say, What's the problem you have in this tribe, or What government funding do you need? I never do that. So that's not an interview.

LB: *So you speak as one person to another with everyone that you write about. This is in complete harmony with your definition of a writer as someone who becomes what he writes about. Tell me something about when and why you felt you were becoming part of the lives of the Indians, the Chicanos, the ranchers, the cowboys. . . .*

SS: I became part of the West in 1945, and I have become more and more part of the West ever since. But I am still not the West. I'm not a spokesman for ranchers; I'm not a spokesman for Chicanos; I'm not a spokesman for Indians, or for anyone else I write about. I'm just reflecting what I consider the major cycles of American life, which are to me in the West. The sources for American strength and life are in the West. Sources of energy are in the West. The sources of the worst racism are also in the West. Everything, it seems to me, is in the West. So, I became part of this. I didn't plan it. When I first came West I just followed my thumb. I wasn't looking for Indians, for anything; I just wandered into it and became part of this whole process.

LB: *What brought you to the West in 1945? How old were you then and what were you doing in those days?*

SS: I was born on January 1, 1925, and brought up in the peaceful countryside of New Jersey and not-so-peaceful New York. When my parents moved to Manhattan in 1945, I went to work first as a printer. Then I went to the University of Wisconsin, but after a few months there I decided to change my life. So, in 1945, following my thumb with a friend, I hitch-hiked across the West and began to write.

LB: *Why did you react so strongly against the university? Did you think that the professional approach puts limitations on one's interest and understanding?*

SS: If you examine the physical aspects of society, that's a science. But it's a very limited science. The things that you can examine, what you know about a society, are limited by you, by your methodology. In a university people make themselves a center of their own world and reduce the world down to their size. And they're often frightened to have to go beyond that into the unknown. The examining of other people, other societies, or examining parts of their societies, is all based on a reductionist principle of breaking these down into their smallest parts. I believe in the truths that are larger than myself; the larger concepts, cosmoses, cycles and circles of life. I don't have to understand them. If I thought I understood them, I might destroy them. But I seek them.

LB: *Can you recall some of the events that helped you to understand the importance of the American West?*

SS: Oh, yes! I always thought I was Huckleberry Finn. In fact, I began to rewrite Huckleberry Finn when I was twelve years old because I thought it was out-of-date. And I always was happier in small-farm country, like the place in New Jersey where my folks had a house. So, that was my kind of life when I came out West. Here it was again. It was like being born again. I was a born-again farmboy, even though I'm a city man. I need the freedom of the West, the sky, the space, the mountains.

LB: *When you decided to be a writer, what did you have in your mind? What did you write about?*

SS: The first thing I wrote after I came back from hitch-hiking across West was a book of poetry, a glorification of the American West.

LB: *What are those qualities you found in the West that brought you back and back again before you settled down here?*

SS: I think I enjoy people who have a lot of gusto, a lot of emotion, a lot of fire in their blood. Who, even when they do terrible things, do it with passion. And I think such people live in the West. I write about people I love. I like Westerners.

LB: *So, you are thinking about a series of important qualities that—according to your view—are essential to life. Why do you associate these qualities with the American West?*

SS: Maybe because people here define themselves as part of a place. In this country this is very rare. But in the West there is a continuity, a sense of place, that affects human quality. And there is also something else, an edge, a frontier that still exists. There is an edge of civilization—there is an edge of Anglo civilization, and an edge of Indian civilization and an edge of Chicano civilization that all meet. There is a borderline. And it's not only defined territorially, but individually, too. And sometimes you go over the edge and go from one civilization into another in a single person or in a single family. You can have all three of these in a single family, but the edge is still there.

That's one of the reasons why people in the West have such strong characters—distinguishable, recognizable characters. In the East if people have that diversity, it's mostly a residue of being European. In the West people are defined entirely differently. They are defined by the line at which Turner's frontier thesis becomes a personal thing between individuals. And they are sharper. They know who they are more clearly and they act out their civilizations, their culture, more clearly. And so there is much more contradiction—there's much more tragedy and paradox, and irony, and anger, and love, and rape, and everything else in the West. There is that edge that is especially exciting. It's more essentially part of the core of America than anything in the East. So here is not only that strong sense of place, of belonging to a place, but also a sense of challenge and danger that, I think, is essential for life. That makes life exciting.

LB: *What you say reminds me of the early twentieth-century American humanism that was represented by writers like Jack London. Tell me, who are your favorite authors and what are your favorite writings?*

SS: When I was young, I read Jack London, Mark Twain and Herman Melville. *Moby-Dick* is one of my favorite books. I don't think it's about ships and whales. The ship is really a prairie scooner and the sea is the prairie. And I think it's really about a confrontation of European civilization with the American West. And the whale is really a white horse. It is an essentially American book, intrinsically American. But I also like Emerson, and Thoreau, and the Bible. I read the Bible often. I like the directness of Elizabethan English, and the St. James version of the Bible is the most beautiful English ever written. I don't like most modern authors. Among them, though, I like Hemingway's short stories about Michigan, and I like Sinclair Lewis's *Main Street*. But I don't like Norman Mailer. He has no appreciation of the language.

LB: *When did you start to write?*

SS: My first professional book, *The Last Horse*, was published in 1961. Then I was very involved with writing *The New Indians*, as well as with other things and people in the West. I edited a series for Crown on contemporary Indian tribes.

LB: *Where did you live in those days? When did you move to Santa Fe?*

SS: First we lived in New York, and then in the late '60s we rented a house in Santa Fe and moved back and forth for several years. Finally in 1970 we bought the house I'm living in now.

LB: *Why did you buy this particular house?*

SS: I could see as soon as I came up the driveway that you could not see the house because of the trees. There were two acres of land. There were no other houses nearby, though it was in the middle of the city. And it was old, it was falling apart. I liked that.

LB: *Why did you move to Santa Fe? Why not, for example, to Albuquerque?*

SS: Santa Fe has more of the qualities of a city than Albuquerque—more theaters, museums and so forth. However, I don't like the way Santa Fe is changing. It's becoming an imitation of itself. People move to Santa Fe now because they want to live in a place like Santa Fe.

LB: *What is a typical day on the job for you?*

SS: Sometimes I wake up maybe six or seven o'clock. I like to work in the morning. I work until twelve o'clock, then I do other things, maybe work around the house. Then I make supper. I like to cook; it relaxes me.

LB: *Tell me something about your working method. I've seen some of your note cards in your studio. How do you develop your writings?*

SS: The act of writing promotes its own thoughts and ideas. I write paragraphs, sometimes twenty pages of them, until they are ready to give birth to a chapter. But very often when that happens, it's not together, it doesn't fit somehow. Then I will stay up for nights; I find I have to go beyond my mind. . . . You need something that breaks through the material and beyond your own capacity. You have to go beyond your own experiences.

LB: *What do you like to do? I know you like to spend part of your time gardening. And I've also seen you watching football on the TV.*

SS: I hate football. I played football. Now it has become so brutal. It's all done for money now. And it disgusts me. But I watch it with complete fascination.

LB: *Is there anything that annoys the hell out of you?*

SS: Anything? Oh, many things! I think the worst crime, to paraphrase Oscar Wilde, is being bored. There are people who have nothing to say but keep on talking. I can't stand them. I think being bored is about the worst thing in the world.

LB: *Could you name some things that please you?*

SS: Emotion, passion and expression of belief. I believe in close human relations. Honest, direct human relations are hard to achieve in this world. I believe that one must try to defy the obstacles that surround you, regardless of what they are. I believe in standing up for things you believe in, because I think that changes you. And if you don't do that, you're wounded forever, as if you lost an arm.

LB: *Could you tell me about some significant changes in your life?*

SS: One day, when I was walking home from high school, I walked past a bookstore where they were selling books for seventeen cents a pound. And I bought two books—poetry by Keats and Shelly. I'd never bought a book before. I was a football player. That was a significant change. I began to write poetry, which I couldn't tell my fellow football players about because they would have thought I was "queer." And, of course, the biggest change and the most lasting was that summer in 1945 when I went West. That was probably the most profound change in my youth and in my life. Wandering free across the country. I still remember that summer very clearly.

LB: *At that time, when you first came to the West, you had already decided to be a writer, and after that summer you wrote a book of poetry, a glorification of the West. But what did you want to write about when you decided to be a writer?*

SS: Oh, America! I was always in love with America. I have an almost religious feeling of patriotism about America.

On my first trip across the country, I got a ride somewhere here in New Mexico with a family of Okies who had gone to California during the Depression and had worked and bought a pickup truck. And I and the mother and two little children were sitting

270

on all their possessions, and they were driving back to Oklahoma to get their farm back. That was about the same time that Woody Guthrie came to New York. The Okies were going back to Oklahoma and Woody Guthrie, who was an Okie from Oklahoma, was becoming a star in New York—presenting this real America to fake America.

LB: *So, at the same time when challenge and gusto were bringing you to the West, you were also breaking away from a gradually distorting image of America. Tell me, do you think the West still provides those qualities that first put a spell on you?*

SS: The West, I think, is dying. It is dying very quickly. The energy sources of America are here, and because of that we will be industrialized and we will be destroyed. When that happens, the mythology of the West—it's already happening—will move away from the West to the East. And the East will emulate the West, while the West will look more like the East. This is the last period, the last years of the West. There are already more cowboy boots in New York than in all of the West. An enormous paradox.

LB: *Your writings bear vivid witness to the fact that America and the West's identity are still part the Mexican American and Indian heritage. How do you think their role will change when the West disappears? Will there be any opportunity left for them?*

SS: The changing face of the West is a great opportunity for all of us. Maybe our country is unique in that this part of it is a reservoir, a treasure house of ideas, and myths, and beliefs. The myth of the country is here; the Jeffersonian and Emersonian ideas combine here with the ideas of the Chicanos and Indians. So, the strongest roots and the strongest understanding of what all that is here in the West. Thus, when the center of gravity of the country moves in the direction of the West, that puts the Chicanos and Indians in a very strong position. Stronger than they have ever been in. What will they do? I have no idea. What can they do? I have no idea either.

The rest of the country is trying to recreate, to reinvent the myths it doesn't understand, and we in the West—the Anglos, the Chicanos and the Indians—do understand them. It's our tradition. That doesn't necessarily mean that it will do us any good, but it could; it could do us and the country a great deal of good.

A VOICE FOR
THE WEST

❖

I N T E R V I E W

W I T H   S T A N   S T E I N E R

B Y   D A V I D   K .   D U N A W A Y

David K. Dunaway is a professor in in the Department
of English Language and Literature at the University of
New Mexico. The December 16, 1986 interview is the last
Stan gave before his death on January 12, 1987. The interview is part of a radio series, titled "Writing the Southwest." It begins with a few excerpts from one of Steiner's
conversations about being a writer.

SS: A writer's job is to write. I spend a good part of
my day, every day, writing. When someone asks
me what a writer does, I tell them a writer writes.
I found out early on that if one is to write about
something he'd better get his experience firsthand.
I try to stay as close as possible to the land I live
on. When I have to go to town, even if it's only
a few blocks away, I feel uprooted.

Natural things excite me. There are certain
times when a small plot of land, because of the
light, becomes magical. I think about my writing
all the time. Even when I'm doing things around
the house, I am writing in my head. Someone once
told me that by the time a writer gets to the typewriter most of his writing should be finished. All
that remains is to put it down on paper, and to a
certain extent I believe that. Books are like plants;
they both start from seeds, you tend them and give
them attention, the attention they deserve, and with
some luck they grow and bear fruit.

The most exciting thing about being a writer
for me is that we share in the work of creation.
Not every day is that totally successful, but when
the dawn comes, I know I have the opportunity to
create a world all over again from the beginning.
Every morning, every morning is the first day of
creation and I find myself more and more drawn
to writing fiction. Maybe it's that feeling that im-
pels me, the feeling that when I'm starting on a
blank page, it's the chance for something new,
something better.

DD: *You manage to integrate an oral voice, the sound of people speaking, into your writing. Does this come from your interviewing skills?*

SS: I think they're probably several thousand ways to interview—or maybe two or three. There are journalists who write about things from the outside. There're academics, who analyze things, and then there are writers. I don't interview people, I talk with them, initially. In a ranching book I visit with them. You never interview a rancher, or a Chicano, or anyone; you visit with them, and you let them talk, and you become who they are. If you can't do that, if *I* can't do that, I can't write.

When I began writing *La Raza*, I would tell everyone—Cesar Chavez, Rich Taylor, everyone— I'm your *hermano* [brother]. I may be your older brother or your younger brother, but I'm your *hermano*. If you can't understand that and be part of it, if you can't let an Anglo be a Chicano, I can't write about you. I have to become who you are.

It doesn't mean I believe what you believe, or speak the way you speak, or come from the same culture, but as much as possible I'm like a novelist: You become the person you're writing about. I've been asked that question about interviewing every time I've taught in a writing class. I keep telling people, don't interview anybody, talk to them like a *hermano*, like a member of the family, and then you can perhaps get some glimmer of their soul, and if you can write that down you've gone way beyond an interview. The other reason I don't do interviews is that if you have a machine recording what someone says, they're very conscious of what they're saying. I'm not interested in the superficialities—the what-they-had-for-breakfast—I'm interested in who they are, and you have to remove the barrier between the person who's doing the interviewing and the interviewee. You have to remove the machine. You have to take the damn machine and throw it out the window.

I don't believe in oral history. My cold line is, and it always gets a laugh, is that's some kind of social disease, probably sexual. Oral history to me is a kind of demeaning term, and it creates a mess.

When I was on a panel with a bunch of historians from the UNM [University of New Mexico] history department, they were talking about myths of the American West and myths of the cowboy and myths of the Indians. I told one of these distinguished professors afterwards that I once asked a rancher what he thought about the "mythic West" and he said, "If someone else ever comes up to me again and calls me a myth I'll kick him in the ass."

DD: *When you have these conversations for your book, some people are more eloquent, more powerful, in their speech than others. How do you know when you've got a good talker?*

SS: Well, I don't pick people by their opinions or their ideologies. I pick them 'cause they *are* good talkers. I can't care what their ideology is. If they can express themselves and express themselves forcefully, then that's what I go for.

How do you know? What are the criteria? You're talking to an Old Westerner, an old-time rancher, and you ask him something, he's bound to say, "I reckon I don't know much about that," then you know you have a good interview, 'cause he's going to talk for eight hours about what he don't reckon he knows much about. The only thing that is a better interview is if the man says, or the woman, says, "I don't have what you would rightly call education." Then you know he's mad as hell and he's gonna talk for three days.

DD: *Supposing you're in a situation where someone isn't really anxious to speak with you? How do you get a hard interview started?*

SS: It goes back to being the person you're with and respecting the person you're with. I did an interview for this new book, *The Waning of the West*, with Archbishop Sanchez. I've known the archbishop for some time and we're kind of friends. We were gonna talk for half an hour and he talked for two hours; it wasn't a question of me interviewing him, it was a question of him feeling comfortable enough to go as deeply as he wanted into the nature of the Church of the future, the Church, his own Catholicism. At the end he said, "You know, Stan, I think you're a closet Catholic." I knew I had a good interview.

DD: *Let me ask another craft question. Could you give us an overview of what is involved in starting a nonfiction book. What stages do you go through?*

SS: My own method, which I don't recommend to writers—I don't think most writers would take it even if I recommended it—is to take several years. The people I've written about in the Indian books and in the ranching books are people at least some of 'em, I've known for twenty, thirty years. Some even started off with a visit and interview with strangers. It sometimes takes two or three years to get the kind of story you want, which is the story that they don't want to tell—their philosophy of life, not just what they do.

I once had an interview with the governor of Puerto Rico, for *The Islands*, who was a Cuban. I tried for two years to sit down with the governor and say, "What is your philosophy of life?" I tried through the governor's offices, through his secretaries, even through the CIA in San Juan. It took two years before he would sit down on the veranda at Forteleza and tell me why he was a St. Augustine Catholic, not a St. Thomas Catholic, and what he believed and what he felt. It took two years.

I didn't agree with most of the things he said, politically. We came from a different political philosophy entirely. But I wrote an exciting interview because he was an exciting man.

On the other hand, if the governer hadn't had on his cologne, you'd have thought he was Robert Kennedy. He combed his hair like Robert Kennedy. He gave me a nothing interview, which I couldn't include in the book because it would've embarrassed him. I said at one point, "When you become governor"—which he became right after my interview—"are you going to rule a commonwealth by contradictions?" He looked at me very angrily and he said, "You're trying to trick me." I said, "No, Governor, that's from Shakespeare."

So some interviews you can't get. There was one very important interview I needed for a book on a congressman, and I tried for more than two years to get it, just to sit down with him and talk, and he offered to take me on a political tour with him to his precinct and show me how he met the people, what his programs were, and I kept saying, "No, no, no. I want to know who you are." After two or three years, his executive secretary said to me, "Stan, give up. He drives home every weekend from Washington with his wife and he hasn't talked to her yet. He's not gonna talk to you."

DD: *How does the idea for a nonfiction project gel for you?*

SS: If I'm writing about American Indian people, or Hispanos and Chicanos, I ask them first—before the project starts—do they trust me to write it, do they want me to write it. If they don't, I won't write it. I just signed a contract for a book that gives me about one-quarter of what I'd get if I were on welfare, and the only reason I signed the contract was a lot of Indian people asked me to write the book because they wouldn't write it.

Sometimes that backfires. I don't think you can write about people without respecting them, without them respecting you, without their permission that this is something you should do. When what I call the generation of new Indians came on the scene in the sixties and seventies, most had been veterans in Korea and Vietnam. They were a new Indian, they

279

had a world, they had all the world in their head, and they had their feet in both worlds.

I knew a lot of Indians who were very fine writers and I kept asking them and asking them to write a book about what their generation felt. They said, "You write it." I had the feeling I was like an Indian who'd been hired by Custer as a scout, except history had reversed itself and here the white guy was the scout for the Indians. One of these Indians, Vine Deloria, was a dear friend of mine, and he kept insisting I write this book called *The New Indians*, and I kept insisting he write this book called *The New Indians*. Then he sent a letter to two hundred and fifty tribal chairmen saying, "Stan Steiner will visit you soon and write what is in your heart." I blew up because suddenly I was committed to two hundred and fifty tribal chairmen to write what was in their hearts. And I told him, I can't even write what's in my own heart, much less two hundred and fifty tribal chairmen's. I was stuck. I had to write the book.

DD: *When do you know a book is done?*

SS: The people who you're writing about may have one opinion, and if they're old friends they may have a feeling towards you. The publishers back in New York have no opinion at all, no idea. They don't care. When [my wife] Vera was on the IREX [Information Research Exchange Board] exchange in Budapest, just before the hostage crisis in Iran, I had a meeting with a very prominent publisher, an editor-in-chief and publisher in a big publishing house. He said to me, "Stan, I hear you're going to

280

Budapest. You know that's pretty close to Iran. Why don't you write a book about Iran?" And I said to him, "Hal, the thing about Iran is I've never really been there. I really don't know Arab people, or Persians in the case of Iran." He said, "Well you wrote about Indians, didn't ya?"

Fortunately, I turned down a big contract—because I would be in prison or dead by now. So you have the opinions of the people you're writing about, plus the publishers back East.

When I wrote *La Raza*, Reies Lopez Tijerina [a land-grant activist] and some of the old farmers had taken over the courthouse [in northern New Mexico]. They didn't raid the courthouse, as popular fiction has it. They took over the courthouse and elected a sheriff, elected a community leadership and reclaimed their land. And they elected a mayor—that was their purpose. I had no intention of writing about that.

You know, I'd been out in the northern villages for many, many years, but it's still a very private place and I had no intention of writing about those villages. And I recall an editor in New York saying, "Stan, you know about these 'chicaynos' out there. Would you write a book about these 'chicaynos'?"

So you have these two worlds to deal with when you're launching a book. . . .

DD: *What kind of reactions have you had from the people you write about?*

SS: I had one very sweet reaction from an old Hispano farmer up north whom I wrote about and sent my chapter to. He lived in a real valley, and [when] I drove in, he knew immediately I was there, 'cause everyone in the valley knows if any stranger drives into the valley. He came down in his pickup truck and said, "Stan, you got me just right. I give you an acre of land." And that's the best literary criticism I ever got. Of course, he never gave me an acre of land.

In *La Raza*, I wanted to do something about the Brown Berets [a Chicano activist group], who are very strong in L.A. and some of the other big cities. Most of these guys were ex-cons or ex-drug addicts who had really had a hard road. And suspicious, very suspicious of anyone who wanted to write about them. I said I wanted to sit down with four of these guys, leaders of the group, and write their story in their words. We had a case of beer and some ham sandwiches and we sat in the basement of the Drug Rehabilitation Center.

It took me two years to get to that point, because they would call me up and say, "Stan, come down, I think we're going to talk to you." I would come to L.A. and I'd be met, and the guy would say, "Drive me to the corner of such and such," so I would do that and he'd say, "Park your car and get into that other car," and he'd mean the car across the street, and he'd take me somewhere else. We'd go to another corner and I'd get into a blue car and then I'd finally get someplace and he'd say "You go out here down the alley, and you go through the basement window out on the porch and across the field and someone will talk to you."

I'd do that. I'd go down the alley through the basement across the field and when I got there, there would three huge police dogs ready to chew me up. I did that three times. The fourth call came finally—this also took about two years—and we went through the same procedure, but this time they talked. They gave me the Marine Corps treatment, but they talked.

I came home and wrote the chapter about them. I sent it back to L.A. and waited and waited and waited and, finally, a guy named Fred knocked on the door here. I could see he was carrying the chapter, and I said, "Want to come in?" He said, "No, I just have a message from the *hombres* for you." I said, "What's the message?" He said, "Either you change it, or we'll kill you." So I changed it. That was harsh criticism.

DD: *So, on a nonfiction book, you take the time to get to know the people you're writing about. You even show them the manuscript. At what point is the book over, done?*

SS: Never. I never read a book of mine that's been published for at least six months. 'Cause I won't dare read it, it's so goddamn awful, there's so many things I left out, so many nuances I've missed. It's never done. The only thing that makes it done is the publisher's contract and when he or she decides that your book is ready to be published. If it were up to me . . .

I spent about a year or two writing *The Ranchers*, but I spent thirty, forty years thinking about it and talking to these ranchers, and finally I got to the point where I said, "For God's sake, stop bellyaching and scrounging around, put it down on tape and let the world hear it. That was not a decision—that was like the thirty or forty years of knowing these people, knowing what they want, what they didn't want, how they talked: If you do that it takes a lot of time. It's nothing like sitting in your study in Beverly Hills turning out manuscripts from newspaper clippings and telephone conversations.

It takes a long time because you can't schedule people's lives. You know, that's why I say you don't "interview." If you interview someone, you make an appointment, you go there with your tape, you sit down, you do the interview and you leave.

If you "visit" with someone, on the other hand, you go there and it's forty miles out of town, and it's ten miles down the county road, and it's five miles down the ranch road, and when you get there they're not home. Cousin Gus or Cousin José died in the next county, and they went to the funeral, and no one knows when they're going to be back. I used to, when I was younger, like most writers do, set appointments and schedule out a plan and go from state to state, long distances. I stopped doing that a few years ago. I just see what happens. I figure if the interview doesn't come off, God didn't want it to. Who am I to defy God?

DD: *When did you come out to New Mexico from the East Coast?*

SS: When? Well, I grew up mostly in Brooklyn and partly in a small farm town in New Jersey. The Brooklyn I grew up in was rural. People don't believe it, but we had a farm right across the street from us. It was an entirely different place.

When I was about eighteen or so, my folks moved into Manhattan, and I couldn't believe it.

284

That to me was not the New York I knew. So a friend and I just bought Army surplus blankets and old khaki uniforms with no insignia—we weren't impersonating officers, we just wore khaki uniforms—and we hitchhiked [in 1945] out West, mainly to get away from Manhattan, or to figure out where America was. I think I found it out West.

I used to go anyplace they fed me. I used to [visit] Navajo country a lot, because Navajos always fed you in those days, especially if there was a sing. They made a lot of mutton stew and a lot of wine.

DD: *You ended up in New Mexico after the Second World War?*

SS: 'Forty-five, 'forty-six—somewheres around there. I commuted back and forth—a long commute—almost every year when I first left. Didn't care much for the East. It wasn't till I married Vera that we came out here to live permanently. But in the intervening period—perhaps fifteen years—I just wandered around. It was a different world. I'm one of the last writers I know who isn't pushing ninety that has ever ridden the rails. Ridden the boxcars, ridden underneath the boxcars. The railroad bulls and police in those days, most of 'em, had great sympathy for a kid on the road, unless it was a particularly mean town—and there were some especially mean towns. They'd feed you and chase you off the train, but they would feed you. In-state police would do the same; it was a different world.

I remember once we got into Des Moines, Iowa, in the middle of the night and we were so

285

tired we couldn't make it to an alleyway just to fall asleep, so we fell asleep on the sidewalk in the middle of Main Street. Sure enough, around five in the morning, some state policeman appeared and tapped me on the bottom of the soles of my shoes with his billy and said, "Get in the patrol car," and my buddy and I got in the patrol car, and they drove us out to the farthest diner on the highway and gave us a nickel apiece for a cup of coffee and talked to us in a fatherly way, saying, "Don't you ever come back."

It was a kinder world, a much kinder world. And I liked that, naturally I liked that. Not only did the Indian people feed you, but Hispanos fed you and Anglos fed you. I know a great number of ranchers that'd pick you up on the highway, which they won't do these days; they'd not only give you a ride, they would take you home and their wife would cook you Rocky Mountain trout for dinner and give you biscuits and a bunk in the barn. I don't think that happens to hitchhikers nowadays.

DD: *How is it that you ended up in New Mexico as opposed to Arizona or California?*

SS: I liked New Mexico when I first came here in 'forty-five, 'forty-seven, 'forty-six, whenever it was. Santa Fe was a little dirt town. Albuquerque was mainly known for its whorehouses. Life was easy: poor, very poor, but easy. New Mexico wasn't that much different from Colorado and Arizona. But it *was* different because it had so many Indians and Hispanic people, who gave it a more dignified quality; in some ways people were more dignified. They were easy.

I remember, in those years right after the war, how the whorehouse business declined because all the guys got out of the service. There were bases, like the bases near Albuquerque and Phoenix and Tucson, but they were empty. See, you could always get a bed in a whorehouse. They never charged you for the bed. They charged you for the woman, but not for the bed. And I didn't really want the woman, I just wanted the bed. I remember particularly in Albuquerque, they used to make two-story whorehouses down where First, Second, Third and Fourth Streets are now, across from the old Alvarado. They'd have a jukebox downstairs and a bar and beds upstairs, and there were endless guys coming back from California to Oklahoma and Texas. They had left during the Dust Bowl to go West. And they'd worked in the war industries, made a little money, and they were going back home in their pickups with all the furniture in the back of the truck.

These guys would come up to me in these bars in these whorehouses and they would say, "You got two bits? I'm going home to Tulsa." And I'd say, "How's it gonna help you get home to Tulsa on two bits?" And they'd say, "Oh, that's all I need is two bits and I'll be home tommorra." I've thought about it since. The land in the Northeast Heights of Albuquerque was selling for seventeen cents an acre. Instead of giving these guys two bits in these whorehouses, I should've bought land.

New Mexico was a great place to be. The people tipped their hats to you and said "*Bueno*." And people you never knew who passed you in pickup trucks would wave at you. If you got stuck on the highway it was really dangerous. Say you stopped on a two-lane road down to Albuquerque 'cause you were tired, or the car gave out, or you wanted to piss, or whatever. Someone immediately would stop behind you, and they wouldn't mug you. They'd say, "Can I help you?" So it was dangerous to stop—all these people were always trying to help you.

DD: *What makes New Mexico different to a writer?*

SS: Well, I'm not a mystic, but a lot of people do feel a mysticism out here. They feel a power, an energy out here. D.H. Lawrence said the Rio Grande—from Albuquerque north to Taos—was the umbilical cord of the world. There is a kind of energy. And there was then. People come here now for different reasons, but there was a peace out here then. Writers didn't come out here to get recognized, they came out her to get unrecognized. The first thing they would buy, or rent, was a fallen-down adobe for fifty bucks a month. You could buy it for two thousand, if you happened to be real rich. But even for fifty dollars a month you could rent yourself a house, and people respected writers. There wasn't the conflict that there is now between the Beverly Hills and Westchester County pseudo-artists who came out here because it's the place to be. Then, it was *not* the place to be. It was the *last* place in the world you wanted to be. It was a very, very poor state. But you could be unknown here. You could be Hispanic, you could even be Indian. The restrictions hadn't been laid down. The society wasn't polarizing, as it is now.

I wouldn't come out here now, never. I sometimes feel like weeping about what's happening in
New Mexico.

Anyway, I think writers wanted that freedom
and they wanted the sky and the sun and they wanted
what they got here, which they didn't get anyplace
else: They got a community. There were no federal
grants for writers. You didn't have to fill out any
application forms for the Humanities Council. You
scrounged around making your living anyway you
could. People helped you; if were hungry they fed
you. It was a community of writers.

I think that New Mexico's one of the three
places in the history of the United States where
there ever was a community of writers. One was
Ripley's Brook Farm, back in the 1840s. One
was the MGM lot, where they had writers like
Faulkner and Scott Fitzgerald, and all these people
were commiserating about their drunken scripts.
Then there was New Mexico, where writers really
were a community. People were very community
conscious.

They're still very family conscious, but they're
not community conscious. People here in Santa Fe
would do anything to protect their family, their
nephews and their cousins. But they don't do anything to protect Santa Fe.

DD: *Two or three years ago, after the National Writers'
Congress, you helped get a group of writers together as
the Writers' Cooperative of Santa Fe. What's the point?
Why do writers need a special community?*

SS: Well, I think it was Abe Rosenthal [former editor-in-chief of] *The New York Times*, who said, "The country stops west of the Hudson." We, of course, live a little west of the Hudson. We have a hard time living out here and trying to communicate with the publishing world. The publishing industry exists in one city, New York, and there's no other industry in the country that exists in one city. There are a couple of publishers scattered around the West.

So Western writers are really foreigners. At *The New York Times*, about two years ago, one of its editors said that people who live outside of New York are more remote than European peasants. *We* don't think of ourselves as European peasants; *they* think of us as European peasants.

So, the co-op was really formed so we could get our voice heard, get our rights protected, get cash in the bank account. That was the rational reason. But I think the underlying reason, the reason it's gone on for three years, is that it has helped build a small community of writers. It's given them some self-respect, and it's even given some people courage to write books they would have never dared write before because they didn't think they were up to it.

I think that's the main reason I formed the co-op. There were all these very practical, businesslike reasons, it's true. Some of them worked and some didn't. But the main reason was to have a community of people you could communicate with on something more than a supermarket level. Or a cocktail party level. The Writers' Co-op never has cocktail parties.

290

DD: *Is the difficulty of reaching readers connected to the Writers' Co-op?*

SS: Oh, a couple of years ago I met a book representative. I met him down in Albuquerque in a bookstore, and he was representing forty publishers. He'd come out here to place books in the bookstores, and he was going to two bookstores in Albuquerque and he was going to see two other, three other bookstores in Santa Fe and then he was going to Denver.

And I said, "You ever been in Roswell?"

He'd never heard of Roswell. It was almost like the rest of the country to him consisted of illiterates. The publishers make no effort to reach people they don't think exist. If they think we're illiterate, they're not going to try to sell books out here. Most towns don't have bookstores; some don't even have libraries. If there is a bookstore, it's like a church bookstore and New York publishers won't visit it. So we're not people. I've never seen anything to indicate that any publisher has ever done a marketing survey of readers in the West, or tried to determine how to reach the Western reader.

When the Writers' Co-op was trying to figure out how to reach the most people in the state of New Mexico, it came right to everybody: the state fair. More people attend the state fair than live in the state. And when we put up a booth at the state fair, there was a lot of incomprehension; we were told it was the first time a booth for writers—not of Lutheran books, or Baptist books, or evangelical books, but writers period—was ever built at the state fair.

The writers actually built a booth and put it next to the cow pavilion—imagine selling books to cowboys. Everybody thought we were crazy. But that's a Western marketing technique. It also shows some respect; a lot of cowboys bought books.

Of course we had some disasters, not knowing how to sell books at a state fair. We had a book a day that we raffled. We even had the author of the book sitting there to autograph it for whomever won the raffle. One writer had the bright idea one day to get one of the rodeo queens to come and pick the winning raffle for the book. Well, she let her horse pick it and the horse stuck his nozzle into the barrel we used for raffle tickets and ate the goddamn tickets. So there are many problems in marketing books, but there are also opportunities if you're willing to look for them.

DD: *What do you think people in New Mexico want to read most?*

SS: Oh, I don't know, almost anything. It's surprising what people will read. When we took the caravan —we had this van that we decked out with books— to Los Alamos, the biggest seller was a book on wildflowers. Why that was I haven't the vaguest notion, but it was a big smash in Los Alamos. In Questa we sold two books. When National Public Radio put us on their hookup, the producer called the day before and asked, "What do you people do?"

"Well, we just sold two books in Questa," I said. And there was silence, and then he said, "That doesn't sound like a hell of a lot." And I said, "Those are the only two books that have ever been sold in

292

Questa." I think people *will* read. The same people are interested in Hispanic culture, Indian culture, ranch culture, particularly if it's native. They're interested in anything. There are more science-fiction writers in Albuquerque than practically any city I know of. People read science fiction, they read romances, they read radical books, and they read conservative books—if they have the books in hand to read them.

DD: *What other things have you and the Writers' Co-op done to try and open up new audiences in the state?*

SS: Everything we do has never been done before, so its chances of working are pretty slim, and its chances of surprising you are built in. We had a program to bring writers into church congregations—if not to the pulpit, then afterwards in the church community house, to talk about books, their books and other books. My original thought was that very few ministers would want a writer in their church. If I were a minister I wouldn't want a writer lecturing at my church. It turned out we were completely surprised and completely wrong.

DD: *Do you think that the distance of the publishing industry from Colorado, from Arizona, from New Mexico, will ever be narrowed?*

SS: I think the publishing industry will go exactly the way the Hollywood movie industry has gone. Although Hollywood is still the center of the movie industry, there are more production units out of Hollywood than in it. There isn't a city in the country

293

that doesn't at one time or another have some production project, or company, or just the civic filler.
I think that's going to happen to the publishing industry. Publishers' representatives need to come out
West to build a Western market. The publishers
will have to do it with a new kind of book, like the
old French paperbacks that used to sell for a few
francs, not these Skaggs [drugstore] paperbacks
where the cover costs more than the book. A book
in paperback costs four or five dollars today because
the cover is so expensive, what with all the gold
naked women and silver passion and whatnot. Out
here you need really cheap books.

One of the main things that happened at the
state fair was not how many people bought books—
we did sell four hundred books, which put two thousand dollars into the pockets of the writers—but,
more important, the number of people who wanted
to buy a book and couldn't afford to. I distinctly
remember one lady who wanted a book. It was three
dollars and fifty cents, and she only had five dollars
to spend at the fair, and she said, "Well, I'm gonna
try and get lunch for a dollar-fifty." You can barely
get a hot dog for a dollar-fifty at the fair, and so she
couldn't buy a book. She couldn't afford it.

DD: *What is it that makes New Mexico or New Mexican
writing unique?*

SS: Well, it's not as unique as it should be. It's very
imitative. Since the publishing industry isn't here
and we have no ready access to the market, most
people here don't write for New Mexico, they write

294

for back East, for the audiences back East. That does not make for New Mexican writing.

If *The New York Times* wants to run a page on the wonders of Santa Fe—which it has done endless times by now—and you write a piece on what Santa Fe's really like, then *The New York Times* won't print it 'cause it isn't romantic. If you say to 'em, as I've said, "Well, you've printed all these really romantic pieces with nothing to do with New Mexico. Why don't you print something that's factual?" They'll say no one's interested. They want to believe in the myth in New Mexico. So the writers give in, writing falsely—falsely to themselves, falsely to their subject, falsely to their market—to please the publishing industry back East.

This fact doesn't just destroy New Mexican literature, it forces writers like Rudy Anaya to publish his own books, or to go to small presses to publish books. The fact that Rudy's *Bless Me Ultima* sold over a hundred thousand copies shows that you can write a book that is truthful about New Mexico and still get a huge audience. Most writers aren't as bold as Rudy was in doing it by himself. Maybe they don't have the courage, maybe they need the money too quickly, but they lie.

DD: *Are there any themes or stylistic elements that unite New Mexican writers?*

SS: I think New Mexico offers a writer the most dramatic subjects possible in this country right now, and also many unwritten stories. If you took all those themes and put them together instead of each writer doing his own little schtick, you'd have a panoramic view of not only historic but also contemporary New Mexico (it's been done in plays, it has not been done in novels).

I think the West in general, and New Mexico in particular, is the source of the next great American literature. It has never been Literature; it's been a genre, a faddish kind of thing about Zane Grey cowboys or Spanish cowboys or Indian cowboys or whatever. But to describe the real power in New Mexico, you would need a Homer, a Shakespeare. This area needs someone who can capture, elaborate and go beyond the drama that's in this state. I think probably New Mexico's waiting for Herman Melville. I don't know where he is, but we're waiting for Herman Melville.

Some little old lady, some Hispano Indian lady up in Pecos, is gonna turn out a manuscript that will be the epic of New Mexico. We have epics all around us, but we don't write about 'em.

DD: *Who would be in that epic of New Mexico?*

SS: Who?

DD: *What?*

SS: You have the combination, not of three cultures, but of two dozen cultures in this state; the cohesion and the conflict between those cultures in the past and in the present is exceedingly dramatic. Everyone who is writing is trying the best he or she can to please the [believers of the] myths and get published on that basis, knowing damn well that the truth, which is much more powerful—and [would] make a much greater book and probably attract a greater audience—is not acceptable.

In the case of my own books, a colleague of
yours from UNM, a Hispano professor, came up
to do some work here at the house with Vera, and
when she was leaving Vera said I should meet her
and say good-bye to her, and I did. She said, "Oh,
you're Stan Steiner. I always thought you were a
Chicano." And I said, "Where'd you get that notion?
I never said I was a Chicano." She said, "Well, you
know so much about us, but you never write the bad
things." Well, none of us ever write the bad things,
but that's where the human drama is. We try to
justify ourselves, to prove ourselves, to get a review
in *The New York Times*. Our main problem is our
self-depreciation. And with that attitude, you can't
write masterful works, powerful works, works that
get people so goddamn angry they read the book.

DD: *I noticed that you work on a manual typewriter and
still use old-fashioned scissors and pots of glue. Do you
think there's a different relationship between a writer
and his work depending on his tools?*

SS: Well, of course. There's an Indian arrowhead over
there on the table some woman from Santa Clara
gave me. Between that arrow and an atomic bomb
there's a big difference. The person who made that
arrowhead chipped it out by hand; and the person
who works in the labs is a different person. You are
not governed by the technology you use, but you
certainly are influenced by it.

My own personal approach is very old-fashioned and conservative. I suppose it's to get as close
to the material as possible. That's why I use a manual

typewriter; I can feel every word and every letter with my finger. I only use one finger to type. When my finger splits, which it does, I'm out of commission. I could work on an electric typewriter, which is one step up, but if I'm writing and I'm angry—which I very often am when I'm writing—and you hit a key on an electric typewriter, it goes "Whooosht!" right across the room. I've never written on a word processor or a computer, but I think the word processor and computer influence what you write, the way you write and, eventually, the way you think. The process is terribly insidious, of course, 'cause you don't feel it. If you're riding on a horse and buggy or riding in a Mercedes, you know the difference immediately. With these machines, the difference creeps up on you.

I use an old Olympia. Can't get parts for it. My typewriter repairman said I must be a fool. Even if he sent to Germany, he couldn't get parts for it. But nothing will ever destroy that Olympia. My wife once went back to New York to fulfill a teaching contract. I went with her, and about three hours after we got to New York City, I went insane. I stayed insane for the two years we were there. I was staring at this brick wall three feet from me out the window one morning, and I stared at it and stared at it, and I couldn't take it any more. I picked up my Olympia and tossed it like a football across the room. It bounced off the floor, hit the door, bounced off the table, landed back on the floor. I put it back in front of me and went on typing. I defy anyone to do that with a word processor.

ACKNOWLEDGMENTS

Emily Skretny Drabanski and Vera John-Steiner would like to thank all those involved in assisting the publication of this, Stan Steiner's last book.

Our deepest appreciation is extended to the children of Stan Steiner and Vera John-Steiner and their spouses: Paul and Patricia Steiner; Sandor and Janet John; and Suki John. They spent many hours organizing Stan's files, notes and manuscripts. They also compiled a literary list of his writings.

We'd also like to thank the editors at St. Martin's Press, who guided this book and saw it through to completion. Joyce Engelson first began working on this book with Stan Steiner. After Stan's death, it was through the perseverance of senior editor Robert Weil that this book was published. We'd also like to thank assistant editor Bill Thomas for his help.

We greatly acknowledge the publishers and editors who granted permission to reprint some of Stan's earlier writings in this book. "The Chinese Railroad Men," from *Fusang: The Chinese Who Built America*, was reprinted by permission of Harper & Row Publishers, Inc. "Jewish Conquistadors: America's First Cowboys?", from *Dark and Dashing Horsemen*, was also reprinted by permission of Harper & Row Publishers, Inc. (World rights granted.)

We thank *American West* magazine for its ongoing support and publication of Stan's writing in that magazine.

We also appreciate receiving permission to reprint several stories that appeared in the magazine. "Real Horses and Mythic Riders" appeared in the September/October 1981 issue; "Jewish Conquistadors: America's First Cowboys?" appeared in the September/October 1983 issue.

Across the Board, the Conference Board magazine, granted permission to reprint two articles. "Space Cowboys: Notes on the Cosmic Cowboys" appeared in the February 1984 issue. "Mother Earth and Father Energy" appeared in the July/August 1983 issue.

An earlier version of "Going West" was published by the *Santa Fe Reporter*. The story, titled "Billy the Kid Was Born in Brooklyn, Too," was printed in the March 26, 1986, issue. We thank publisher Hope Aldrich for granting permission to reprint the story.

We extend our gratitude to Sarah Nestor, editor of *El Palacio* magazine, for granting permission to reprint László Borsányi's interview with Stan Steiner. Borsányi's interview, then-titled "The Challenge and Vitality of the West," was published in the Fall 1982 issue of *El Palacio*.

The interview with Stan Steiner copyright © 1987 by David K. Dunaway is used by permission. We also thank David K. Dunaway for making a copy of the transcript of the memorial service for Stan Steiner available to us for background material.

Finally, we greatly appreciate LaVon Alt's assistance with typing the manuscript. We also extend our gratitude to John Drabanski, Emily's husband, for help with numerous errands as well as his ongoing confidence and support.